Genghis Khan

Genghis Khan—from the collection of portraits of the Mongol
Emperors in the National Museum of China, Peking (Li Tai
Ti Wang Hsiang).
(Photograph kindly supplied by the Percival David Foundation
of Chinese Art.)

Genghis Khan

R. P. LISTER

Cooper Square Press

Published by Cooper Square Press,
An Imprint of Rowman & Littlefield Publishers, Inc.
150 Fifth Avenue, Suite 911
New York, New York 10011

Distributed by National Book Network

Library of Congress Cataloging-in-Publication Data

Lister, R. P. (Richard Percival), 1914–
    Genghis Khan/ R.P. Lister.
        p. cm.
    Originally published: New York : Stein and Day, 1969
    Includes bibliographical references and index.
    ISBN 0-8154-1052-2 (pbk.)
        1. Genghis Khan, 1162–1227. 2. Mongols—Kings and rulers—Biography. I Title.

DS22 .L52 2000
950'.2—dc21
[B]   00-022820

☉™ The paper used in this publication meets the minimum requirements of American National Standard for Information Sciences—Permanence of Paper for Printed Library Materials, ANSI/NISO Z39.48–1992.
Manufactured in the United States of America.

CONTENTS

Now however we shall also tell what these first Tatars resembled, for the first who came to the upper country were not like men. They were terrible to look at and indescribable, with large heads like a buffalo's, narrow eyes like a fledgling's, a snub nose like a cat's, projecting snouts like a dog's, narrow loins like an ant's, short legs like a hog's, and by nature with no beards at all. With a lion's strength they have voices more shrill than an eagle. They appear where least expected. Their women wear beautiful hats covered at the top with a head shawl of brocade. Their broad faces are plastered with a poisonous mixture of gum. They give birth to children like snakes and eat like wolves. Death does not appear among them, for they survive for three hundred years. They do not eat bread at all. Such were the first people who came to the upper countries.

—the Armenian monk, Grigor of Akanc'

INTRODUCTION

This book is mainly an account of the early life and rise to power of Genghis Khan, up to the time of his elevation as Ruler of the Steppes in 1206. It is based on a Mongol chronicle, *The Secret History of the Mongols.* This remarkable work was written in 1240, thirteen years after the Khan's death, and was then lost to history for seven hundred years, until its restoration in the present century. It was written at a time when many of his companions still lived, and when the knowledge of his early career was still well preserved among a people whose illiteracy conferred on them the benefit of a good memory, and a fondness for repeating such stories. It deals with his early years in great detail; the last twenty years of world conquest are passed over quite summarily. I have followed the same plan, dealing in detail with the early years and cursorily with the years of conquest, partly because (perhaps like the Mongol chronicler) I find the early life irresistibly fascinating, and the later conquests a tediously repetitive tale of rapine and slaughter. But there is also a further reason: that the story of the conquests is widely known, while that of the early years is not.

Many books have been written about Genghis Khan. As far as the later years are concerned, where he and his armies emerge from the steppes to make a shattering impact on world history, they are full and accurate, within the limits of historical controversy in matters of detail. But in dealing with the early life they are misinformed. This is no reflection on the scholarship of their authors. They simply had not the material at their disposal. They had to depend for their information on the work of historians, mostly Chinese and Persian, of a much later period. These incorporated in their accounts material from the *Secret History*, but it was inextricably mingled with legend and falsehood. The *Secret*

History is the sole contemporary record of the great Khan and his people, and without it none of the later historians was equipped to give a credible account of either.

It is clearly desirable, in view of the fundamental importance of this work, and my own dependence on it in writing this book, to give here an account of its compilation, loss and recovery, and the way in which I have used the material in it. These matters are dealt with in this Introduction. They are not, I think, without interest in themselves. But I should point out that the reader who is interested in the career of Genghis Khan, and does not wish to trouble himself about how the details of that career came to be known at all, can safely ignore the remainder of this Introduction and pass straight on to Chapter I.

The book itself, though based on the *Secret History*, is by no means a translation of it. It is a re-telling in my own words of the story of Genghis Khan's rise to power. The original work was written for the information of Mongol princes, and is largely incomprehensible except to the specialist in the period. I have re-told it as it might have been written if the scribe had had an intelligent Western audience in mind. Much material has been added from other sources to give the story meaning; much that was of little general interest has been omitted. The basic narrative is that of the *Secret History*, but the manner of telling it, except for reported speeches, is my own. The occasional comments on larger matters or life in general are similarly mine, but they are comments that I believe might well have been made by an intelligent Mongol of the period. The Mongols emerge from the *Secret History* as a down-to-earth people with a dry wit of their own, and the chronicler is very much a human being.

In the notes at the end of the book I have enlarged on various matters that appear to deserve further comment, where this would be out of place in the main narrative. I have also given there some explanation of my interpretation of doubtful points in the original chronicle.

One question which may trouble the reader should

certainly be answered. The *Secret History* is a work of astonishing richness, giving with overwhelming conviction a detailed picture of a forgotten people and a forgotten way of life, and a full account of the desperate struggles by which the son of a small Mongol chieftain finally achieved immense power. Would it not have been better merely to have published a translation of it, rather than base an entirely new book on it?

The question is justifiable, and the answer simple. The *Secret History*, as it stands, is virtually unreadable. It was not until I had laboured over it for some time, and read a great deal elsewhere, that I began to perceive its quality. As I got to know it better, it reminded me in many respects of the *Morte d'Arthur*. It gives the same vivid picture of a world living by a clear logic of its own, of idiosyncratic human beings inhabiting a wide and illimitable landscape. In contrast to the *Morte d'Arthur*, the story it tells is true, and all the characters in it were living people. But no pains were taken to make it comprehensible, let alone entertaining. It is rough notes for the *Morte d'Arthur* combined with a manual of infantry training and the London Telephone Directory. My own part in writing this book has been to dig the nuggets out of the dross, to polish them up, and to arrange them in a coherent setting so that their meaning is perceptible.

It would be impossible to achieve complete accuracy in a book dealing with a period so remote, unfamiliar and largely undocumented. All I can claim is that I have made every effort to ensure that the story is true; or, if it is not true, that it represents what a Mongol born in the time of Genghis Khan, and with access to all the surviving companions of his younger days, firmly believed to be true.

THE SECRET HISTORY OF THE MONGOLS

Genghis Khan died in 1227. He was succeeded by his son Ogodai. Ogodai was a powerful warrior and a heavy drinker. When he was forty-six he had a stroke, which made him stumble in his speech, but he lived on for ten years after it. Towards the end of that time, feeling that he had not long to live, he summoned the Mongol leaders from all parts of his vast empire to a council. This council was held in the autumn of A.D. 1240 on the banks of the Kerulen river, in the original Mongol homeland.

The Khan commanded that during this council an account should be written down of the origins and rise to power of his great predecessor, of his conquests and deeds of war, and of the measures of military organisation and government initiated by Genghis Khan and continued under Ogodai. This is the work referred to here as *The Secret History of the Mongols*, from its original Mongolian title, *Mangqol'un Niuca Tobca'an*.

It is a reasonable assumption—though it is nowhere stated—that the direction of the work was entrusted to the prince Shigikutuku, the principal lawgiver of the empire. No other person among the Khan's leading advisers was so well qualified by his intimate knowledge of the events described, his authority among the princes, and the wide respect in which he was held.

The actual author is unknown. He was quite probably an Uighur, since writing had been known among this people for some generations. There may, however, by that time have been a few literate Mongols capable of the task.

The work was by no means intended for general perusal, but was reserved for the use of members of the ruling house. It is for this reason that the word 'secret' was incorporated in its title.

It was originally written in a variant of the Uighur script which had been adapted for writing Mongolian, a related language. Of the original manuscript, or any early copies of it in the Uighur script, there is no trace.

During the hundred years of Mongol rule in China, under Khubilai Khan and his successors, decrees were promulgated in the two languages, Mongolian and Chinese. The Uighur script, which ran horizontally, was ill-fitted for this purpose, and a new form of writing was developed, the

Phagspa script (from the name of the Tibetan lama who invented it). This used Tibetan characters running vertically, so enabling the columns of Chinese writing and Mongolian writing to be set side by side.

These attempts to force on the Chinese a familiarity with the language of their Mongolian rulers met with little success. The Chinese had to carry on the administration of the empire under rulers whose language, for the most part, they did not understand. In these circumstances the device was hit on of rendering the Mongolian language phonetically in Chinese characters, using for each Mongolian word a set of Chinese characters whose sound corresponded as closely as possible to the Mongolian sounds. The message would be accompanied by a Chinese commentary or paraphrase. A Chinese bearing a message or instruction from one Mongolian ruler or official to another could then read out the message in a semblance of Mongolian, and even give some rendering of its contents in Chinese if some passages of the Mongolian proved incomprehensible. Since Chinese characters are ill-adapted for the phonetic rendering of Mongolian this must have been necessary fairly often.

In the closing years of the Mongol dynasty the *Secret History* was transcribed into Chinese characters according to this by now familiar system. It is to this transcription that the survival of the *Secret History* is due. When the Mongol dynasty was overthrown and replaced by the Chinese Ming dynasty, in 1368, there followed a widespread destruction by the Chinese of all relics of the hated alien rulers. Apart from a few stone tablets, from which the Uighur and Phagspa scripts are known, all Mongolian writings were destroyed. The imperial archives no doubt contained copies both in Uighur and in Phagspa of the *Secret History*. All were lost.

The phonetic transcription, however, being in Chinese characters, was assumed to be a Chinese work, and so survived. It was even printed, in the first years of the Ming dynasty, as an official record. Some fragments of this printed edition were found in Peking in the 1930s. Further handwritten copies survived, finding their way into the libraries of scholarly noblemen and administrators. For them, however, it was merely a curiosity, since the main work was incomprehensible to them.

The continued existence of the *Secret History* was unknown to the rest of the world until the nineteenth century. Then, in 1847, the Chinese paraphrase was published. This is the work entitled *Yüan-ch'ao Pi-shih, The Secret History of the Yüan Dynasty, Yüan* being the name by which the Mongol dynasty is known to the Chinese. It was translated into Russian by the orientalist Palladius in 1866. It must be emphasised, however, that this translation of the *Yüan-ch'ao Pi-shih* is made, not from the Mongolian original, but from an extremely abbreviated Chinese paraphrase of it, often hardly more than a summary, containing numerous inaccuracies and misunderstandings of the original material.

RESTORATION OF THE SECRET HISTORY

Clearly what was needed was a reconstitution of the main work. This was not without difficulty in itself, and the final reappearance of the text was further delayed by a series of remarkable misfortunes.

The first scholar to address himself to the task was the Russian, Palladius. After his publication of the Russian translation of the Chinese paraphrase in 1866 he was able to obtain, in 1872, a copy of the complete work, i.e. one including the Mongolian text written out in full in Chinese characters. He was aided by a wide knowledge of both languages and of the cultures of both China and Mongolia. It is believed that by 1878 he had completed the reconstruction of the text and possibly its translation into Russian. Unfortunately, on his way home from China, he died, and his work was lost. The original document, however, survived and was used later by the German scholar, Erich Haenisch.

In the early years of this century the Chinese bibliophile, Ye Teh-hui, published a complete copy of the Chinese version of the *Secret History*, including both the transliterated main text and the paraphrase. The work was now generally available to scholars for the first time.

During the First World War the French orientalist, Paul Pelliot, produced a complete transliteration of the text in Mongolian, in Roman characters. He worked principally from a manuscript of the Ming period in his possession, but also used the Ye Teh-hui text and others. Pelliot also embarked on a translation into French of the entire *Secret History* from his own reconstructed manuscript, but unfortunately died when he had completed only the first half of it. This has been published, together with the transliterated Mongolian text.

Finally, Haenisch undertook the restoration of the Mongol original from various texts, and published his own version of it in 1937. His translation of the *Secret History* into German was completed in 1940; most of the first edition was destroyed by fire, but a new edition was published in Leipzig in 1948. Haenisch's work was based principally on the Ye Teh-hui text, supplemented by others, including the Palladius text and the Ming fragments discovered in Peking in the thirties.

It is these two works by Pelliot and Haenisch, the first giving a translation of the first half only of the *Secret History* and the second of the complete work, that I have used as the principal source material for this book.

OTHER SOURCES

There are several other early works which, in the absence of the *Secret History*, have had to serve historians as the only sources of information available until the most recent years.

The earliest is *The History of the World-Conqueror*, by the Moslem historian 'Ala-ud-Din 'Ata-Malik Juvaini. A native of Khorasan, Juvaini served under the Khan Hulagu, and wrote his book between 1252 and 1260. As a work of such early date, it is of immense interest. Unfortunately it is unreliable in its accounts of the Khan's youth and rise to power, the background and circumstances of the time being so alien to the writer as to be incomprehensible to him.

During the reign in China of the Mongol Khan Ghazan (1295–1304), the Persian historian Rashid-ud-Din was permitted access to the original Mongol *Secret History*. This was the only use made of the original chronicle before its disappearance. His work was extensively drawn upon by subsequent writers, but his viewpoint was also alien, and he was aiming at the glorification of Ghazan rather than at the truth.

The writers of the official history of the Mongol dynasty, compiled in the Ming period, also had access to the imperial archives, but their information was drawn from the Chinese paraphrase, with its numerous inaccuracies and misunderstandings of the original text.

There are two Mongolian sources, but both date from the seventeenth century, four hundred years after the events described. One is the *Altan Tobci*, or *Golden Book*, the official Mongolian history of the imperial family, written in 1604; the other is the history of the Mongol rulers written in 1662 by Sanang Setsen. Both these works were written at a period so remote from the events they describe and contain so many allusions by their pious Buddhist authors to improbable supernatural interventions into mortal affairs that it is impossible to disentangle the truth from any distorted reflections of it they may contain.

Then there are the accounts left by Western travellers: Giovanni Piano del Carpine, who visited the court of Güyük; William of Rubrouck, who visited Möngke; and Marco Polo, who visited Khubilai Khan. These are fascinating, and contribute valuable impressions of Mongol life and customs, but their accounts of early Mongol history are unreliable.

Such were the sources on which Western historians of later centuries had to draw. Given the inadequacy of their information, they performed miracles of scholarly labour and speculation. However, in the absence of any contemporary record, that labour and speculation could not

xiv

prevent their deductions from being frequently erroneous. I have read with interest and attention the works of Howorth, d'Ohsson, Vladimirtsov, Grousset and others; but there is little in their accounts of the early period that can be relied on, however sound they may be on later events.

One point, though, must be stressed. The *Secret History* undoubtedly contains the only reliable account of the period; but there is no guarantee of its completeness. Indeed, it is quite certainly incomplete. In view of this, some of the statements of Rashid-ud-Din and others, though uncorroborated by the original history, may have to be regarded as possibly valid. Where, however, their accounts differ from those of the *Secret History*, the latter have a better claim to be regarded as authentic.

I have derived useful information concerning the country and the period from a number of sources. For the most part I have regarded these as too remote from the essence of the subject, besides being too numerous, to merit inclusion in the bibliography. This gives details of the works mentioned above, and of a few others which have provided more extensive assistance.

Of these, I must make special mention of three. One is a work published since the issue of the rediscovered *Secret History*, entitled *The Rise of Genghis Khan and his Conquest of North China*, by H. D. Martin. This work is, and will remain, indispensable for any student of the period.

Another work which gave me immeasurable aid of a different kind was the collection of writings by Owen Lattimore entitled *Studies in Frontier History*. This brilliant book is essential to the understanding of such wider matters as the emergence of a feudal system from the breakdown of an earlier clan system, and the interaction of settled and nomadic civilisations, in Asia and elsewhere. These matters lie behind the whole story of the Mongol conquests.

The third work to which I must express my special debt is the only one in existence, apart from the *Secret History*, which gives a contemporary view of the Mongols of the time of Genghis Khan. It is the account by Ch'ang Ch'un, a

Taoist adept, of his journey to the camp of Genghis Khan near Samarkand in 1220–3. This, in its translation by Arthur Waley, under the title *Travels of an Alchemist*, is an extremely vivid and readable work. I have drawn on it for some pages at the end of the book, in the hope that it may illuminate for others (as it did for me) something of the world-conqueror's state of mind in his closing days.

INTERPRETATION OF THE SECRET HISTORY

As the sole credible source of information concerning the early years of Genghis Khan, the *Secret History* has to be regarded with immense respect, but also with caution. A collection of tales repeated by word of mouth for up to fifty years, though frequently corroborated by people actually present at the events recounted, is still a collection of tales that may have been embroidered and improved on in the telling. Much of the credence accorded to them has to depend on a judgment of their inherent probability.

The first part of the Mongol chronicle is an account of the ancestry of Genghis Khan. Most of this is obviously legendary. I have dealt with this, and a few other passages where fancy has clearly been preferred to fact, by supposing that the chronicler was as sceptical about them as I am. This seems to me a reasonable assumption. The Mongols of that time believed in a vague presiding deity resident in the sky, and lesser spirits who inhabited the rocks, trees and rivers, but the intervention of these into human affairs was limited. The world encountered every day was the real world; visions and magical occurrences were regarded as exceptional.

I think it unlikely, for instance, that the chronicler believed that the Mongols were descended from the union of a grey wolf and a white doe. He may have thought it more likely that the grey wolf was a Tibetan prince, whose name, Burte Chino, has that meaning. As for this Tibetan prince, he quite probably had much the same relation to reality as Hengist and Horsa. There may have been Saxon

xvi

chiefs who bore these names, or there may not. If there were not, there were, nevertheless, some unknown chiefs who roughly resembled them.

Although the early ancestors of the Mongols, as named, probably did not exist, the account of them is useful in that it gives a clear idea of the degree of relationship between the clans, which is a matter of some importance. For this reason, I have extracted from the chronicle a genealogical table of Genghis Khan's ancestry as the chronicler describes it. It may safely be assumed that the names of the chieftains within a few generations of Genghis Khan represent real men and women, and that the most remote ones do not. Those in between inhabit a doubtful region. The chronicler is certainly convinced that the beautiful queen Alan-qo'a was a real person; but even her sons, born at a time when she had no perceptible husband, are represented as sceptical about her assertion that their father descended from Heaven through the roof of the tent on a moonbeam, and it is unlikely that the chronicler, accustomed to the facts of life on the steppes, believed it either.

The chieftains of Genghis Khan's own line, from Kaidu Khan down to Bartan Ba'atur, Genghis Khan's grandfather, must be regarded as historical personages, and the vicissitudes of the Mongols during this period correspond closely enough with Chinese accounts of their relations with the steppe peoples. With the advent of Yesugei, Genghis Khan's father, and his contemporaries, there can be little doubt that the persons named are real, and the details recounted of their lives substantially true.

In the latter part of the chronicle, the account of the Khan's words and actions after his elevation as Ruler of the Steppes becomes noticeably vague, and the account of the campaigns of conquest is highly condensed and occasionally difficult to adjust to the known facts. I do not regard this as throwing any great doubt on the credibility of the preceding events which form the main subject of the chronicle. The Khan was by now a great ruler, and remote from other men, even from his closest advisers. There was no longer a knot of friendly though respectful tribesmen standing near his tent when he came out, to note his actions and repeat his words. As for the conquests, the vagueness of the account of them merely indicates that the Mongols, like any other people, were devoted to their own way of life and thought little of anyone else's. They rode over vast tracts of the world, sacking cities and defeating the armies of their enemies, without caring much what the cities were called, or what king they were defeating. There is a much greater immediacy in the narrative where it concerns the affairs of their own homeland, or of people whose actions and ways of life they could comprehend.

NOMENCLATURE

It has been a major difficulty to effect a satisfactory compromise between accuracy and readability in reproducing the names of people and places. Even consistency proved undesirable.

(1) The guttural sound, as in Scottish 'loch', rendered often in English as 'kh', but in Pelliot's reconstructed Mongolian text as 'q' (Haenisch uses the guttural 'ch'), is of frequent occurrence. I have reproduced it as 'kh' where possible, but in certain words this seemed undesirable. 'The leafy trees of Qorqonaq' conjures up a pleasant impression; 'the leafy trees of Khorkhonakh', in my opinion, does not. Where such repeated gutturals occur I have stuck to the less familiar 'q'. I have also retained the 'q' in some words such as Qorolas, for a similar reason: it looks pleasanter than Khorolas. Qahan I have rendered throughout as the more familiar 'khan'. In some names of lesser importance in the narrative I have dropped the guttural entirely where its presence appeared to me distracting. I believe the average reader would be happier with Kutula Khan than with Qutula, or even with Khutula. Qo'aqčin, in a book not intended for the scholar, would be an outrage; Khoakchin has to do. Major characters, such as Jamukha, I have left

with their guttural, for the sake of accuracy in the naming of such important personages. I have been comforted in perpetrating these inconsistencies by the reflection that the average English or American reader will, in any case, render either 'q' or 'kh' by a hard 'k'.

(2) Inflected vowels offer a similar difficulty. I have again given readability precedence over pure accuracy, and sacrificed consistency where I had to. I have most frequently rendered 'ä' by the diphthong 'ei', which sounds not dissimilar, as in Chileidu for Čilädü; but Yeikei for Yäkä was unattractive, so I condensed it to Yeke. The distortion is not too great if it is remembered that all vowels are sounded. 'Ö' presented even more formidable difficulties. Hö'älün, the mother of Genghis Khan, could not very well be represented throughout as Heu'eilun; I fell back on calling her Hoelun. The Khan's wife, Börte, is a little easier; I call her Berta, which is no great distance from the true pronunciation. As for 'ü', nothing can be done with it in English; so the Khan's father Yäsügäi has to be Yesugei.

(3) Clan names such as Tangut, Mangqut, etc., are plural forms. Where I use them in the singular I do so in order not to cause confusion by introducing too many different forms of the same word.

REPORTED SPEECH

There are numerous occasions in the *Secret History* where speeches and conversations are reported as they were spoken by the persons concerned. The speeches clearly may not be what the characters actually said, but they represent what the witnesses of the scene reported that they said, as it was remembered after frequent re-telling. In direct translation they often sound a little stiff to modern ears. I have gone on the principle that, except where formal speeches were concerned, these people expressed themselves in racy, colloquial Mongolian, and their speech should therefore be rendered in racy, colloquial English. I believe I have on no occasion taken undue liberties with the sense or feeling of the dialogue in attempting to give the impression of living speech.

Some speeches are more formal in character, though it is astonishing how often they still reflect the character of the speaker. An outstanding example is Dai Sechen's address to Yesugei, recommending his daughter Berta as a wife for Temujin. This, in the original, is masterly, and my rendering of it, as of many other more considered speeches, is very close to a literal translation.

One occasion on which I felt some trepidation in my handling of a speech was on the occasion of Temujin's delivering himself of an invocation to the mountain Burkhan Khaldun, after the theft of his wife Berta by the Taijiut. This is expressed in the original in extremely high-flown speech: in fact, in alliterative verse. I thought the only thing to do with it was to render it in blank verse form. The result falls short of the highest poetry, but Genghis Khan was no poet. I have preserved all the repetitions, and the poem, such as it is, sticks quite closely to the original.

Some speeches I have condensed considerably, notably Hoelun's tirade to Temujin after his murder of his half-brother. Repetition was a bad habit with the Mongols, who had plenty of time for it.

But I must make it clear that there is no dialogue in this book of my own invention. Every speech reported in the book is based on a speech reported in the *Secret History*, and though I may have taken occasional liberties with the manner of expression in my desire to convey a feeling of living actuality, I have taken none with the substance.

The same remark applies to the book as a whole. I have enlarged on the bare recital of facts, to make them meaningful, and I have omitted a great deal, such as the endless details of military organisation and appointments and the rotation of guard duties, which are of slight interest to the general reader. I have deduced from the text much that lay hidden in it: for instance, in the ride to recover the stolen horses, the chronicler does not mention the riders' shadows stretching ahead of them across the steppe. Since it was late evening and they were riding east, the shadows were undoubtedly there; and it seemed to me that those shadows would do more than anything else could to make this long-ago scene seem vivid and actual. I have used my imagination to the extent of trying to identify myself with the Mongol mind, in order to find convincing reasons for the actions of the characters, where these were not made clear; but, down to the smallest matter of fact, I have invented nothing.

REASONS FOR WRITING THIS BOOK

A few years ago, in a small restaurant in the Sirkeci quarter of Istanbul, I shared a table with a Turk who informed me, during the course of a long conversation in my inadequate Turkish and his inadequate German, that he was a student of Chagatai. By the time I had, on my return, fully informed myself on what and who Chagatai was, the writing of this book had become inevitable. But its inevitability was not apparent to me until the positive suggestion that I should write it was made to me by Elaine Greene, to whom my thanks are due in this as in many other things.

My chief aid in writing it was an intense interest in, and sympathy with, Mongols in particular and nomads in general. By good fortune I have had glimpses of steppe life and of the Gobi itself; these have been brief, but a brief glimpse is better than nothing. As has been truly said, after a day in Rome you know it well; after a week you are beginning to get to know it, and after a year you hardly know it at all.

As for nomads, I have been happy to make the acquaintance of various Lapps during my travels in their delectable country. These people come from the same region as the Mongols, and speak a language distantly related to theirs. They have much of the same down-to-earth character, a refreshing absence of all pretension, and a common-sense attitude to life which is the reverse of romantic. Take away the reindeer and substitute a camel, and many of my

Lapp friends were virtually indistinguishable from my later Mongol friends, whom I know largely through the medium of their thirteenth-century chronicler.

I owe my acquaintance of the Istanbul restaurant, a farmer from Erzerum, a great debt for a fascinating experience. I regret that I do not know his name.

R. P. LISTER

Genghis Khan

I

The Country of the Mongols

The country of the Mongols lay in north-east Asia, where the two rivers Onon and Kerulen[1] ran down to the east and north-east from the mountain massif of Burkhan Khaldun.

It was a harsh land, covered with snow in winter and intensely hot in summer.[2] There were forests in the river valleys, but between them stretched great expanses of bare steppe. Most of the land was arid steppe, and to keep alive in it at all a man needed a horse, weapons, flocks and the company of his clansmen.

To the west and east lay the lands of other steppe peoples, the Keraits and the Tatars. To the north-west were ranges of high mountains, with ice on their summits. Beyond these, three or four hundred miles away, was the great lake, Baikal; and beyond it a country of hills covered with woods, where the forest peoples lived.

To the south-east was the true desert, the Gobi. Beyond this, five hundred miles away, there were more mountains, bare and rough, a jumble of mountains; and running among them, swooping and diving from summit to summit, was the Great Wall. The Wall stretched for thousands of miles, from the eastern sea to the Nan Shan, on the borders of

Tibet. The Chinese built it to keep the steppe peoples out; sometimes it did, sometimes it did not.

These mountains fell away again to the patterned plain of China, and in this plain, half encircled by the distant mountains, lay Peking.

When Genghis Khan was born, in 1167, north China was ruled by the Chin Emperors. Their power was felt a long way beyond the Great Wall. They were originally nomadic people themselves, forest people from the north. Having conquered northern China, they had settled down there and adopted Chinese ways and customs.[3]

This had happened many times before, and it would happen again. Usually the tribes were disunited and fighting among themselves for the leadership. Then whoever ruled China at the time had power over them. The emperors did not station soldiers north of the Wall, outposts with fortified camps and watchtowers. They did not want this country; it was bleak and bare, and no crops could be grown on it. They traded with the nearer people, and sent armies against them if they made trouble; they made treaties with the tribal leaders, and played one people off against another. So they kept what they called peace, and the Wall protected them.

But now and then some leader arose among the nomads who united the clans and the nations. The Chinese were more numerous, and richer; they had bigger armies, better weapons and walled cities to defend themselves in. But they quarrelled among themselves, like any other men, and because they had so much wealth to make their lives easier they did not like to lose their lives defending it. So the poor nomads, with everything to gain and nothing to lose, could sometimes defeat them if they were agreed among themselves and well led.

The latest nomads to do so had been those Jurchen, who provided the Chinese with the dynasty of Chin Emperors. At first they were fierce fighters who ruled the Chinese firmly, and kept the nomads beyond the Wall in order with ease, since they were the same kind of people themselves.

2

But in the course of time they became used to a more leisured and luxurious way of life.

Naturally the Chinese, and the Chin Emperors who ruled them, regarded the nomadic peoples as barbarians. The Mongols and others had no cities. They did not make beautiful pots or paint pictures or build houses, or even put together much in the way of furniture, since they could only make a living off the land they lived on by moving constantly over it with their animals, and they could not carry such things about with them. They had a language in which they could say anything they wished to say, but had so far seen no need to find out how to write it down. They had history and traditions, legends and songs, and rules of behaviour which governed the way they lived, though not perfectly. They quarrelled and fought and stole from each other, as men have done in other countries. They had certain skills in tending animals, providing themselves with fire, food and shelter, making clothes and weapons, and such matters. So they were able to survive in a country where most men, lacking these skills, would swiftly die. But the Chinese had money, and the Mongols had none; and this alone proved, in the eyes of the Chinese, that they themselves possessed all the cultivated virtues, and the Mongols were nothing but brutish savages.

The Gobi formed something of a barrier between the Chinese and the steppe peoples, but it was not an insurmountable one. There were wells here and there, sometimes more than a day's march from each other, but never so far that a man would necessarily die before he reached the next one, as long as he knew where it was. People even lived there, after a fashion; but they lived better on the steppes that surrounded it.

On the steppes there was grass for the animals to graze on, and though the grass was not superlatively good, it was good enough. But soon the grass would become exhausted. So at certain seasons of the year the clan grazing in that area had to pack up its tents and move on. The ropes that held the felt tents to their wooden frameworks were untied,

3

and the felt tents folded; ropes and felts and frameworks were loaded on to the covered ox-wagons, together with the cooking-pots and milk-churns, the anvils and the pestles and mortars, and the women and children. The men mounted, armed with bows and arrows and swords, ready for any trouble they might meet on the way; and the whole clan moved off across the steppes, for days or weeks, to whatever fresh grazing-grounds the chieftain, having taken counsel with the knowledgeable old men, and considered the movements of other clans in the region, might decide on.

The bare steppes alone could not support such a way of life. There had to be wood, for the bows and arrows, the tent-frameworks, the eating-vessels and churns, the beds and the wagons. But in this borderland country, between the deserts in the south and the forests in the north, there was plenty of wood growing along the river valleys, from scrub to tall trees. However bare the steppe might be, the forest was never so far away that wood could not be obtained when it was needed. And however arid the steppe might be, the water was never too far away, if a man knew where to look for it. It was the combination of forest and steppe that made the nomad way of life possible. The steppe would not grow crops, but it nourished beasts, and the beasts nourished the men.

There also had to be iron, for the swords and arrow-heads and cooking-pots. This was obtained by trading, from the neighbouring peoples, who got in exchange for it skins and furs and such things, which they could not readily find for themselves. But there was never enough of it. In these early times the sign of a great chieftain among the Mongols was that his stirrups were made of iron;[4] common men made do with leather or wood.

THE DECLINE OF THE MONGOLS

The Mongols were a small people, but once, long ago, under Kaidu Khan (who was Genghis Khan's great-great-great-great-grandfather), and again under Kabul Khan,

4

Kaidu's great-grandson, they were powerful above all the nations of this region.

The Chin Emperors regarded the Mongols, and the other steppe peoples, as their subjects. The steppe peoples fell in with this idea when they were obliged to, or when it was profitable to them. Kabul Khan received some support from the Chin Emperor of the time, Wukimai, in his struggles against the Tatars and others. Then in 1135 Wukimai died. His subject Kabul Khan was summoned to the court to attend the ceremonies on the accession of the Emperor's successor, Holoma.

After the ceremonies he set off for home. Holoma, after permitting him to depart, took counsel with his advisers and came to the conclusion that the Mongols by this time were growing a little more powerful than was desirable. He sent messengers after Kabul Khan, demanding his return, but Kabul Khan thought it wiser to stay where he was, and treated the messengers with disrespect. The Chin Emperor sent an army after him. It was not large enough, and Kabul Khan defeated it.

From this time on, the Emperor sought more faithful subjects among the Tatars. And it was not long after this that Kabul Khan died; as some say, of poison. He had seven sons, but they were still young, so he nominated as his successor his father's cousin Ambakhai, the head of the Taijiut clan.

The Mongols elected their rulers, rather than condemn themselves always to have the eldest son of the late Khan to rule them, even if he should be a fool, a weakling or an infant. This was an excellent practice, as long as the number of possible claimants was not too great, and the choice of the best among them was fairly clear. It was unfortunate that Kaidu Khan had had many descendants, and because the times had been good, many of them were still living.

Ambakhai was of irreproachable birth, being a grandson of Kaidu Khan, and his clan, the Taijiut, was powerful. Kabul Khan had no doubt made the best choice of a successor that he could. But his seven sons were not happy about it, and there were many others who had reason to speculate whether the right choice had been made.

Moreover, Ambakhai soon began to have trouble with the Tatars. There is unfortunately no way of knowing whether a ruler is going to be successful or not, whatever his apparent qualifications are, until he has started to rule; and by then it is too late. It may be that any other ruler would have encountered the same trouble, given the circumstances of the time; but it was Ambakhai who was in that position, and who proved unlucky in it.

The Tatars, who lived eastward of the Mongols, were much the same sort of people, leading a similar way of life and speaking a similar language. In later years there were so many of them in the armies of Genghis Khan that some western peoples gave their name to the hordes that invaded them. But for this last fifty years or so, they had lacked effective leadership, and the Chin Emperor, when he exercised his influence in those distant regions at all, had been inclined to send them punitive expeditions rather than subsidies. When there was trouble on their western borders, such as springs up from time to time between neighbours, they had had to yield to the superior strength of the Mongols.

Now, observing that there was dissension among the Mongols, and that the Chin Emperor no longer regarded their enemies with favour, they began to reassert themselves. Kaidu or Kabul Khan would have assembled an army and fallen on the Tatars; Ambakhai Khan could not rely on the seven sons of Kabul, or the other Mongol leaders, to give him the support he needed. Casting around for some other means of warding off these incursions, he hit on the device of offering his daughter to a prince of the Tatars who lived away to the east in the region of Buir Nor,[5] the big lake beyond the bend of the Kerulen, five hundred miles or so from its source.

The Tatar prince was by no means reluctant to accept Ambakhai's daughter. A man's good name depended to a large extent on his lineage, as well as on his other attainments; and it would bring honour to his descendants, and increase their standing among their fellow-Tatars, to have a great-granddaughter of Kaidu Khan among their ancestors.

Ambakhai set off for Buir Nor with his daughter and what he considered a sufficient retinue. If he had got there, no doubt the Tatar would have received him well, and feasted his new father-in-law according to custom before sending him off home. After that he might have gathered other Tatar chiefs around him and attacked his father-in-law's dominions as he thought fit. But there is no reason to doubt that this prince was well enough disposed towards Ambakhai, for the time being.

Unfortunately other Tatars were less well disposed. Ambakhai Khan, misjudging the situation, had taken too small a retinue with him. The Juyin Tatars,[6] whose grazing grounds lay at that time westwards of Buir Nor, across the Khan's path, swooped down on his party and took him prisoner. They saw no reason to seek the advice of the Buir Nor Tatars on how to dispose of him, but sent him off immediately to the Chin Emperor, who put him shamefully to death.

Nothing is known of what happened to Ambakhai Khan's daughter. Khan's daughters were useful bargaining counters, but once they had failed to serve in this regard, as little was thought of them as of any other woman, unless she happened to be some important person's wife or mother.

Ambakhai Khan, before he died, was able to send off a couple of Mongols to the west with a message. The message ran:

'I am the Khan and the ruler of all the peoples. I was seized by the Tatars; punish them for me. Though you wear the nails of your five fingers down to the quick, avenge me. Though you wear all your ten fingers down till you have no fingers left, avenge me.'

Everybody agreed that this was an admirable message, and it went far to restore the people's opinion of the late Khan, which had appreciably declined. It was widely repeated, and even a hundred years later large numbers of Mongols could still remember it word for word, having learned it from their fathers and grandfathers. It inspired future generations of Mongols to the slaughter of innumerable Tatars and Chinese. Few Khans about to be impaled have composed such far-reaching words. But Ambakhai added to the efficacy of his message by commanding that it should be delivered to one of his own sons, whom he named, and also to Kutula, one of the seven sons of Kabul Khan.

Since the Khan had chosen these two by name, it was clear that he intended one of them to be elected as his successor. The choice was thus narrowed down to two; and nobody was likely to dispute this, since the candidates had been named in such portentous circumstances. The choice between the two was not difficult. Even the powerful Taijiut clan, in the enthusiasm of the moment, agreed that a prince of the line of Kabul Khan would be more likely to restore the unity and greatness of the Mongols than a son of Ambakhai, despite the nobility with which that prince had met his end.

KUTULA KHAN

The clans assembled on the wooded banks of the Qorqonaq, where it joins the river Onon. Without audible dissent they elected Kutula as Khan. It was readily assumed that Kutula would recreate the glories of Kabul and Kaidu. After the election there was an immense feast, with dancing. Everybody ate and drank as much as he wished. It was one of the great days of the Mongols. They danced round the leafy trees of Qorqonaq with such zest and renewed hope that, as the old men remembered years afterwards, those dancing on the beaten earth round the fires danced in dust up to their knees; and some claimed that they stamped waist-deep furrows round the trees.

The memory of the feast did not fade, but things did not turn out as well as the people had hoped. If the spirit of the Mongols was refreshed by the noble death of Ambakhai Khan, so was that of the Tatars. They came pouring down from the east, scattering the Mongol clans, slaying the people and driving off the cattle and the horses from the grazing-grounds around the ruined camps.

Kutula Khan and his five surviving brothers (the eldest, Okin Barkak, had been impaled along with Ambakhai) fought bravely against them. Defeated in battle, they reassembled the scattered tribes and fought again. They fought thirteen major battles against the Tatars; thirteen times they were defeated.[7] No reproach was ever levelled against the valour of Kutula Khan, but under him the Mongols became a ruined and powerless people. Kutula, it seemed, was the last Khan of the Mongols.

And so, in truth, he was. When Genghis Khan first became Khan, he was not Khan of all the Mongols, but only of a few of them; and by the time he became Khan of all the Mongols, he was Khan of several other peoples as well.

Under Kutula the greatness of the Mongols came to an end. Not that they were completely annihilated. This was not what happened in these steppe and forest wars. When a camp was attacked or an army defeated, the chieftains fled, such of them as survived. Such of the men as had un-wounded horses fled too. The Tatars would pursue them, and kill some of them when they caught up with them; but they had not the patience to pursue them for ever. Some of the men, too, would be able to load their women and children into wagons and drive them off, and some of these would get away in the confusion. Other people would run as far as the forest and hide in its depths till the Tatars went away.

So there were plenty of Mongols left in the country between the Onon and the Kerulen, but they were hardly a people any more. Some of the leaders, too, were left; a chieftain was expected to fight harder than the others, but, on the other hand, when it came to fleeing, he had the best horse.

One of the princes who survived these thirteen battles was one of Kutula Khan's brothers, Bartan Ba'atur. This title of Ba'atur meant that Bartan was a particularly powerful and noble warrior, a strong prince. The word was taken over

9

in later days by the people of the Indus, who called it Bahadur.[8]

Bartan, the strong prince, was the eldest surviving son of Kabul Khan. He was, therefore, older than Kutula; but Ambakhai had sent him no message, so he had not been elected Khan. This was the will of the Khan Ambakhai and the people, and Bartan Bahadur served Kutula loyally in this bad time.

His principal wife bore him four sons. Of these, the third was Yesugei, the father of Genghis Khan.

II

The Birth of Genghis Khan

Yesugei was a young man, barely more than a boy, when his uncle Kutula was elected Khan; but he was old enough to get drunk and dance round the leafy trees of Qorqonaq with the rest of them. He was old enough, too, to fight in the first of those thirteen battles against the Tatars;[9] and in the course of time he fought in them all, gaining a great reputation and the title of Bahadur, which was given to few.

But he was still quite a young man, living in the camp of Bartan Bahadur, his father, and going off with him to battle as the need arose, when the event occurred by reason of which men still remember him: namely, his fathering of Genghis Khan.

Bartan Bahadur strove to preserve the standards of his princely house, but these were bad times to bring up sons in. Apart from the danger of their being killed, the moral atmosphere surrounding them was not good. In time of war it is expected of every man to be fierce and ruthless, and kill without hesitation if he senses any danger, in case he should be killed first. A young man learns courage and swift decision, but hears little in favour of prudence and compassion. These boys were taken off on raids deep into Tatar territory, at an age when they should have been learning wisdom and the proper customs from the old men; but every hand that could pull a bowstring was needed. They rode down on Tatar camps, full of people much like themselves, and saw how, after killing or driving off the men, their kinsmen would drag the women and girls out from the tents or from the covered wagons where they had been hiding, and do whatever they liked with them. They saw their second cousins and uncles do this, men who had been telling them round the fire only the other day that they must not steal anything they saw lying around, and must treat their female cousins with respect.

So their moral standards were low. The times were exceptional. In a prolonged war moral standards suffer, and armies do these things the world over.

Yesugei and his brothers grew up bold, dangerous and poised for instant action. If they saw anything they wanted, they were inclined to think they had a right to it; they were more wilful and impulsive than their fathers or uncles had been at their age, when things were peaceful and prosperous, under Kabul Khan.

Yesugei went out hawking by himself one day, along the banks of the Onon. He must have been about twenty then: fierce, proud and highly-strung, like a noble horse. It was a pleasant scene: the young prince trotting along by the banks of the river, through a sparse wood, with his hawk on his wrist; the sunlight coming through the leaves, and the bare hill above.

Coming to the edge of the wood, he saw in the distance a single horseman coming down the hill, riding beside a single wagon, towards the river.

This was how it still was in those long-ago days, though the times were beginning to be a little uneasy, and the Tatars were growing bolder. The country was still quiet enough for this man, a foreigner from a northern tribe, to make a journey alone, several hundred miles and back again, to bring himself a wife from among the Olkunut. As it turned out, the horseman was over-confident, like Ambakhai, but this was due to an unusual combination of circumstances. Yesugei thought it as well to lurk among the trees for a time, since he had learned caution in battle against the Tatars. He watched the little group come down to the river, at a shallow place where the wagon could cross to the northern bank. He recognised that the horseman was a Merkit, one of a people living across the mountains northwards, between the Mongol lands and Lake Baikal. He was a handsome young fellow, well dressed, with particularly fine hair done with great care in the steppe fashion: two long plaits coming down on each side, by the ear, and a tuft over the forehead. He was clearly a man of good birth, though Yesugei did not know who he was; he would have known his name if he had heard it, since anybody of any education knew the names of the leading families and their members for hundreds of miles around.

HOELUN

What attracted Yesugei's attention more was the woman. He should not, by convention, have had this opportunity to look at her. She should have been sitting inside the covered wagon, while the young man drove it, with his horse tied to its tailboard by a halter. On those occasions when she had to emerge, she should have been well wrapped up, so as not to excite other men and give rise to the possibility of blood-feuds.

This is no doubt how they had started off from the Olkunut camp, in the correct fashion, after the bridal negotiations and feasts had been concluded. But they had been travelling now for several days, and Hoelun was a high-spirited girl. She saw no good reason to remain cooped up in that wagon when there was nobody in sight and the sun was shining; if somebody did come into sight, which might happen every day or two, she could always huddle back into the wagon till they had gone away again.

The young man easily concurred in this, since he preferred riding a horse to driving a wagon; and as the Merkit

13

had no quarrel at that time with the Mongols, or with the Tatars, he could expect a friendly reception everywhere. So Hoelun was permitted to emerge from the wagon and drive it. And since the day was hot, she was by no means wrapped up, but wore a kind of shift or smock, a brief and revealing thing, and very little else.[10]

Yesugei thought he had never seen such a girl. His admiration was reinforced by the hot blood of youth, but it was probably justified. Hoelun was an altogether exceptional woman. As a middle-aged and elderly woman, the great Khan's mother, she was vast and magnificent, and still wild. Genghis Khan was terrified of her till the day she died. As a young girl she was a good deal slimmer, and must have been an unusually handsome sight, driving this wagon along in her shift with her customary exuberance.

Yesugei's mind was instantly made up. He wanted this girl, whatever the consequences. This was not a light matter. A man could not take another man's woman, let alone his wife, and a girl of good birth into the bargain, without starting a great deal of trouble. Yesugei, if he did not think about this, was aware of it; it was the custom and tradition he had been brought up in. But it weighed for nothing against his wish. In this he was like his as yet unborn son, who similarly was a reasonable man enough until he really set his mind on something, when nothing in the world could stop him.

He was also like his son in another way. Many men, with their minds so made up, would have charged out of the wood and fought the young nobleman for the girl. But there was in Yesugei, as in Genghis Khan, a cold streak of calculation along with his courage. Knowing what he wanted, he did not do the first thing that came into his head, but thought first about the best way to obtain it. He did not want to fight this young nobleman; he merely wanted to kill him in order to take his woman from him. And he could kill him more effectively if he had help.

He rode back to the camp and found two of his brothers there, Neikun and Daritai. He asked for their aid, and they agreed to give it. A man was either for his brother or against him. While he was for him, he was for him in everything; if he showed doubt or hesitation, his brother might remember this later, when he in turn needed help. Neikun and Daritai instantly rode off down the river, with Yesugei.

When they came out of the wood, the wagon was just across the river, and the young nobleman, Chileidu of the Merkit, was giving a hand with the bridle to haul it out. He saw three horsemen come out of the wood, and disliked the look of the situation. They might be friendly, but they looked too purposeful. They were three to one, but if he drew them off, and they were careless and strung themselves out, he might be able to deal with them one by one. So he struck his horse on the haunch and galloped off, making away from the river, diagonally up the hillside.

Yesugei and his two brothers splashed across the shallows and galloped after him, taking no notice of Hoelun and the wagon, on the bank.

Chileidu had a very good horse. He kept ahead of them, and increased the distance; but they followed him in a tight group. Galloping up the side valley that led away from the Onon, and doubling round the back of the hill, he returned down the next valley to the riverside, and rejoined Hoelun. The three brothers were out of sight, behind the hill.

Hoelun had not expected to see him back.

'Do you know who those three men are?' she asked him.

Chileidu did not. He was not quite sure that there might not be some better way out of this situation than running away; but Hoelun had no doubt on the matter at all. 'You can tell by the look of them, they intend to kill you,' she declared.

Chileidu still hesitated.

'There are plenty of girls who can perch up on the box and drive a wagon,' she said. 'There are women in all the black wagons.[11] As long as you stay alive, there are other girls and other women. When you find one, call her Hoelun. But stay alive.'

Just at that moment, the three horsemen came round the

shoulder of the hill. Hoelun tore her shift off over her head, and held it out to Chileidu. 'You can take the smell of me with you,' she shrieked. Chileidu reached out and took the shift from her, struck his fallow horse on the haunch and galloped off, up the river.

Such was the manner in which the mother of Genghis Khan was stolen from her Merkit husband.

The three brothers galloped after Chileidu, who bore away from the river across the rolling steppe, northwards. They chased him across seven hills and across the valleys between, but they could not catch him up. Because of that swift fallow horse, a lot of trouble came later for Yesugei's son; but, as was his way, in the end he turned it to his advantage.

Yesugei and his brothers gave up the pursuit at last and rode back to the river, where they found Hoelun. She was still sitting there on the coach-box, by the river bank.

They turned the wagon round and drove it back across the river. Yesugei pulled the horse along by the bridle, while Daritai rode alongside the shafts, and Neikun went ahead to find the best way for the wagon through the woods.

Now there was someone to hear what she had to say, Hoelun began to cry out, not for herself, but for Chileidu.

'My husband, my handsome Chileidu, you never had to ride across the steppe with your tuft of hair and your tresses uncombed; you never had to camp hungry on the steppe. What will you do now, with no one to comb your beautiful hair for you, and no one to cook your food? Who will comb your hair so that one plait hangs down behind, and one in front?'

Hoelun wept for her husband, and his beautiful hair. Her lamentations were so vehement that it is said she made the waves on the Onon rise up with the sound of her voice, and the wooded valleys resound.

Yesugei bore this in patience, having got what he wanted. But Daritai had gained nothing, and saw no reason why he should put up with it. Finally he spoke to her, in a reasonable way.

'He whom you long to hold in your arms has crossed over many passes by now. He for whom you weep has ridden through many rivers. However much you call for him, he will not turn round and see you; however skilfully you search for his tracks, you will never follow the way he has gone. Be quiet, woman.'

Nobody could recall being told how much effect this speech had on Hoelun, but those most knowledgeable about women in general, and Hoelun in particular, agreed that it probably had very little.

Nevertheless, Hoelun soon resigned herself to her loss. Nobody remembers just what Yesugei's hair was like, and in this respect he probably could not come up to Chileidu, but he was a more considerable chieftain. Moreover, he was there, and Chileidu was not; and a man in the tent is worth twenty on the steppe. What is more, he did not take her as just another woman to bear him sons who might be useful, but would lack lineage; he made her his wife, which was more than she could have hoped for.

There were no trifling limitations in those days as to the number of women a man could take into his tents. Most ordinary men could only support one woman and her brood; those who could afford more often found one quite enough to cope with. A chieftain would usually have several women. These would be respected by his people, and their children properly looked after, but he had only one wife, whose sons were his heirs.[12] Genghis Khan's favourite woman was the lady Hulan, who was honoured by all for her position, and he held the ladies Yesui and Yesugen in high esteem, but his wife was Berta, and no other woman was ever his wife; nor could Hulan's children, or those of his other empresses, be considered as the true sons of Genghis Khan.

Yesugei had some sons already, but they were not his heirs.[13] They would in due course serve the chieftain like other men, according to their capacities. But so far he had no wife. The custom was that a man of good stock must seek for his wife from far away, among another tribe or people. Bartan Bahadur had not yet made any such arrangement for Yesugei, and since Hoelun was a girl of a good Olkunut family and suitable in every way, he made no objection to Yesugei's marrying her. He no doubt regarded Yesugei's way of getting hold of her as rash to the point of stupidity, but it was done, and there was no way of undoing it.

So Yesugei married Hoelun. She was a woman of strong passions, and, having wailed for her former husband all the way across the river and through the trees, she considered that the past had received its due tribute, and transferred her passions without reservation to Yesugei and the children she bore him.

She bore him five. At the time of the birth of the first, Yesugei was away, fighting the Tatars in the east. Like all those battles, this one ended with the Tatars slightly better off, and the Mongols slightly worse off, than before; but this is not to say that certain good blows were not struck for the Mongols. On the fringes of this battle Yesugei captured two Tatar princes, Temujin Uge and Khori Buka. They were bound and brought back with the army to the Mongol camps, to give some illusion of success to what everyone knew had been failure.

When Yesugei came back to the camp at Deili'un Boldak on the Onon, he found that Hoelun had given birth to a son. This son was born clutching in his fist a small lump of blood, the size of a knucklebone. It was clear from this that he had every chance of becoming a great hero, if he lived.

It was the custom for the son of a leading man to be named after some auspicious event associated with the time of his birth. The capture of the two Tatar chieftains would have been regarded as an adequately auspicious stroke of good fortune, even if it had not been the only one available at the time. So the boy was named Temujin,[14] after the chief of the two Tatars.

This boy Temujin grew up to be, in later days, Genghis Khan, the World-Conqueror.

III

The Betrothal of Temujin

There were three more sons. The next after Temujin was Kasar. He was barely two years younger than Temujin, became his principal comrade as a boy and a youth and served him well as a man. Much later in life, when they were elderly men and should have known better, there was trouble between them, and grief arose from it. It is often so in families, since as they grow older people grow more sombre and find it harder to forgive. It is also said that they grow wiser, but the evidence of this is not always easy to find.

Then there were Khaji'un and Temuga, and a daughter Temulin. Temuga, the youngest son, was called Temuga Otchigin, the hearth-prince, since the custom was for the youngest son to inherit the homeland, while the elder sons went out to seek their way in the world.

When Temujin was nine years old, Yesugei decided it was time to go and find a wife for him among the Olkunut,[15] the tribe from which Hoelun came.

All this time, things among the Mongols had been steadily deteriorating. Kutula Khan, the last Khan of the Mongols, was dead, killed in some fight with the Tatars. Nobody remembered the fight in which he was killed, or the manner of his death. There was a lot of confusion then,

19

and straggling fights here and there. It may be that in this small fight every one of the Mongols was killed, or else they were scattered, and it was not until the news went round the camps, later, that it was realised that Kutula had never come back. There were no battles any more, like those thirteen battles in which Bartan Bahadur and Yesugei had won renown. It was not possible to assemble a Mongol army to fight any more battles.

Nor could the Mongols assemble to elect a new Khan. If they had been able to assemble, they would still not have been able to agree on who the new Khan should be. They were wandering round in their separate clans by now, and since there was no strong ruler to guide them, quarrels sprang up here and there, about pasturage, or women, or just as a result of some drunken fight between two men of different clans in the same camp. There was no Khan to judge these things, and small wounds festered.

Bartan Bahadur was dead too. He died, somewhere. If Temujin had known, later it would have been told how Bartan died. But Hoelun never told him. It may be that on whatever occasion it was, she was so relieved to see Yesugei riding back that she never took in what had happened to his father, who did not ride back.

Yesugei inherited the camp from Bartan Bahadur. There were other men who might have led it, such as his cousin Prince Altan, the son of Kutula Khan; or even his own brothers, two of whom, Menggetu and Neikun, were older than he. Prince Altan was known to be a courageous warrior, as were other men, such as Targutai, chieftain of the Taijiut. But Yesugei was recognised by all to be the necessary leader in these difficult times.

There were men of many different clans in the camp, men who adhered to Yesugei Bahadur for protection. These clans were formed when some son of a noble family left his father's camp, with selected warriors and retainers that his father would grant to him, and set up his own camp, which moved about the country under his command. These men would in the course of time become a separate clan, and even if, in later generations, it was split up into separate groups, the men of each group still called themselves by the name of their clan, and obeyed the most respected member of their clan among them as their immediate chieftain.

The men of Yesugei's camp all belonged to clans which had hived off in earlier generations from the great clan called the Borjigin, which was descended from a great chieftain of ancient days called Bodonchar. Many clans had since sprung up from the Borjigin stock, such as the Noyakin, the Barulas, the Uru'ut, the Mangqut, the Taijiut, the Basut, the Qongqotan and the Ganigas. Yesugei himself was of the Kiyat clan, which was descended from the eldest sons of the Borjigin, from Bodonchar right down to Kabul Khan. But in the camp he inherited from Bartan Bahadur were men from many of these clans, including a strong body of the Taijiut, the clan to which the Khan Ambakhai had belonged.

Other clans, such as the Olkunut, Hoelun's people, had had their origin from the ancestors of the Mongols in even earlier ages. And there were other people, such as the Merkit, who had sprung up so long ago, and been so long separated, that they were now regarded as a different people. Such people as the Tatars and the Kerait must have come from the same original stock in distant days, before the time of the grey wolf and the white hind.[16] There were other steppe peoples too, the Huns of long ago, and the Turkish peoples, such as the Naimans and the Uighurs. It may be that many other peoples who were by this time living in remote lands had come from these same steppes, which bred good warriors and agile horses.[17]

BERTA

It was the custom for a chieftain to select a wife for his sons from some people far away. This kept the ruling stock strong, besides ensuring that they had useful friends and relations in many different quarters.

So Yesugei decided to look for a wife for Temujin among the Olkunut. And although the country was by no means as peaceful as it had been, he set off to visit the Olkunut with quite a small party, because he had friends and relations everywhere. The people he ruled were still powerful, though their power no longer extended over all the Mongols, and no one would lightly pick a quarrel with them.

He travelled east, down the Kerulen, and then south, since these people lived on the eastern fringes of the Gobi, far to the south of Buir Nor. He was threading his way between two mountains, called Chekcher and Chikurku, when his party came to a camp of the Onggirat. These people were related to the Mongols, and Yesugei had more recent relations among them, owing to this policy of marrying off sons and daughters in distant parts. In the camp of the Onggirat he was greeted by the chieftain, Dai Sechen.

Dai Sechen was a stately man with a proper awareness of his own worth and position. His people, whom he led, lived among these rugged mountains, not far from the land of the Chin Emperors. He had preserved his independence and self-respect, though this had necessitated careful dealings with the emissaries of the Chin Emperor. Chinese merchants came to trade with him, and he had learned to negotiate with them with a decent slowness, avoiding any appearance of haggling, but arriving at a good price by restraining his impatience and maintaining his reserve.

All this had given him a great dignity, and his manner of speech' reflected it. He spoke well, and in a considered fashion, after due thought. He had found that an effective way of adding weight to his utterances was to say everything twice.

This custom was not at all unusual. If a man had something worth saying, and considered he had said it well, and there was plenty of time, he said it again. A thing worth saying is worth saying more than once; and a man could show his mastery over his thoughts and his tongue by saying it the second time in a slightly different fashion.

Having greeted Yesugei, and given him refreshment,

Dai Sechen said: 'Where are you going, Yesugei, my kinsman?'

Yesugei replied: 'I am going to ask for a girl for my son from among the Olkunut, his maternal uncles.'

Dai Sechen reflected on this for a time, and took a good look at Temujin, who was fiercely gnawing a bone and washing it down with fermented mare's milk.

'Your son Temujin has fire in his eyes and a bright power in his face,' he commented. 'Yesugei, my kinsman: last night I had a dream. A white gerfalcon, holding the sun in one of its talons and the moon in the other, flew down and settled on my hand.

'I told my uncles and brothers about this dream, saying: "Up to this time, I have only seen the sun and moon from far away. But last night a white gerfalcon carried them down in its talons, and settled on my hand. The white gerfalcon brought them down to me!"

'Yesugei, my kinsman, was not this a good dream? It foretold to me that you would come, bringing your son by the hand. It was a sign that you would come from among your Kiyat people, bringing in your hand great fortune.'

Yesugei listened to this discourse with attention and patience. Among the Mongols of the Onon and Kerulen there had not been much spare time lately for such stately usages, but he was familiar with them, and realised that Dai Sechen would come up with some important proposition, in his own good time.

Dai Sechen, having refreshed himself, continued.

'From the earliest times, no man has dared to deny that among us, the Onggirat people, the girls are beautiful; and the sons of the girls are well-made sons. Now, we do not part with our girls for gain, selling them for profit. When some one among you becomes Khan, and asks for one of our beautiful girls, we send her to him on a fine Kasakh cart, drawn by a black camel-stallion, to sit beside the Khan on his high seat. We do not demand in exchange lands and people; we bring up these smooth-cheeked girls, and send them to you in the best of our covered wagons, drawn by a dark, high-pacing camel, to sit beside the Khan on his throne.

'So it has been from the earliest times: our women have been bound to your Khans in wedlock. This is because our women are brought up to be worthy of such high positions. They know how to speak wisely to the Khan, and intercede with him on behalf of his people.

'As our ancestresses were prized for their beauty, so are our daughters for their shapeliness. Our sons are sought in marriage for their manly bearing, our daughters for their beauty.

'Yesugei, my kinsman, we will go into my tent. My daughter is still quite small. Come and look at her.'

So saying, he rose. Yesugei rose too, and went with him into the tent, where he was seated in a place of honour.

Dai Sechen's daughter was brought to him. She was ten, one year older than Temujin; and her name was Berta.

Berta was beautiful, though in later years Genghis Khan came to prefer the lady Hulan. Berta had a great deal of natural dignity, like her father, and it is an excellent quality, but a man can have too much of it as a daily diet.

Yesugei liked the brightness of her eyes and the nobility of her small face.[18] He took to her at once, and abandoned his projected journey to the Olkunut immediately. Naturally he did not say he had abandoned it. With a man like Dai Sechen, it was better to do things at his own pace. He praised the girl, and went outside to drink some more mare's milk; and allowed Dai Sechen to press him into staying the night.

In the morning, he asked Dai Sechen for the hand of his daughter, for Temujin.

Dai Sechen could not accede to such a request without making his position clear, twice if need be. He said:

'If a man, on giving away his daughter, asks a lot for her, he is doing himself too much honour. If he asks only a little, he is despised. But this is the fate of a girl: she does not grow old in the tent in which she was born. Her fate is to be given to a man, not to grow old sitting at the door. I shall ask for nothing: I shall give you my daughter. When you ride away, leave your son here, to be my son-in-law.'

They agreed on this easily, because they both gained from it. Dai Sechen, for all his fine words about giving his daughter away for nothing, made an excellent bargain. He could have asked for cattle or servants, but he had enough of both, and they could not be of much help to him if he was in trouble. What he did get was an alliance with a man who was the leader of the most powerful group currently operating among the Mongols, and a son-in-law who looked strong both in temperament and in physique. Either could be the saving of him if he came up against more trouble than he could cope with from the Chin Emperor, the Tatars or anyone else.

Yesugei was also pleased, because not only was his son provided with a wife of great promise, but also he could leave him behind here in this relatively safe corner, in the care of a cunning old chieftain who knew how to look after himself and his people.

This was also the custom: a boy who had been betrothed was often left with his future in-laws, to be brought up by them until it was time for him to marry and come back to the clan.

They held a betrothal feast. After it, Yesugei prepared for his departure. He selected a good spare horse from his train and gave it to Dai Sechen as a betrothal gift. Also he cast around in his mind for some word that would help to make his son's stay at Dai Sechen's camp more comfortable. He remembered that a short time before, as it seemed to him, Hoelun had mentioned to him some trouble about dogs. There are a lot of dogs roaming loosely about a Mongol camp, and sometimes they knock small children over, out of curiosity and a sense of fun. They are not savage; they are working dogs, used for herding, and highly intelligent, of all kinds of mixed breeds.[19]

'Dai Sechen, my kinsman,' he said in an anxious, fatherly way, 'my son Temujin is afraid of dogs. Do not let him be frightened by the dogs.'

This is often how it is with parents, for whom time goes so quickly that they do not bear in mind that what is true when a boy is three, and no bigger than most dogs, is no longer true when he is nine. So they suddenly come out with the belief that one of their children dislikes mutton, because six years ago they used to have trouble with him about it; whereas in fact for the last five years the boy has eaten it eagerly.

This odd remark, which was repeated with some amusement in Dai Sechen's camp, and so was remembered years later, when these matters were written down, is the only evidence available that Genghis Khan was afraid of dogs. He was afraid of one or two things, notably his mother Hoelun, and to a lesser extent his wife Berta, but it is doubtful whether after the age of three he was ever afraid of dogs.

THE DEATH OF YESUGEI

Yesugei Bahadur rode away, and his homeward journey was less fortunate. On the yellow steppe north of the mountain Chekcher he came across some Tatars gathered round a fire, feasting.

'Yesugei, the Kiyat,[20] is come,' they muttered to each other, round the fire. Yesugei did not know who the Tatars were, but they knew who he was. He and his people had ruled over them in recent years, and it is one of the basic truths of human society, and a great handicap to good government throughout the ages, that the ruled know the rulers, but the rulers do not know the ruled.

They invited Yesugei to join their feast. Yesugei was not eager to join them, but in view of their greater numbers it would be unwise to seem discourteous. So he joined them round the fire, and the Tatars, bearing in mind that Yesugei and his father Bartan Bahadur had pillaged their camp in former days, slipped something into his drink that would serve as a revenge. There were plenty of shamans among all the steppe peoples in those days, wizards knowledgeable in the ways of natural and supernatural powers, who combined an unwholesome interest in religion with a devout study of poisons.

Yesugei, riding onwards, began to feel ill, and travelled with increased haste, riding day and night.[21] Arrived at his camp, he took to his bed. He was by then so ill that he could hardly see. He peered round at the women standing in distress round his bed, and said: 'I have a bad sickness inside me. Who is that standing by the tent door?'

'Munglik the Qongqotadai,' they told him.[22]

Yesugei told them to bring Munglik in.

'Munglik, my boy,' he said, 'I have children, small children. I gave one of them, Temujin, to be a son-in-law.' He collected his thoughts with an effort. 'On my way home the Tatars poisoned me. I have this bad sickness inside me. My small children, my widow and my brothers, my sisters-in-law . . . I am worried about them, leaving them behind. I am sure you understand this.'

Munglik assured Yesugei that he understood how things were. He was a simple man who regarded his chieftain, Yesugei Bahadur, with awe; and he was full of grief to see him in this condition. But he gathered what the chieftain was driving at.

'Go quickly, Munglik, my boy, and bring my son, Temujin. Go quickly, Munglik.'

Munglik rushed from the tent, saddled his horse, stuffed some cooked meat and a skin of mare's milk into his saddlebag, and rode off. Before he left the camp, Yesugei was dead.

Munglik rode across the steppe and through the mountains to Dai Sechen's camp. He was a thoughtful man; in much later days he saved the life of Genghis Khan through this capacity he had for brooding on things, and observing caution in his actions. It seemed to him that it might be best not to reveal to Dai Sechen that Yesugei was dead. Alive, Yesugei stood at his back; dead, he could not influence Dai Sechen from a long way off.

He said to Dai Sechen: 'Your kinsman, Yesugei, greets

you. He is sick at heart. He yearns for his son, Temujin. I have come to bring Temujin home.'

Dai Sechen was taken aback. Such a request was unusual, when Temujin had been formally confided to his care. But, as Munglik had worked out for himself during that long ride across the steppes, he did not want to go against the wishes of so powerful a chieftain, believing him to be still alive.

He said: 'If my kinsman is yearning for his son, let Temujin go to him. But when he has seen his father, let him be brought back again swiftly.'

To anyone as humble as Munglik, Dai Sechen did not make the effort to say anything twice.

Munglik, the thoughtful man, rode back with Temujin to Yesugei's tents.

This was the way in which Temujin came back to what might have been his inheritance, if he had been a few years older and able to prove his fitness to inherit it. He came back as a boy with no power, among the powerful chiefs. As one of the possible successors they had every reason to regard him with suspicion.

If Dai Sechen had known that Yesugei was dead, it is doubtful whether he would have let Temujin go. By keeping him, he would at least have had a son-in-law; as it was, he had a betrothed daughter, who could not be betrothed to anyone else without causing bad feeling, as long as Temujin lived. And Temujin was far away, powerless, and in a precarious position. Dai Sechen, when he heard the news that Munglik had not told him, must have considered that the betrothal had turned out a very bad bargain.

IV

The Outcasts

After Yesugei died, there was no leader who could hold the camp together. Just as the Mongols could find no Khan on whom all the people could agree, so even this one camp who had followed Bartan and Yesugei could not agree on anyone else to follow.

The strongest chieftain among them was Targutai, the Taijiut. His clansmen obeyed him, but the men of the other clans in the camp had their own leaders. These might follow Targutai while it suited them, but they did not regard him as their true chief, or allow him to rule over all matters concerning their own people. So the camp was badly governed. In the absence of a strong leader, all kinds of unseemly disputes sprang up; the men of different clans quarrelled, the women bickered, and no one could keep the peace.

For a time Hoelun was treated with respect, as the widow of the late chieftain. But there were other distinguished widows in the camp, such as a couple of haughty ladies called Orbai and Sokhatai, who were the widows of Ambakhai Khan. Like other women, they were pernickety about their social position and precedence, particularly since their claims were shaky. They were not of much use to anyone now, but long ago they had been wives of the Khan of all the Mongols, and they considered their standing greatly superior to that of a woman who had merely been married to a small chieftain.

They were devoted to religious practices. It is proper enough for any man to pay his respects to the gods, when the occasion demands it, and to honour his ancestors. But these women were not so much concerned with the gods as with the details of the ritual, and with bolstering up their own importance. Instead of accepting their true status and making themselves useful, busying themselves among the children and the sick and old people, they fussed about with the gods, who had more important matters to attend to, and made trouble.

One morning, this spring, they let it be known among the other noble women in the camp that they were going to make a big sacrifice to the ancestors, in the place set aside for that purpose.[23] But they made sure that Hoelun was not included in the arrangements. Either they managed to keep the affair dark from her entirely, which seems improbable among such babblers, or they merely told her that the sacrifice was at noon instead of at dawn. No man in his senses would bother his head with the details of such an affair, and no man did.

However it may be, all these women, Orbai and Sokhatai and the women of Targutai and the other chieftains, went off and made this great sacrifice, leaving Hoelun behind. It seems that if the ancestors depended on the sacrifice to keep them going, wherever they were, they must often have gone hungry, since the food offered to them was then eaten by those who had offered it. A lot of this eating and drinking goes along with religions of all kinds; and the various gods are supposed to set great store by it, though they are otherwise credited with some measure of intelligence.

However, even among the Mongols, or at least among the women, meat and mare's milk were solemnly offered to the ancestors and then taken away again and eaten by the worshippers. And while these distinguished ladies were stuffing down the offerings, Hoelun came along, having at last heard rumours of what was happening. She was a sensible woman, but she, too, was concerned about her social position, and up to this time it had been the custom for her to be in charge of these arrangements, first as the wife of the ruling chieftain, and then as his widow.

So she came storming along, to this place on the steppe where they had set up the shrines of the hungry ancestors, and found them finishing the feast. And she gave tongue, being adept at it.

'I see that Yesugei Bahadur is indeed dead. My sons are small; are you not afraid that one day they will grow up? What kind of behaviour is this, that you set me aside, when you are eating the sacrificial meats, the cakes in the shape of whetstones, and the holy drink? You know that this is the last sacrifice, before we move on to the summer pastures. What do you mean by holding this feast without waking me to take part in it?'

Orbai and Sokhatai, sitting among their friends, had no hesitation in speaking their minds.

'You are one of those who do not need to be invited to the sacrifice,' Orbai said. 'You are one of those who may be offered a share in the sacrifice, if they happen to come along. That is the rule.'

She would have said this twice, but Sokhatai, sitting by her, repeated it for her, and added: 'Anyone can tell that the Khan Ambakhai is indeed dead, when a person like you can come and speak to us in this fashion.'

This is what they said, squinting and leering up at Hoelun. And Hoelun, seeing that there was nothing to be gained by remaining there, was about to retire, furious but helpless, when Orbai, out of a natural inclination to have the last word, spoke again.

'What's more,' she called after Hoelun, 'if it suits us to move off to the summer pastures, leaving you behind, women and children, and anyone else we care to leave behind, we shall move off, and not take you with us.'

This was not so brief a quarrel, but to repeat the whole of it would be boring as well as unedifying. Anyone who knows the ways of women will realise that the shouting match went on on the steppe for quite a long time, before Hoelun went back to her tents. But this was the essence of it, and all that men cared to remember.

Hoelun, after a little reflection, spent the rest of the day in sounding the feelings of her people about this new development. About half of them took a realistic attitude. They were not enthusiastic about Targutai and his Taijiuts, but he was the best leader they had for the time being, and offered them some protection. It was best for people to stick together in this big camp, until something better turned up. The other half were more inclined to be faithful to the memory of Yesugei, and stand by his widow, having some hope that the sons of Yesugei might turn out to be capable chieftains, if they lived long enough. But this was a big gamble to take, and even these idealists maintained that they would do better to trail along behind Targutai, giving him no allegiance but co-operating when they had to, rather than go off on their own as a small, weak camp with a woman as its leader.

Hoelun fell in with their plan, since it was the best she could do. In the morning, without including her in their arrangements, the Taijiut set off up the Onon, in the usual long line, with the men riding ahead as advance guard, protecting the flanks and bringing up the rear. Half of Hoelun's people joined up with the main body, making it clear to Targutai that they regarded themselves as supporters of his party. The faithful half who adhered to Hoelun milled around their tents, some of them claiming that they ought to pack up and follow the Taijiut, and others uncertain whether to go off with them or stay where they were.

In all this confusion, an old man called Charakha was arguing that some way could surely be found of persuading Targutai to adjust matters with Hoelun to the satisfaction of them both, since Targutai was a Mongol and so, by definition, a reasonable man. Charakha was a Qongqotadai, and the father of Munglik, that thoughtful man who had gone off at Yesugei's request to bring Temujin back from

32

the camp of Dai Sechen. Though there was little support for his belief, he went off on his own, on his old horse, and trotted forward, past the slow-moving cortège, until he came up with Targutai, riding at its head. Targutai took little notice of him, but Charakha rode along by the side of Targutai and his men, appealing to the chieftain's better nature, and saying how if he would only stop for a time while everybody got together and talked things over, some happier solution might be found.

Targutai would not even speak to him, but one of his attendant chieftains and kinsmen, Todo'an Girta, became bored with this old man badgering them, and put the matter clearly and succinctly to him.

'The deep water is dried up,' he said. 'The bright stone is broken.' Yesugei was dead: what was the use of going on about his widow and children?

Charakha did not take this for an answer, but went on talking across at Targutai from the flank of the little party. Todo'an Girta, as the most effective way of silencing him, raised his spear and drove it into the old man's back. Charakha fell from his horse, and the party moved on.

A few of the Qongqotadai who had followed after Charakha to see how things went spurred up to him, lifted him up and set him on his horse again. They led him back to the tents, where he was hauled off his horse and laid on a bed. Somebody went off to tell Hoelun what had happened. It was a man's matter. The head of the household, Temujin, who was ten, went to see Charakha.

Charakha was lying on his bed, dying. He said to Temujin: 'All the people, all the people whom your good father led, were gathered together, going off to the summer pasture. I tried to hold them back. Look how they treated me.'

Temujin, weeping, ran back to his tent. His mother, Hoelun, took up the banner of his father Yesugei, and went out of the tent. Mounting her horse, and grasping the banner of Yesugei, she commanded that her people should follow her to summer pasture. They broke camp and followed her up the valley of the Onon, towards the high summer pastures. But in the following days, many of those who were with her left and moved on with their women and cattle to join the Taijiut, making such arrangements as they could with them to preserve something of their independence and self-respect.

The old man, Charakha the Qongqotadai, died, and his son Munglik, the thoughtful man, went to join Targutai. Many years later Munglik came back to join Genghis Khan, and served him well. Genghis Khan accepted his service, and bore him no resentment; too much cannot be expected of most men, and loyalty has its limits.

Before long Hoelun had no people left, except her immediate household. There were her sons Temujin and Kasar, and her two other sons and her daughter, but these last three were still very young. There were one or two other widows, of Yesugei's men, and their infants; and two boys who were half-brothers of Temujin. These two, Bektair and Belgutai, were Yesugei's sons by some other woman, before he met Hoelun; they had no kinsmen, and Hoelun had brought them up with her own sons. The mother was part of her retinue. Then there were a few servants, who were not much good for anything, except perhaps the old woman Khoakchin, who was at least shrewd and energetic. Any serving man who was capable and loyal would sooner or later be granted weapons, but Hoelun had none who were fitted for it.

THE SMALL CAMP ON THE ONON

When the last of Hoelun's people abandoned her to follow Targutai, they took their own beasts, and left her with only Yesugei's personal flocks and herds. These were small enough for so large a brood; in normal times his followers would contribute to the chieftain's household from their own herds, and he had no need for great flocks of his own. Targutai could have taken away what little they had with no great effort; but killing Hoelun and her sons would

be a great matter, calling for revenge from Yesugei's kinsmen, and to leave them alone on the steppe without any
sheep or goats, and with no horses, would be tantamount
to killing them. As it was, they had so little to support them,
and were so short of people capable of tending the animals
and guarding them against human and other predators, that
they could be abandoned in the confident expectation that
they would all die of their own accord without too much
delay.

Hoelun, however, was a woman of resource. She crammed
her cap[24] on her head, tucked up her skirts into her belt,
and dashed up and down the Onon the whole of that
summer, gathering what food she could find and bringing
it back to the camp, so that the gullets of her sons and all
the others should have something to work on. She gathered
burnet and other plants that would make a kind of salad,
and, using a trowel of juniper wood, since they had no iron
to spare for such a purpose, dug up the roots of sedges and
rushes along the river, and wild onions, and brought them
back to the tents, where the old woman Khoakchin made
what she could of them, over the fire. Later on in the season
she gathered wild apples and cherries, juniper berries, hazel
nuts and the edible fruit of the pine that flourishes in those
regions.

In this way the noble lady Hoelun nourished and kept
alive her sons, who were destined to become the great ones
of the earth.

In the winter they killed off some of their small flock,
and others died, so that they had even fewer. One or two
of the women and children died too. The blizzards howled
over the steppes, the Onon was frozen over, and they
huddled in their squat tents, hard put to it to find enough
wood and dried dung for the fires.

When the spring came, Temujin and his brothers were
hungry, but they were gaining in strength. They applied
themselves with new seriousness to the task of keeping
alive; in the previous year they had made some haphazard
attempts, but they were very young, and accustomed to the

aid of their clansmen. Now they asked their mother for some needles, which were a rare treasure. They bent these into fishhooks, and sat on the banks of the Onon, fishing. They caught a few small fish, which went into the pot along with the wild onions and sedge-roots. As they grew in skill, they occasionally caught a sizable grayling, but it did not happen often. Hoelun showed them how to make a net; and with this, such as it was, they caught a few more fish, those that had not the energy or the wit to avoid it.

They set traps, and by and large caught very little.

Kasar was in later life a superb archer, famed beyond other men for his range and accuracy in shooting. Necessity nourished this gift. At this time, when he was only nine, his skill was not great, but he was improving. He succeeded in shooting a few voles and other small steppe-mice. These successes encouraged him, and his aim grew more confident. One day, as he was wandering across the steppe with his bow and arrow, he saw a lark descending from the sky and wildly loosed an arrow at it, since he was by now in the habit of shooting at anything that moved. By chance he hit it. As he ran up to it, and took out the arrow that transfixed it, Bektair and Belgutai, his half-brothers, came up. They were both bigger than Kasar; they were also bigger than Temujin, being older, though since they were not the sons of Yesugei's wife, Hoelun, they had little rank or position.[25]

There was not much meat on this lark, but there was more than Bektair and Belgutai had seen since the last time one of the animals was killed, in the spring. Since then they had lived on roots and wild leeks, with a few small fish, and a vole or two, lost in the big pot. They took the lark away from Kasar, pulled the feathers off it and ate it, before it could go into the common stock.

Kasar went off and told Temujin about this, and they both complained to Hoelun. Hoelun scolded Bektair and Belgutai, but she did not take the matter very seriously. A lark was not much to lose, and she had a lot on her mind, with the necessity of keeping her small camp alive. She had to do the major part of the food-gathering and keep some sort of order in the tents; besides this, she was trying all the time to teach Temujin and his brothers as much as she could of Mongol law and custom, the history of their ancestors, and correct ways of behaviour, so that they would grow up to be worthy chieftains, as she did not doubt for a moment that they would. She did not perhaps realise to what extent they were growing up like wild men, always hungry and hardly in control of themselves.

A few days later, those four, Temujin, Kasar, Bektair and Belgutai, were sitting on the banks of the Onon, fishing. They quarrelled often, but, as is the way with children, their quarrels were soon forgotten. By misfortune, they caught an unusually splendid fish, a golden *sokhusun*, a kind of trout. The temptation was too much for Bektair and Belgutai, who fought the other two for the fish, and, being bigger and stronger than they were, took it away from them. They went off to some distant corner of the steppe to eat it in peace.

Temujin and Kasar, rubbing their bruises, went to complain to Hoelun. They were in a furious temper, and their sense of natural justice was outraged.

Temujin burst into the tent, saying: 'A golden fish that took the hook has been stolen from us by Bektair and Belgutai.'

Hoelun was in a bad temper too, and had no time for these childish dissensions.

'Enough of all that,' she said. 'What do you mean by it, you four brothers, going on at each other in this way? You are old enough now to know how things are with us. We have no friends but our shadows, no whips but the tails of our horses. You ought to be thinking all the time how we can avenge ourselves on the Taijiut. Instead of that you quarrel among yourselves like Alangoa's five sons. Get out of here and leave me in peace.'

Alangoa was a beautiful Mongol queen of long ago who had five sons. One of them was the great chieftain Bodonchar, ancestor of the Borjigin. When these five were always quarrelling, she took a bundle of sticks tied together,

37

and tried to break them. Then she separated them . . . Similar stories, proving to men that when united they stand, but when divided they fall, are to be found among many nations, so there is no need to tell it again here. Hoelun had been telling her sons this story lately, and it is indeed edifying, though widespread.

Temujin and Kasar went out muttering to each other, not at all tranquillised by the legend of Alangoa and her five sons.

'Only a few days ago they took that lark from me,' Kasar said.

'And now they take the fish,' Temujin replied. 'How can we go on living together, if they behave like this?'

THE MURDER OF BEKTAIR

Temujin was conscious, at the age of eleven, of being a chieftain. There are times when a chieftain can overlook small infringements of his authority without endangering it, and times when he must act to preserve it: Temujin judged that this was one of the times when he had to act. His judgment was perhaps not quite mature. A year living wild on the steppe, in perpetual hunger, in the care of a woman, however powerful of personality, is not the best way of instilling discipline into boys. The memory of Genghis Khan is properly to be revered, but it is true that at this period, in the point of self-restraint, he stood about on a level with the average wolverine.

He and Kasar picked up their bows and went out on to the steppe. In the distance they saw Bektair on a hillock, keeping watch over nine mares and a silver-grey gelding. Somebody among the women had found him wandering on the steppe, replete with fish, and told him to sit there doing something useful.

Kasar, obeying Temujin's instructions, stayed where he was while Temujin crept round to the other side of the hill. Then they came forward, the two of them, drawing out their arrows and fitting the nock on to the strings.

Bektair saw Kasar coming towards him and got up to run away, but when he turned round he saw Temujin coming up from the rear. Bektair, if he was frightened, did not show it; he, too, was Yesugei's son. He laughed at Temujin and called out to him: 'Is this how you revenge yourselves on the Taijiut?' Temujin, as the chieftain, was always telling them how they must devote their thoughts to this revenge.

Temujin made no answer, but kept on coming nearer.

Bektair called out: 'What do you think I am? Do you mean to treat me like an eyelash in your eye, or a fishbone stuck in your throat?'

But Temujin kept on coming nearer.

'Ought you to be doing this,' Bektair said, 'when we have no friends but our shadows, no whips but the tails of our horses?'

As he could see that Temujin was not open to reason, Bektair sat down, crossing his legs, with his arms folded.

'Don't wipe out all my family,' he said to Temujin. 'Don't do any harm to Belgutai.'

Temujin was now quite near, twenty or thirty yards away. He raised his bow with its nocked arrow and shot Bektair in the chest. As Bektair toppled forward, Kasar shot him in the back. So he had a swift and merciful end, and when Temujin and Kasar went up and pulled the arrows out of him he was already dead.

Then they went back to Hoelun's tent. Hoelun, as soon as she saw their faces, knew what they had done, without asking.

'Murderers!' she shrieked, leaping at them. They stood there with bowed heads, and she ranted and raved at them, but she did not hit them, they were too old for it. 'You, born with a black bloodclot in your hand! You, Kasar, like a *qasar* dog that snaps at its own afterbirth! What kind of animals are you, that came out of this hot womb of mine? Panthers that cannot hold back their anger? Snakes that swallow a beast alive? Eagles that stoop on their own shadows? Sly jackals that creep on their prey in silence? Camels in rut that savage their own mates? Wildfowl that eat their own brood? At such a time, when we hardly know how to live, when we have no friends, no means of defending ourselves, cannot you even live with each other?'[26]

Collecting herself, she made them sit down, and lectured to them sternly. She told them old legends, concerning unnecessary violence and the sorrow that came from it, and she quoted the words of wise old men. Temujin and Kasar listened obediently.

It might be said that this first and early murder committed by Genghis Khan proves him to have been a wholly savage and ferocious person, and it is certainly difficult to approve of it. Even among the Mongols, for a boy of eleven to murder his half-brother was, to say the least of it, unusual. Men killed each other for self-preservation, or out of a desire for power or wealth, or in a fit of sheer bad temper, but small boys rarely killed each other for a fish.

It is true, though, that after this regrettable incident there was peace in Hoelun's camp, and no one challenged Temujin's authority from then on. Perhaps his unusual instinct for ensuring that people would obey him was already developed at that early age. Bektair and Belgutai, both bigger and stronger than he was, were a constant threat to him. With Bektair out of the way, his position was secure, over these few people. Belgutai alone could give him little trouble, whatever feelings of resentment he might have.

As it turned out, from then on Belgutai was a useful and co-operative member of the clan. Quite possibly he had never liked Bektair much, but allowed himself to be persuaded into making trouble because it seemed even more troublesome, and somehow unmanly, to stand up against him. Such half-unwilling acquiescence in mischief is common enough. He mourned his proud and bad-tempered brother in the correct fashion, and buried him on the steppe with the proper rites and observances, but it may be that he was secretly as glad to get rid of him as Temujin was.

V

Temujin in Captivity

The hard life went on for Hoelun's small camp. Somehow they survived the next winter; the summer came, and the nuts and berries, and then they survived another winter, most of them. Hoelun's children grew up lean and hard and hungry. It is one way to make a strong ruler: to take a boy of suitable character and send him out on to the steppe to fend for himself for a few years. But he will be a hard ruler, and people who want an easier time of it should bring up their princes more gently.

They avoided meeting people as much as they could, and many people avoided them, thinking it unwise to be friends with them. But now and then somebody would pass by. So it was known among the other clans that in some uncanny fashion this undesirable relic of Yesugei's rule had remained alive.

The news was unwelcome to Targutai Kiriltuq, the Taijiut chieftain. Someone came to him in the spring, in the Year of the Tiger, 1182, after three or four hard winters had gone by, and told him how he had seen this little camp, and a capable-looking youth who could be no one else but Temujin.

Temujin was tall and broad, and at fourteen he was a

man. He had cat's eyes, and a fierce face, full of authority.[27]

Targutai held a council.

'The evil brood is fledged,' he told the assembled chiefs. 'The serpents have sloughed their skins.'

It was not easy to decide what to do. Temujin had many kinsmen. Nobody would have minded if Hoelun and her sons had died in the wilderness, but killing them was a dangerous business, calling for retribution. It was agreed that Temujin must be captured, but not killed.

There were men in Targutai's camp, even among the Taijiut, who had been faithful followers of Yesugei, as Targutai had been. Now they followed Targutai, but they still remembered their old loyalties. One of them slipped off and warned Hoelun. Temujin and his people struck camp and rode off into the wooded mountains, south of the Onon, with their loaded wagons, driving their flocks before them. It was no great matter to move camp in this way, in a country where often a man would take his women and children and all his beasts and goods into battle with him, rather than leave them unprotected. But they could not, hampered like this, travel as fast as Targutai's punitive expedition, a band of warriors on horseback.

They found a place deep in the forest, backed by rocky cliffs. Belgutai hacked down saplings and small trees and built a palisade or abattis, with the branches pointing outwards, in a semicircle in front of the cliffs. They found hiding-places for the small children in crevices among the boulders. When Targutai and his men rode up through the woods, they found this stockade confronting them. It was a difficult place to attack, if a skilful archer was concealed behind it; and rumours had circulated on the steppe concerning Kasar's marksmanship.

The place could be taken by rolling boulders down the cliffs, from above, but then somebody would be killed, and this they wished to avoid. They sent a man forward to speak to them. From a reasonably safe distance he shouted: 'Send us out the elder brother, Temujin. We have no need of the others.'

Temujin and his people took no notice of this. The Taijiut settled down to keep watch. Inside the stockade, they discussed the situation. They could not go out to forage, or to bring in meat or milk the mares; in a few days they would be starved out. Moreover, the Taijiut might lose patience and decide to kill them. A few arrows or boulders from the cliffs would soon finish them off.

Temujin, who was accustomed by now to having the final word on such matters, said that the only way of avoiding this was for him to escape alone. The Taijiut, finding he was gone, might keep their word and spare the others. After nightfall, he saddled one of the horses inside the stockade and mounted. Belgutai pulled away some of the saplings from the stockade, and Temujin rode quietly out.

Some of the Taijiut had crept closer to the stockade in the darkness. They saw Temujin go, and ran forward, shouting, to catch him; but Temujin kicked his horse forward and galloped off, crashing through the woods. The Taijiut scrambled for their horses in the darkness and rode after him.

Temujin could not hope to outride these men, with the small lead he had. He rode across the rough mountainside, where sometimes the trees were quite sparse, and sometimes in clumps, growing closely together, until he saw what looked like a dense thicket, with one opening leading into it. He dismounted and led his horse into this opening, and crouched there, in the heart of the thicket.

The Taijiut had seen him go in, but they did not like to follow him. This was a place where he could kill several men before they laid hands on him, and it was a thankless death. They rode round the thicket, but there was no way of telling where Temujin was hiding and where his arrows might come from. They spaced themselves out round the thicket and settled down to keep watch.

Temujin stayed in that thicket for three days, and the Taijiut lay round it, watching. On the third night he thought he would try to slip away; but as he led his horse towards the one way out, the saddle fell off. Temujin was superstitious, and by now he was a little light-headed. He said to himself: 'How did that happen? The saddle might slip round with the girth still fixed; but with the girth still fastened, and the breast strap into the bargain, it could not possibly fall off. This must be a sign from Heaven that I am meant to stay here.' He went back again to his hiding-place.

Some nights later he was making his way out again when he saw a boulder across the entrance that he was sure had not been there before. He took this as another sign from Heaven that he was intended to stay in the thicket. At last, after more days and nights had gone hungrily by, he said to himself in desperation: 'Am I to die without a name?'

He led his horse to the entrance, cutting down a sapling or two that stood in his way, because he was convinced that the boulder sent by Heaven was blocking the exit; and he was feebly trying to mount his horse when the Taijiut, who had been eating as much as they pleased all this time, came forward and seized him. He was too dizzy with hunger to put up a fight.

In later life Genghis Khan always swore that he had been in that thicket for nine days and nine nights, and nobody liked to contradict him. But it is possible that he lost count. No evidence could be obtained from the Taijiut, because the men concerned had all been dead for a long time, leaving no descendants.

Having captured Temujin, they let the others go. Even at this time it was only Temujin that they were afraid of. Kasar was also a son of Yesugei, and skilled with the bow, but he was just one more potential chieftain among others. Temujin was more than this. Men had to follow him or fear him, and already when he was only fourteen they could see this.

Hoelun, with Kasar and Belgutai, and the other youths and children, and the surviving widows and servants, set off south and west, into the mountainous country nearer the sources of the Onon and Kerulen, where the living was harder but they might have securer refuge, further away from Targutai's people.

The Taijiut took Temujin to their camp, and here they fixed on him a wooden collar. The Chinese used this device, which they called a k'ang, to keep their prisoners under control. The hands were fastened to the collar, and the prisoner wearing it could not lie down to sleep, so that although he might harbour rebellious thoughts he was too uncomfortable to act on them.

The Taijiut did not know what they intended to do with Temujin in the long run. He might meet with some accident; or in the course of time he might grow so weak that disease or illness would carry him off. For the time being, it was enough to have him in captivity and under constant surveillance.

But Targutai was still nervous about Temujin. He did not want him to be always in the care of the same group of people in case he should talk them over to his side, arousing old loyalties which were best forgotten. He commanded that Temujin should spend one night only in each group of tents, in the charge of the chief of that group, and then be taken over by another group. The camps were always organised in this way, each man belonging to an *ail*, or fellowship, living in a group of tents with a recognised leader who was responsible for this group to the higher chieftain.

So Temujin was passed from tent to tent. Sometimes his temporary host would be reserved but friendly, and sometimes openly hostile, according to his clan and his personal feelings. One relatively pleasant night he spent in the tent of Sorkhan Shira of the Suldus clan, a dependent clan of the Taijiut. Sorkhan Shira had no quarrel with Targutai, but he was a humane man who had good memories of Yesugei Bahadur and considered that some ways of dealing with potential rivals were more admissible than others. He treated Temujin well, as far as the rules allowed. His sons, Chimbai and Chila'un, took a warm liking for the young prisoner. In the night, when Sorkhan Shira was asleep, they

45

crept up to Temujin and unfastened his collar so that he could get a good night's sleep. In the morning they quietly fastened it on again, before Temujin was taken off to the next group of tents.

Temujin passed some weeks in considerable discomfort and anxiety, seeing no obvious way out of his predicament, but watching out for one.

TEMUJIN ESCAPES

The spring went by, and the first moon of summer came up over the steppe, a thin moon, fattening every day, until on the sixteenth day it was at the full. This day, the sixteenth day of the first moon of summer, was called the Day of the Red Disc; it was one of the major feasts of the year among the Mongols. Towards the end of the day, all the Taijiut and the other people of Targutai's camp gathered on the banks of the Onon to eat and drink.

The chief of the group in charge of Temujin that day did not want to miss the feast. He and his men took Temujin with them down to the river bank, leading him by a strong cord fastened to his collar, like a pack-horse. As the feasting went on, any man who had charge of Temujin passed him on to someone to whom he could give orders. So Temujin was passed from man to man, always going on to some less important person, until finally he found himself anchored to a weak, thin youth who was so inconsiderable that he had no authority over anybody.

This young man remained on the fringe of the feast, as befitted his humble station, but near his own people. Temujin sat there and watched the feasting, taking no part in it. The sun grew a deeper red, and sank towards the steppe; and at last, when everybody was considerably drunk, it sank below it, leaving a red patch in the sky, and darkness elsewhere except for a white patch in the east, where the moon was about to rise. The chieftains and leading men arose, laughing and shouting incoherent talk at each other, and staggered off across the steppe towards their tents.

46

The young man who had Temujin on his lead respectfully allowed the others of his group to go ahead. All at once there seemed to be hardly anybody about. Temujin jerked away from the young man, snatching the cord from his grasp. As the young man blundered forward, stooping to clutch at the cord again, Temujin threw himself forward, so that the k'ang struck his keeper on the skull. The young man collapsed on to the steppe. Temujin ran off, along the bank of the river. There were still a few stragglers about, and although it was dark and they were moving away from the bank, Temujin judged that they must have seen him. When the news of his escape reached them, they must remember having seen a shadowy figure running upstream, however drunk they were. In any case, he had no horse, and could not hope to escape across the steppe.

He came to the edge of the woods, and after making his way through the trees along the bank for a time found a small, deep inlet, well shaded by undergrowth. The moon was rising, and its rays were beginning to light up the wood. Temujin clambered down to the inlet and lay down on his back, with only his face showing above the water, under an overhanging bush. His collar floated; he had to force his head back to keep it from lifting out of the water. The cord trailed away in the current, floating on the surface; he got his fingers to it, and gradually wound it in.

Back in the camp, the young man, having been temporarily stunned, sat up rubbing his head, and raised his voice weakly.

'The prisoner has escaped!'

Nobody heard him, and he made his way up to the tents, repeating his faint cry. Someone listened to him at last, and confusion arose. Men seized their weapons and rushed unsteadily out of the tents, some thinking there was a Tatar raid, others hardly thinking at all, but prepared to defend themselves. The flight of Temujin was at last established. Someone thought he had seen a man running along the bank. The moonlight seemed as bright as day. The re-assembled clansmen went along to the woods, spreading out in a line leading inland from the river.

Sorkhan Shira of the Suldus clan took up his station on the extreme right of the line, and went along the river bank, beating the bushes and peering here and there, like everyone else. Looking over the edge of a small inlet, as he moved round it, he saw Temujin's face in the water, watching him expressionlessly from under an overhanging bush.

He looked round and saw that the next man was a little way ahead, inland from the head of the inlet, having gone past it. He leaned over and spoke in a soft voice to Temujin.

'Your kinsmen, the Taijiut, are a little jealous of you. They say you have fire in your eyes and power in your face. I see you are also a man of resource. Stay where you are; I shall not say anything.'

He went on, and caught up with the line of searching men. They ransacked this wood, and came out beyond it on to the steppe, where a few men were pacing up and down on horses. There was a gap here along the bank, where no trees grew, and it seemed unlikely that Temujin could have got across here before the horsemen reached it. They decided to go back and search the wood again.

Sorkhan Shira spoke to Targutai. 'I suggest that every man should go back by the way he came. Since he has been over that ground already, he will be more likely to look out for any places he has missed the first time.'

Sorkhan Shira was respected by all for his sound judgment, and they agreed that on this occasion his advice was, as usual, excellent. They went back through the wood in the same positions, Sorkhan Shira on the extreme left of the line, by the river bank. As he approached the inlet, carefully beating every bush and peering about him, he went ahead a little.

Leaning over the edge of the inlet as he moved round it, he spoke softly to Temujin's upturned face.

'Your kinsmen are coming along, gnashing their teeth. Stay where you are, and be careful.'

He moved on, and the next man inland, seeing that Sorkhan Shira had searched this inlet thoroughly, walked past it without a glance.

48

They came out of the wood, back near the camp, all very tired and bad-tempered. There was some argument about whether they ought to go back and look again. Sorkhan Shira spoke up, respectfully tendering his advice.

'Princes of the Taijiut: we could not find this man when the moon made the night as bright as day. Now the moon is sinking. How can we hope to find him in the darkness? I suggest that we wait until it is daylight before searching again. A man in a k'ang cannot run very far, and if he does, the men watching round the wood will catch him.'

Nobody had had any sleep, on top of all the drink, and they had been beating about in the wood half the night. They thought Sorkhan Shira's advice even better than before. But Targutai, who was more personally concerned, and had his authority as a chieftain to think of, commanded that they should search once again.

They went once more through the wood and back again, but they had little heart left for it. Sorkhan Shira managed to get down to the inlet when nobody was too near, and spoke to Temujin again.

'They have decided to have this last look and then go to bed. They will look again in the morning. Wait until we have all dispersed. Then get away and find your mother and brothers, if you can. If anybody catches you, don't tell them I saw you here.'

After he had gone, Temujin waited until the wood was quiet, thinking things over. He did not believe he had the slightest chance of getting away across the steppe to join his people, with no horse and no food, and wearing a k'ang. He remembered the friendly attitude of Sorkhan Shira; and the sympathy of his sons, who had taken his k'ang off during the night. Now Sorkhan Shira had found where he was, and passed by without giving him away. It seemed to him that these people might save him, when he had no hope of saving himself.

He climbed out of the inlet and went back to the camp, along the river bank. There were no guards about in the camp; the men appointed by Targutai to watch out for him were all pacing about the farther steppe, on their horses.

He was not quite sure where Sorkhan Shira's tents were, having stayed in so many. Behind one group of tents he heard the sound of churning. When he stayed there, in Sorkhan's tent, the servants, having skimmed off the cream, had worked at the churn through the night, till the day whitened. It was dark now; the moon had sunk behind the hills. He made for that group of tents, going round about a little, so that he would not pass too close to the churns. Here there was a tent he knew. He stopped and went in, pushing aside the door curtain.

Sorkhan, waking at once, saw the shadowy figure in the doorway, misshapen by the unnatural hump that the k'ang made round its neck, and knew it for Temujin.

'What did you come here for?' he said softly. 'I told you to go and look for your own people.'

Temujin was silent. So was Sorkhan's family, sitting up and holding its breath. This was sudden disaster for them; the stranger coming into their tent brought death for them all, within a few minutes, if he had been seen.

In the darkness Sorkhan's son Chila'un spoke.

'When a bird, escaping from its cage, flies into the bush, the bush gives it shelter,' he said. He and his brother Chimbai went up to Temujin and untied his k'ang. They put it on the dying fire in the middle of the tent. Chila'un knelt down and blew the cinders into life. As the flames licked up round the dry wood of the k'ang, Sorkhan Shira looked round the tent. The others in there were all grown women, except for his small daughter Khada'an.

'Do not tell any living person that you have seen this man,' he warned her. He took Temujin out to a cart that stood behind the tent, not far from the churns. It was full of wool. He gestured at it silently. Temujin climbed up into the cart and buried himself under the wool at the farther end, away from the opening.

Sorkhan Shira went back to bed. Within an hour or two, when the day lightened, he got up again. He and his sons went silently out to join the Taijiut in the search for Temujin.

They ransacked the woods around the camp for three days. At the end of that time Targutai was convinced of what he had suspected all the time; someone in the camp was concealing Temujin. He ordered that all the tents in the camp should be searched, each group searching the tents of another group.

The men of another clan came into Sorkhan Shira's tent and rummaged around, even looking under the beds. They went outside and looked into the carts; one of them was full of wool. Two of the men climbed into it, and started pulling the wool out, throwing it through the rear opening on to the ground. Sorkhan Shira stood below watching them.

In this first month of summer the nights were cool; they were glad of a fire in the tent in the evenings. But the days were hot; the sun burned down on Sorkhan Shira as he stood watching the men throwing the wool out of his cart.

'You think a man could lie under all that wool for three days, in this weather?' he called up at them.

The two men looked at each other and laughed. They were sweating like pigs there, in the hot black inside of the cart, and they had cleared all the wool out of it except the pile against the far wall. They climbed down out of the cart and went on to ransack the rest of Sorkhan Shira's tents.

That night Sorkhan Shira's women cooked over the fire in the tent a fat lamb that had been suckled by two ewes. They filled a large goatskin and a leather bottle with fermented mare's milk. Sorkhan Shira went out soon after dark and brought Temujin in.

'You nearly had us all scattered to the winds like ashes,' he remarked. 'Now go off and find your mother and brothers.'

Chila'un brought to the tent door a straw-yellow mare with a white mouth.[28] They gave Temujin no saddle; and also no flint and tinder, because Sorkhan Shira thought he would be tempted to light a fire in the cool evening, and give himself away. But they gave him a bow and two arrows, so that he could hunt some game for himself if the meat they had given him was insufficient. Then he rode quietly off. The men who had been guarding the steppe had given it up after this last day's search. Temujin had simply disappeared. Perhaps he had gone up to Heaven along a moonbeam, like the lover of the beautiful queen Alangoa, in the old legend; perhaps he had tried to swim the river and drowned, though it seemed too much to hope for.

Sorkhan Shira and his sons continued to serve Targutai for some years; but they came over to Genghis Khan at what Sorkhan judged to be the right moment: not too soon, and almost too late, but not quite. He was granted lands and people along the Selenga, and the two extraordinary privileges of paying no taxes and sharing the emperor's cup. His son Chimbai rose to command a thousand men in the Khan's army; Chila'un became one of those Four Coursers, the great generals whom Genghis Khan sent on missions of unusual difficulty or importance.[29] He was then known as Chila'un Bahadur, the strong prince.

Temujin got clear of Targutai's camp and rode upstream, back to the place they had defended under the cliffs. From there he followed the trail of Hoelun's people, by the trodden marks in the grass, as far as the place where the river Kimurkha flowed into the Onon from the west. The trail led up this valley; and high up it, under the hill called Khorchukhui, he found his people.

VI

The First Companion

This was a good place for Hoelun and her family, well up into the hills, several days' ride from Targutai's summer pastures on the Onon, and even farther from any ground he was likely to settle on for the winter. But it was too near Targutai now that Temujin had rejoined them. They broke camp and moved up into the mountains, farther west. There is a great tumbled sea of mountains here, stretching for a hundred and fifty miles in every direction. The three great rivers of these parts all rise there, the Onon, the Kerulen and the Tula. The Onon and Kerulen run down to the east. The Tula runs at first westward, through the Kerait country; then it turns north and flows down to Lake Baikal, joining on the way the Orkhon and the Selenga, which rise five hundred miles farther west, in the nearer ranges of the Altai.

One of the broader heights of the range called Guralgu[30] is a vast mountain seamed on its flanks with precipitous ravines, and with many lesser heads and ridges and outlying spurs. This is Burkhan Khaldun.

They fixed their camp below this mountain, on the banks of the river Sanggur, by a small mountain lake which they called Koko Nor, because it was a greenish blue in colour;

53

there is a big lake which has been given the same name, for the same reason, a thousand miles away to the south at the west end of the Wall, on the way to Tibet.

Here in the black heart of the mountains they could live in comparative security, but they did not live very well. It was a harsh and rugged land. Things were worse than they had been in the old days on the Onon, because there were no wild onions or apples or cherries, though there were juniper-berries and the pine-fruit. The young men were all grown stronger now, and used to this sort of life. They trapped and shot what game they could find, namely, marmots and steppe rats; and these, along with fish, were what they lived on. They had to keep some of the meat they took, dried, for the winter, because there was not going to be much killing of cattle and other beasts this winter. There were not so many left, for all Hoelun's care, and they had to be preserved, so that they would breed and increase.[31]

As for horses, these were even fewer in number. They had exactly nine left.

THE HORSE-THIEVES

However secure the place might seem, it was not secure enough. The news of Temujin's escape and return to the camp was heard on the steppes.

A small band of people, a few days' ride away, decided to steal Temujin's horses. There is no evidence to connect this with Targutai. They may well have conceived the idea for themselves. But if they decided to steal some horses from other people, why did they decide on these horses, so few and far away? And how was it they were not in fear of punishment? A horse was a man's most valuable possession; without it he could not live. Men who stole horses, if it was not in times of war, were regarded as enemies by all men. It is possible to imagine that these people received certain messages from Targutai, leading them to understand that, whereas horse-stealing was never desirable, in certain circumstances it might be condoned. But there is no proof of it.[32]

However this may be, these men rode off, and came one morning over the hill, from where they could see the camp on the Sanggur. There were eight horses grazing in a group by the tents; few people were in sight, and none of them was mounted. The men rode straight down on the camp and drove off the horses. Before Temujin or Kasar could snatch up their bows, the raiders were making off over the hill. The brothers ran after them and loosed one or two arrows, but the raiders were out of range.

The stolen horses included the silver-grey gelding over which Bektair had been keeping watch when they shot him, and the white-mouthed yellow horse that Sorkhan Shira had given to Temujin. All the horses they had were gone except one, a brown with very little hair on its tail. Belgutai had gone off on this horse in the early morning, to hunt marmots. He did not come back until it was nearly sunset; then they saw him coming over the hill, on foot, leading the brown behind him, piled high with marmots.

They went to meet him, and told him that horse-thieves had stolen the rest of the herd.

'I'd better go after them,' Belgutai said.

'You're not capable of it,' Kasar said. 'I'll go after them.'

Temujin said: 'Neither of you is capable of it. I shall go after them myself.'

They took the load of marmots off the brown; Temujin mounted and rode off, following the trail of the stolen horses.

He followed the trail across the mountains and down to the high steppe, riding all day and sleeping wherever he was when darkness came, shivering through the cool night until it was light enough to pick up the spoor again. On the fourth morning, as he was riding across the rolling steppe, he came to a high plain where a large herd of horses was grazing. Some distance away across the plain he could see one man, milking a mare. Temujin left the spoor of his own horses and rode across the plain to him. He stood up as Temujin approached. He was an alert-looking youth, about Temujin's age. Temujin asked if he had seen any men go by, driving some horses, including a silver-grey gelding.

'This morning, before sunrise,' the young man answered, 'some men went by, over there, driving eight horses, a silver-grey gelding among them. I'll show you which way they went.'

He made Temujin dismount from the bald-tailed brown and gave him a fresh horse, a grey with a black stripe down its back. His own riding-horse, a dun, was tethered near by. Before mounting, he picked up the leather bucket he had been using for milk. It was half full of milk. He threw it down again so that the milk ran out across the steppe, and mounted.

'It seems to me, my friend,' he said, 'you have quite a problem here. Well, a man's problems are pretty much the same everywhere. I'll come along with you. My father is called Nakhu Bayan. I am his only son. My name is Bo'orchu.'[33]

This was a remarkable thing about Genghis Khan in those days, that men would follow him right off, hardly taking thought about it. Chila'un, Sorkhan's son, was in a way the first; but he knew who Temujin was, the son of Yesugei Bahadur, the great Kiyat chieftain. Bo'orchu had no idea who the stranger was; he was a young fellow who rode out of the west one morning, asking about some horses. Whereupon Bo'orchu immediately rode off with him. The young Temujin must have had something about him beyond a lust for power not stopping short of fratricide.

The horse-thieves not only had a day's start, they were travelling fast. Temujin and Bo'orchu followed the trail all day without catching them up, and slept on the steppe when it got too dark to see the spoor. They went on the next day, and the day after that. The following day, when the sun was going down behind them, and their shadows were stretching long and thin before them across the steppe, they saw far ahead, in the luminous evening, a camp of people, with a fenced enclosure. They went on slowly, to give the horses a little breathing-space, and as they drew nearer they could see the group of eight horses outside the enclosure, the silver-grey gelding among them. There was no one about; the men were all relaxing round the fires at sundown.

'There they are,' Temujin said. 'You stay here, my friend. I'll go forward and drive them off.'

Bo'orchu said: 'What do you think I came all this way with you for?'

They kicked their horses forward and rode up to the camp. Riding between Temujin's eight horses and the enclosure, they cut them out of the herd and drove them off westwards, towards the red sky. There were shouts behind them and two or three men came riding out of the camp, with half a dozen more following.

As they rode on, the pursuers gained on them a little; but they also became strung out in a long line. It was growing dark. Turning round, they could see that the man in front had a pole in his hand with a lasso on the end of it. The Mongols were skilled at lassoing, using this device for catching their horses; they used a lasso which had the noosed rope attached to the end of a pole, for greater force in throwing.

It would be a grave inconvenience if either of these two, Temujin or Bo'orchu, or his horse, was caught by the lasso, with all these men following.

'Pass me the bow and arrows, my friend,' Bo'orchu said. 'I'll have a shot at him.' He had no weapons himself, having been peacefully milking his mares on the steppe when he suddenly set out on this expedition.

'You could get into bad trouble because of me,' Temujin observed. 'I'll shoot at him myself.'[34]

He wheeled his horse round, and waited until the man was well within range. He was waving his pole in a circle, about to discharge his lasso. Temujin loosed his arrow, wheeled round immediately, and galloped on, without staying to see whether the man had been hit. Looking round over their shoulders, they could see that the man had reined in his horse and was still sitting there in the saddle, waving his pole about, as if he was unsuccessfully striving to point

57

it at them. The other horsemen came up with him, and gathered round him in a group. None of them left the group to follow them farther, as far as they could see. The sun had set now and it was twilight, growing rapidly dark.

They had no need to follow a spoor now, knowing their way. They rode hard all that night; and they did not stop at all, except for brief halts to graze the horses, until they came back to the high plain where Temujin had met Bo'orchu.

Temujin said: 'Without your help, friend, I should never have got my horses back. We must share them out. How many of them would you like to have?'

Bo'orchu thought about this offer for a time, and replied: 'When you came here, I could see you were in trouble, so I came along to help, as a friend. Am I now supposed to claim part of your property? My father, Nakhu Bayan, is a rich man; I am his only son. Everything he has will come to me, and it is quite enough. I will take nothing. What sort of service would it be if I took payment for it?'

They rode down to Nakhu Bayan's tents. The old man was sitting there in tears, weeping for the loss of his only son. When Temujin and Bo'orchu rode up, he jumped up in surprise and started scolding Bo'orchu, weeping at the same time.

Bo'orchu took this very calmly. 'I'll tell you how it was,' he said. 'This good friend of mine came along, in great difficulties. I thought I should go along with him, so I went. Now I've come back.'

Saying no more, he galloped off into the steppe to collect the milk-bucket he had left there. Nakhu Bayan soon calmed down, realising that he ought to be giving Temujin a hospitable welcome, instead of wearying him with his family affairs. He had a fat lamb killed and roasted, so that Temujin would have something to take along for provisions. He was a good man, more given to worrying about Bo'orchu and his independent ways than Bo'orchu thought necessary. Bo'orchu was often more independent than he need be, in order to keep his father's interference within bounds. They were typical specimens of a well-off man, rather old, who has a single son, and an only son of a rich, rather old man. Bo'orchu was impulsive, swift of decision and careless of danger; in later years he was, like Chila'un Bahadur, one of those famous Four Coursers of Genghis Khan.

By the time Bo'orchu came back from the steppe with the bucket, Nakhu Bayan had reconciled himself to the behaviour of his son.

'You two young fellows obviously took a liking to each other,' he observed. 'Since that's how it is, stand by it. Don't either of you ever do anything against the other.'

They gave Temujin his provisions, tied a big skin of mare's milk to his saddle, and sent him off. Temujin rode up into the mountains, and after several days' journey came down into the valley of the Sanggur. Hoelun, Kasar and the others had been deeply anxious, hardly hoping to see him again. His return was the occasion for rejoicing, though there was little to feast on except marmots.

THE SABLE CLOAK

It was not long after this that Temujin decided that something essential was missing from his life. He had borne in mind all these years that he had been betrothed to Berta, the daughter of Dai Sechen, since he was nine. He took Belgutai with him and set off down the Kerulen, to the country of the Onggirats.

Dai Sechen was uncommonly glad to see him.

'I heard that your kinsmen, the Taijiut, had set themselves up against you,' he said. 'I was sad for you: I was almost in despair. I hardly hoped to see you again.'

He brought Berta to Temujin. She was in every way fitted to be the wife of a Mongol chieftain. They held a wedding feast, as custom demanded, but it was brief; Temujin did not want to be away from his camp any longer . than was necessary. They stayed there only one night; the following day, they set off again on the return journey. Dai Sechen accompanied them, with his wife Chotan; but he, too, did not want to be too much away from home in these troubled times. At a bend in the Kerulen he took his leave of them and rode back to his camp, leaving Chotan to escort her daughter to her new home.

She brought with her various presents for the bride and groom, and for Hoelun a splendid cloak of sable.

In the camp on the Sanggur bare necessities were scarce enough; luxury was wholly absent. This cloak was by far the most valuable object in the family's possession. Even for Dai Sechen, whose standard of living was considerably higher, since his trade with the Chinese had brought him some wealth in material things, it was a magnificent gift. A great chieftain, when he gives gifts, should not be close-fisted. Dai Sechen was not in everyone's estimation a great chieftain, but it was all the more a point of pride with him that he should act like one.

Temujin reflected on this matter and discussed it with Hoelun. She, being the woman she was, fell in with his suggestion readily. Temujin, being the head of the family, and the owner by custom of everything it possessed, could have demanded the cloak from her, but his respect for her made this impossible. Fortunately she gave it willingly.

What he needed most was friends. There was no doubt in Hoelun's mind, any more than in Temujin's, that they needed friends more than sable cloaks. He would use this cloak to obtain what he needed. But first he had to see to his camp; as things were, he could not go on a properly attended mission to a neighbouring chieftain without leaving the camp virtually unattended.

As soon as Berta's mother, Chotan, had left, he sent Belgutai off across the mountains to ask Bo'orchu to come to him. His message was brief. It was: 'Let us be bound in blood-brotherhood.'

In former times, so it is said, a man could trust his own family. Brothers were faithful to brothers, and their sons supported them. The case for the virtue of the ancients may be exaggerated. However this may be, it is certain that in more recent times the clans that were kin to each other had taken to quarrelling and fighting among themselves. So, for instance, the Taijiut had quarrelled with their cousins, the line of Kabul Khan. Besides this, some clans were so much reduced in numbers that they had not enough trustworthy warriors to defend themselves. In these more recent generations it had become the custom for a man to increase his strength, and that of his clan, by swearing blood-brotherhood with a man he trusted. This man became his own brother, as much as if he had been born of the same people, and worshipped his new brother's ancestors as if they were his own.

There were other ways in which a clan could make up for the insufficiency or lack of faith of its own kin. A whole clan, knowing itself to be too weak for its own proper defence, might submit to the chieftain of a strong group, even if they were of a different clan. The chief of the small clan would then serve the greater chief just as if he were his own father or uncle. This is how Sorkhan Shira, a Suldus, came to be serving Targutai of the Taijiuts.

So the old idea of a clan as one family, with its chieftain as its head and its fighting-men all related to him, was changing. The leader of a clan would now have serving under him men who were not at all related to him; and if he conquered another people he might pick one of these men of his to rule over it and its land on his behalf, though the man was not of his own blood, trusting in the oath he had taken.[35]

Bo'orchu, when Belgutai brought the message to him, knew at once that he wished to become Temujin's *anda*, his sworn brother. He did not say a word to his father Nakhu Bayan. He saddled his horse, a brown with an arched back, rolled up his grey felt cloak and tied it to the saddle, collected his weapons, mounted and rode off with Belgutai across the mountains. At the camp on the Sanggur he became the sworn *anda* of Temujin.

Before this, there had been three capable men at the camp, Temujin, Kasar and Belgutai. Now there were four. It was a beginning, though a small one.

The camp on the Sanggur had proved insecure. Temujin struck camp and moved up the Kerulen to its farthermost sources, to camp on the banks of one of its tributaries, the Burgi. Behind them still loomed the immense massif of Burkhan Khaldun.

Here they were at the extreme limits of the Mongol lands. Westwards lay the land of the Keraits;[36] it was there that Temujin intended to go in search of his ally. He packed up the sable cloak and, leaving Bo'orchu in charge of the camp, rode off with Kasar and Belgutai across the mountains westwards to the headwaters of the Tula, to visit Toghrul, the Khan of the Keraits.

VII

The First Ally

This Toghrul was better known in later times as Ong Khan, or, as the Chinese called it, Wang Khan, meaning the prince Khan; but at this time he had still not won these titles. His people were like the Mongols in many ways, but in others different. Some of them were Moslems; and others, stranger still, were Nestorian Christians, having been taught that religion by missionaries from the West who had penetrated to these parts.[37] Toghrul himself was said to be a Christian, though no one ever accused him of an excessive piety. Because of this Christianity of his, he won a wide and lasting fame of a singularly illusory kind.

Twenty or thirty years before this time, a Khan of the Kara Kitay,[38] a powerful people living west of the Gobi, had defeated an army of the Seljuk Sultan, in the remote west. Even farther west, beyond the known confines of the earth at that time, some Christian warriors were fighting for the recovery of certain holy places of theirs that had fallen into Moslem hands in the country called Palestine. The victory of the Kara Kitay relieved the pressure of the Moslems on these Christian warriors for a time.

It so happened that although the Kara Kitayans were mostly Moslems, and their rulers were Buddhists, there were many Nestorian Christians in their army. This gave rise to the notion among the Christian warriors of the west that somewhere in the remote east there was a great Christian king, previously unheard of, who would come riding to their rescue and save their holy places for them.

Now there was no such king, and no such Christian kingdom. But there was Toghrul the Kerait; and later, when the conquests of the Mongols had caused the names of the leading men of this region to be more widely known than before, Toghrul's name became identified with that of this mythical king, whom the Christians called Prester John.[39]

Toghrul had as much claim to be called Prester John as anyone else, but he knew nothing of the troubles of his fellow-Christians in the Holy Land, and could have done nothing to help them if he had. He had troubles enough of his own at home, from his own relations, besides having the Naimans and Uighurs on one side of him and the Mongols and Tatars on the other.

He had inherited his power over his Kerait people from his father, Khurchakhus; but he was unfortunate in having innumerable brothers and uncles, and this gave him a sense of insecurity. As a boy of seven he was captured by the Merkit, and had a hard life with them until his father Khurchakhus rescued him. When he was thirteen he was captured again, by the Tatars, along with his mother; this time he got away by the exercise of his own wit, persuading some shepherds to liberate him. As a result of these early experiences he suffered all his life from a lack of self-confidence, and this made him an incorrigible waverer. He was decisive one moment and hesitant the next; from being bold and direct he would turn suddenly cowardly and sly; his cruelties and treacheries were succeeded by periods of futile and unprofitable remorse.

Inheriting the rulership of his people from his father, he concluded that the best way of ensuring that he lived long enough to enjoy it was to reduce the number of his relations. He did away with one or two of his uncles, and had plans for his brothers; but the brother who was next on the list fled, and another uncle, seeing that there was no future in being an uncle of Toghrul's, gathered his men together and came up the Tula to overthrow his nephew.

Toghrul escaped with a hundred men and fled down the Selenga. His uncle chased him into the gorges of the Black Mountains; Toghrul got away over the watershed. This was in the Merkit country, of which Toghrul had unhappy memories; but he obtained the co-operation of the Merkit chieftain, Tokhto'a, by promising him his daughter. Crossing the mountains into the land of the Mongols, he turned for aid to the only person available, Yesugei Bahadur, Temujin's father.

Yesugei, like anyone else, needed allies. He promised Toghrul aid, but the first necessity was for the Kerait to become his blood-brother, his *anda*. This would at least ensure that Toghrul had a clear duty towards him, and an undependable ally is sometimes better than no ally at all. They declared themselves *anda* with due solemnity. Yesugei gathered together an army, mostly of Taijiut people, and chased Toghrul's uncle across the desert till he took refuge in the land of Qashin,[40] the Tangut country, in the bend of the Hwang Ho, the Yellow river, where he was too far away to do any harm.

Yesugei Bahadur then escorted Toghrul to the west and across the mountains to the headwaters of the Tula, where he brought Toghrul's surviving uncles and brothers under control. They were not happy under Toghrul, but it was clear that when he had such a powerful friend they would have to put up with him. The brother, Erke, however, Black Erke, who had been next on Toghrul's list, did not come to submit to him, but fled to the west and took refuge with the Khan of the Naiman.

After this, Toghrul's Kerait people settled down to be ruled by him, since there was no alternative. By the time

Temujin came to visit him he had been reckoned a powerful ruler for many years, but his sense of insecurity was still strong. He was glad to welcome this small party of Mongols who came to pay him homage, particularly since their leader was the son of his old *anda*, Yesugei.

Temujin found Toghrul in his camp in the black forest on the Tula.[41] Having been hospitably received by him and given refreshment, he addressed him formally, with every mark of respect.

'In former days,' Temujin said, 'you were the sworn *anda* of my father, Yesugei Bahadur. It is proper, therefore, that I should look on you as my own father. In these recent days a wife was brought to me, and with her she brought a gift. It would have been right that I should give this gift to my father; therefore I have, as a dutiful son, brought it to you.'

With this he presented to Toghrul the sable cloak that Chotan had brought as a gift to Hoelun.

Toghrul was, as Temujin had foreseen, delighted. From the reports he had heard—and everybody knew something of what was happening on the steppe, for a thousand miles in every direction—Temujin's power was insignificant, and his wealth non-existent, but this was the gift of a great chieftain. It might be that the reports were inaccurate. In any case, the smallest of vassals was better than none, and a princely gift was the mark of a generous character, even if the coffers it came from were otherwise empty.

He was moved to eloquence.

'In return for this gift, I will reunite your scattered people; in return for this black sable cloak, I will bring back to you your straying kinsmen. This thought will remain in the depths of my loins; I shall cherish it in the pit of my stomach.'

For the moment this was sufficient. The time was not ripe for Temujin to ask Toghrul to bring his thought out of the pit of his stomach and act on it; some further inducement had to be offered. He rode back with Kasar and Belgutai to the camp on the Burgi.

They were not alone here in the wilderness, though it was sparsely peopled. Here and there in the remote valleys there were little groups of *yurts*, of felt tents, the dwellings of humble people, with a few sheep or goats and little else. They did not think of themselves as warriors, these small herdsmen, though they could fight if they had to, like any other Mongol; they had nothing to boast of in their lineage. They owned so little, they had no need of a protector. There was no question yet of their regarding Temujin as their chieftain, since he had no power to protect them, and if they were his men they would need protection.

There were also some wandering men who had no home. An old man of the Uriangqadai[42]–distant relations of the Mongols, like the Onggirat—came down to Temujin's camp one morning with his young son Jelmei. The old man was a smith; he wandered, as smiths did, from camp to camp, with his bellows on his back, forging the swords and the axeheads, beating the iron into knives and needles, and making iron stirrups for those few chieftains rich enough to use them.

Temujin and one or two others who were at the *yurt* gathered round to greet him. Visitors were rare, and there was often news to be heard from them. The old man had no news; he had brought something else. They had forgotten him, but he had met them before.

'Long ago,' he said to Hoelun, 'when you were at the hill of Deili'un, on the Onon, when Temujin was born, I was there also. I gave you some swaddling clothes of sable for him. I gave you, too, Temujin, my son Jelmei; but he was too small then for you to take with you. Now I bring him again. Let him saddle your horse; let him open your door.'

This Jelmei was much the same age as Temujin, having been a tiny infant when Temujin was born. He came to saddle Temujin's horse and open his door, since that was as far as the old smith's imagination could see him doing for a chieftain of the line of Kabul Khan. But this was a lucky time for the sons of old wandering blacksmiths, if they came along at the right time and were able men. This boy Jelmei became one of the Four Hounds of Genghis Khan, those fearful warriors who brought death and terror to the Khan's enemies.[43] His own brother Subetai was another of them, but Subetai was a young boy at this time, lurking silently in the background: Subetai Bahadur, the greatest general of them all. It seems that it cannot be so difficult to be a good general, when so many of the men who first came to Genghis Khan succeeded so well at it. It is certainly very easy to be a bad general. Something else must be involved, the men, the training, or the guiding spirit and idea. When one army annihilates another, it is hard to imagine that all the fools are on one side and all the wise men on the other.

Now there were five capable men in the tents. But they still had only nine horses; Bo'orchu had ridden in on a tenth, but one had died. And one of the nine was fit for very little, though it might still serve as a packhorse.

THE MERKIT RAID

The news of everything that happened on the steppe was carried across the steppe, far beyond the lands of the Mongols. Even in the land of the Merkits, far down the Orkhon towards Lake Baikal, news was heard of the little camp on the Burgi. Temujin's exploit in recovering his horses from the robbers may have been spoken of widely, since this was the kind of story all men liked to listen to; or his embassy to Toghrul may have drawn wider attention to him.

A leading chieftain of the Merkit, Tokhto'a, was particularly interested to hear that Temujin, the son of Yesugei Bahadur, was encamped on the distant flanks of Burkhan Khaldun, and was acquiring a certain reputation. Tokhto'a, of the Uduyit Merkit, was the chieftain to whom Toghrul the Kerait had given his daughter, when he was fleeing through the Merkit country from his uncle; and he was also the elder brother of that Chileidu from whom, many years ago, Yesugei had stolen his new bride, Hoelun.

Tokhto'a was not an exceptionally vengeful man, but his nearest family had suffered an outrageous insult from Yesugei, and it was his clear duty to avenge it, over fifteen years later, provided it was convenient to do so. Temujin was virtually defenceless, and any relation of his who might feel aggrieved by his death was a long way from the Merkit country.

Tokhto'a called for assistance from his kinsmen, the chieftains of the two other great divisions of the Merkit people, Dair Usun of the Uwas and Khaghatai Darmala of the Khaghat. They collected together a body of warriors from these three Merkit clans, and set off for Burkhan Khaldun.

They reached the Burgi one evening, after several days' journey, and rode up it by night. Tokhto'a was not restrained by any of those inhibitions that had hampered Targutai; he firmly intended to wipe out Temujin and all his family.

The old woman, Khoakchin, slept lightly, particularly towards dawn, as is the way of old people. The murmur of distant hooves, a long way down the valley, came to her ears as she lay in Hoelun's tent. She was awake instantly, and leaped up from her bed.

'Mother, Mother, get up quickly,' she cried, shaking Hoelun. 'The earth is trembling; it is like thunder. It must be the terrible Taijiut who are coming. Get up, Mother.'

'Wake the children,' Hoelun said, scrambling out of bed.

They ran among the tents, rousing everybody. Temujin and the others ran from the tents, straight to their tethered horses. There were only those nine horses, one of them unfit for riding. There was no doubt in anybody's mind who had to use them. As Hoelun had not protested, years before, when Chileidu rode off and left her, Berta did not protest now. A man could soon find a wife somewhere else, but it took a long time to make a man.

Hoelun mounted, taking with her on the saddle her

69

daughter Temulin, who was not yet ten. Temujin, Kasar, Belgutai, Bo'orchu and Jelmei each had a horse; so did Temujin's younger brothers, Khaji'un and Temuga. They rode off into the hills, leading the other horse by hand, and leaving behind Berta, and Belgutai's mother, and the other women and children.

Khoakchin hurried Berta to an ox-cart to which she rapidly harnessed an ox with speckled flanks. She made Berta climb into the black covered wagon and began to drive it off, up the Tunggelik, the stream that ran down into the Burgi at this place. It was early dawn; a greyish-yellow light lay over the hills. She was hidden here, in the side valley, from the main body of horsemen who were galloping up to the tents; but as she came round a bend in the valley a troop of warriors appeared before her, having cut across the hill to approach the camp from this side. They hardly glanced at the old crone and her ox-wagon as they rode by, but one of them looked back over his shoulder, turned and trotted back again. Two or three of the others followed him.

'Who are you?' the first man asked her.

'I belong to Temujin. I was at the main *yurt* to give a hand with the shearing. Now I am on my way home, to my own *yurt*.'

'Is Temujin at the *yurt*? How far away is it?'

'Just round the bend,' Khoakchin answered. 'But whether Temujin is there or not, I don't know. I harnessed up behind the tents.'

The troop rode off down the valley. Khoakchin, who had so far proceeded slowly in order not to arouse suspicion, waited until they were out of sight, and whipped up the ox to its fastest pace. They had hardly gone a few yards when one of the wheels became lodged against a boulder. The axle broke, and the wagon settled down on its side.

Khoakchin went and spoke to Berta, who was still huddled inside. The best thing they could do, she thought, was to make their way on foot to the nearest patch of forest, and hide there.

70

Before Berta had begun to climb out, the troop of warriors came into sight again, downstream. Tokhto'a had sent them back up the Tunggelik with orders to round up this woman, since she was one of Temujin's people. The leading warrior ordered Khoakchin to climb up in front of him; she sat there with her legs dangling down, one on each side.

'What's in the wagon?' he asked her.

'Wool,' Khoakchin said.

'Get off and take a look inside,' the Merkit told two of his younger kinsmen.

They pulled back the door-cover and saw a young woman sitting inside. They ordered her out, made her mount in front of one of them, and rode back to the camp.

A few of the Merkit were still there, guarding the women and children. The rest had already ridden off in the direction of Burkhan Khaldun, following the tracks of the nine horses, in pursuit of Temujin.

There were several score of them. There was nothing Temujin and his party could do but ride, and escape if they could. They rode up into the recesses of the great massif, climbed over one of its spurs and rode down into the forest in the next valley, doing what they could to hide their traces. After gaining as much distance as they could, they began to ride here and there, leaving false trails to confuse their pursuers. They rode through tangled forest and tumbled rocks in the valley bottom, and up the stream, so as to leave no tracks. The Merkit, casting up and down the stream, found the marks of their hooves in the quagmires by the banks, and took up the trail. The fugitives climbed the farther spur, through the forest, and, crossing the ridge, rode along the verge of precipices until they could pick their way down rock-strewn slopes into the next wooded cleft.

In this way they toiled round the great massif, sheltering at night when and where they could, hungry and exhausted always. High up among its innermost peaks and ravines, they clambered up and down the savage terrain, now making straight ahead across open stretches, now doubling here and there when there was some concealment in the deep valleys and on the shattered mountainsides.

The men of the three Merkit clans at last grew weary of it. In this wild country a small band of fugitives might hide for ever, unless they were unlucky or badly led. The Merkit, exhausted after days and nights of the hunt, rode out of Burkhan Khaldun, down to the camp on the Burgi.

They said to each other: 'We have taken their women, in revenge for Hoelun. It is sufficient vengeance.'

They rode off down the Burgi, taking the women and children of Temujin's camp with them, and travelled back to their own country.

From some crevice in the rocks, high up on a spur, Temujin and his party watched the Merkit withdrawing from Burkhan Khaldun. They might be intending to ambush the Mongols as they descended; Belgutai, Bo'orchu and Jelmei were sent down from the mountain to scout after them. They followed the Merkit discreetly for two or three days, then came back to Burkhan Khaldun to tell Temujin that the Merkit had really gone.

The small party rode wearily back to the deserted camp. The women and children were gone, the tents thrown down, their belongings scattered here and there, much of them burned in the fires. A few herdsmen rode in from round about, now that the Merkit had gone, to help in re-establishing the camp, and in rounding up the beasts.

When everything was in order again, as far as it could be, Temujin gathered his family, friends and neighbours around him. He stood on a small hillock, facing the mountain massif, struck himself on the chest, and declaimed the following incantation:

> Because the ears of Khoakchin
> Are like the ears of a polecat for hearing,
> Because the eyes of Khoakchin
> Are like the eyes of a marten for seeing,
> I have been saved from my enemies;
> I have escaped to Burkhan Khaldun.

72

On my stumbling horse
I have made my way along the paths of deer;
I have built myself a shelter of willow branches
On the heights of Burkhan Khaldun.
I have scurried here and there like a louse;
Burkhan Khaldun has saved me.

On my solitary horse
I have made my way along the trails of elk;
I have built myself a shelter of osier-twigs
On the heights of Burkhan Khaldun.
I have scrambled here and there like a squirrel;
Burkhan Khaldun has saved me.

I have gone in terror of my life;
I have known great fear.
Every day I shall sacrifice to Burkhan Khaldun;
Every morning I shall invoke its name.
Let my sons think always of this;
Let the sons of my sons keep alive the memory of it.

As his mother and his people respectfully watched him, he turned towards the sun, took off his belt and hung it round his neck, took off his cap and wrapped it round his left hand, and, beating his chest with his right hand, prostrated himself nine times, while some of those present poured libations of mare's milk out of skin bags on to the steppe.

All these procedures were those recommended by the shamans for expressing gratitude to the infinite Power. The shamans had given a great deal of time and thought to these matters, and it must be assumed that their prescription was the best that could be arrived at. Who is to say, except the infinite Power itself, which of these observances is the most effective? The greatest shamans do not necessarily approach closest to the gods, any more than the greatest rulers necessarily write the best poems.

VIII

The Expedition Against the Merkit

Temujin, taking Kasar and Belgutai with him, rode off again to visit Toghrul of the Keraits.

His previous visit had been timely. If he had gone now, as a suppliant, for the first time, Toghrul might well have been less than impressed. A stranger has few claims, whatever his misfortune. Temujin could hardly have offered him a sable cloak as a bribe to attack the Merkit.

But he was no stranger, and had come already as a chieftain, offering his services, and a splendid gift. His proposal had to be given serious consideration. Tokhto'a of the Merkit may have considered that his being married to Toghrul's daughter gave him some assurance against being attacked by Toghrul; if so, he misjudged Toghrul, who had old grudges against the Merkit, and had not forgotten how, when he was captured by them at the age of seven, they had dressed him up in a dirty goatskin and made him pound wild millet all day with a pestle and mortar, on the banks of the Selenga. This had been an experience from which he had never recovered, and having Tokhto'a for a son-in-law made him feel no better about it.

74

His decision was an easy one, and he expressed it with a wholeheartedness which was not only politic but genuine.

Temujin said: 'The three Merkit chieftains came unexpectedly and pillaged us. My wife, and all our women and children, have been taken. We have come to you, O Khan my father, to ask you to rescue them and bring them back to us.'

Toghrul, this being a formal audience, expressed himself with proper eloquence.

'Have I not given you my reply already? When you brought me the sable cloak, you said that since in the time of your father I became his sworn *anda*, you looked on me as your father. Then I said, when you laid the cloak before me: "In return for this cloak, I will reunite your scattered people; in return for this black sable cloak, I will bring back your straying kinsmen. This thought will remain in the depths of my loins; I shall cherish it in the pit of my stomach." Did I not say this?

'Now I repeat those words of mine. In return for that black sable cloak I will bring back to you your lady Berta, if I have to destroy the whole Merkit people; we will restore to you your wife Berta, though all the Merkit must be annihilated to do so.'

When Temujin had expressed his thanks for this resolve, Toghrul came down to more practical matters.

'Send a message to the younger brother Jamukha,' he said. 'They will find him on the banks of the Qorqonaq. Tell him I shall start from here with two *tumans* of horsemen. I will fight on the right wing. Ask him to bring also two *tumans* of horsemen, to form the left wing. Let Jamukha fix the time and place of our meeting.'

JAMUKHA

Jamukha was a young Mongol chieftain, the head of the Jadaran clan. He was considered to be a distant kinsman of Temujin's, being descended from a woman stolen by the chieftain Bodonchar in ancient times; but the woman was pregnant when Bodonchar took her, and the Jadaran were descended from the child already in her womb. So the kinship was more of law or custom than of blood.

Jamukha was already, strictly speaking, Temujin's *anda*. As small boys they had played together in the camp on the banks of the Onon, while Yesugei was still alive. They had played at knucklebones on the ice of the frozen river, and in the spring they had hunted together in the woods with their little bows and arrows. They exchanged presents, knucklebones cast in copper, and Jamukha went to the trouble of boring holes in bits of bone antler and fixing them to arrow-shafts, so that the arrows made whistling noises when they were loosed from the bow. These he gave to Temujin, and Temujin, less inclined to take so much trouble, gave him in return some favourite arrows of his tipped with cypress wood hardened in the fire.

The attachment between them was so great that at that early age they were solemnly declared *anda* in front of the amused clansmen. But nobody could take too seriously a bond formed between two children, when it was impossible to tell what the future might hold for them.

Jamukha, having become chief of his clan, allied himself with the Taijiut, the most powerful group among the Mongols at that time. He also entered into an alliance with Toghrul of the Keraits. But he was leader of his own camp, and strong enough not to submit to the dominance of Targutai or any other chieftain if he did not choose to. Unless the Mongols agreed together to elect a Khan over them all, he was likely to remain his own master. His reputation as a warrior was excellent, and if there was a question of electing a Khan at all, Jamukha considered he had as good a claim as anyone else to the position. His claim was not put quite so high by other chieftains. To some extent their doubts arose from his character and temperament. He was a strange, moody, withdrawn man. Nobody ever really understood what he was thinking, and nobody was ever close to him, except Temujin, and that only for a short time.

When Temujin came back from Toghrul's camp, he sent Kasar and Belgutai to Jamukha. 'Tell this to my *anda* Jamukha,' he said. 'The three Merkit have visited me; my bed has been made empty. Are we not of one blood? Half of my breast has been ripped out. Are we not of one kidney? How shall we wash out this injury?'

Kasar and Belgutai, having reached Jamukha's camp on the Qorqonaq stream, gave him Temujin's message, and repeated also the words that had passed between him and Toghrul of the Keraits.

Jamukha replied: 'I have learned that the bed of my *anda* Temujin has been made empty, and there is sorrow in my heart. I have learned that half of his breast has been torn away, and my liver aches for him. We will have vengeance; we will wipe out the three Merkit, the Uduyit, the Uwas and the Khaghat; we will restore the lady Berta to him.

'Tokhto'a is at present on the Bu'ura steppe, where the camel stallions graze. He is a nervous man; every time he hears the saddle-cloths beaten, he thinks it is the sound of drums. Dair Usun is at the island of Talkhun, where the Orkhon meets the Selenga. He is nervous, too; he starts up if he hears someone's arrows rattling inside their covered quiver. Khaghatai is on the Kharaji steppe; this man is seized by palpitations when, in the dark heart of the forest, he hears the grasses of the steppe stirred by the wind.

'Let us cut straight across the river Kilkho. The stiff reeds, the *sakhal-bayan*, are in good condition now; we will use them to bind rafts together. We will take this Tokhto'a by surprise, as if we came leaping in through the roof-hole of his tent. We will cast down his tents and wipe out his women and children until there are none left. We will overturn the shrines of his ancestors and destroy his people till the place is an emptiness.'

All men have some cruelty in them, and there are exceptionally cruel men in all nations. The Mongols were not exempt from this rule. On the whole they destroyed their fellow-men at any time when it appeared to be necessary to enhance their own power, position or wealth. Jamukha went further: he took a greedy pleasure in it, as if he sought some compensation in the heat of destruction for the coldness of his own nature. It brought him no good in the end, because he was smaller in the sight of men for it, not greater, as he imagined. He was a great general, effective both as a strategist and as a tactician. Genghis Khan learned a lot from Jamukha, but he never equalled him in the capacity to dispose his forces most effectively in a battle.[44] What Genghis Khan did have was the ability to attract men to serve him with absolute devotion, and of this gift Jamukha had nothing at all.

Jamukha sent Kasar and Belgutai back to Temujin with this message, to which he added the following words.

'Tell this to my *anda* Temujin, and to my elder brother Toghrul Khan. I have raised my standard of yak's tails, so that it can be seen from far away, and I have made the sacrifices to it. I have stretched the skins of black bulls over my groaning drums, and I have beaten them with a satisfying clangour. I have mounted my swift black horse; I have put on my leather jerkin; I have taken my sharp lance and my curved sword in hand; I have laid the notch of my arrows on the cord. We will ride against the Merkit, and cut them to pieces.

'Tell them this also. When Toghrul Khan has mounted, let him ride by the front of Burkhan Khaldun to join up with the *anda* Temujin. I shall ride from here up the Onon. I have some of Temujin's people in my camp, and I shall bring them with me. I shall have a *tuman* of my own people; with Temujin's people, that will make two *tumans*. We will meet at Botokhan on the Onon, the place where the camel-foals are reared.'

A *tuman* was the Mongol regiment, the largest body of warriors acting as a unit. In the later days of Genghis Khan a *tuman* was very large, numbering ten thousand men; but at this early time, when Temujin first went to war, the greatest of Mongol chieftains could not have raised a quarter of that number of fighting men. Not even Toghrul, Khan of the Keraits, could have raised a single one of the *tumans* of later times. Yet when Temujin became Khan of the Steppes he raised ninety-five of them.[45]

THE MEETING OF THE ALLIES

The two *tumans* that Toghrul brought with him round the north side of Burkhan Khaldun to join up with Temujin were very small *tumans* by later standards. Five hundred or a thousand men they may have been, not much less, and not much more. It is said that the three chieftains of the Merkit had come up against the camp on the Burgi with three hundred men, but it is doubtful if there were so many. It was incredible to the Mongols of later days that a man could ride against his enemies with less. But if Tokhto'a rode against Temujin's camp with three hundred men, he brought more than he needed; and if Toghrul brought two thousand men to this present task he was overstraining his resources.

Nevertheless, Temujin was faced with a problem in matching this force, since his own private army, at the time when he sent Kasar and Belgutai to take his message to Jamukha, numbered exactly five. Some of his Kiyat kinsmen would come with Jamukha to join him, but this would not help him to make much of a showing at his rendezvous with Toghrul.

He sent around the scattered herdsmen of Burkhan Khaldun and the mountains of Guralgu, requesting aid from those that had the heart for it. The response was excellent. Before this, they had seen no particular reason to ally themselves with Temujin. He was a defenceless refugee in his small camp, and had powerful enemies, even though his escape from the Taijiut and his feat in recapturing his horses had given him a certain reputation for valour. But to join him in a large-scale expedition against the Merkit, in alliance with Toghrul the Kerait and Jamukha the Jadaran,

79

was quite a different matter. There was loot to be gained, women and cattle to be shared out among the conquerors. And when they came back, Temujin would be a chieftain with something to defend, and power to defend it.[46]

They were simple herdsmen, but as soon as they took up their weapons and mounted they were warriors. The *tumans* of Toghrul and Jamukha consisted of nothing more. There were no armies then, such as Genghis Khan assembled later, of men trained for war and nothing but war. A warrior was a herdsman on a horse, armed, and obeying his chieftain.

They flocked in to Temujin's camp, and by the time Kasar and Belgutai returned from delivering their message to Jamukha, Temujin was ready. It was not a large *tuman* that he had, but a *tuman* it was, and his first command. Toghrul was riding round the north side of Burkhan Khaldun, the front side, as Jamukha had put it, looking at it from his camp on the Qorqonaq. Temujin rode with his men up the Tunggelik, that same stream that the old woman Khoakchin had tried to escape up, with Berta in the ox-cart. Crossing the watershed, he came down the Tana, and so to the head-waters of the Onon; and at the tributary Kimurkha he joined up with Toghrul Khan.

Toghrul Khan was camped there with his two *tumans*, one of which he led in person. The other was led by his younger brother Jakha Gambu. Jakha Gambu was one of those brothers whom Toghrul, in his earlier days, had been disposed to abolish; but after Toghrul had been restored to power by Yesugei, his surviving brothers and uncles, except Black Erke, bowed to his authority more or less willingly. Jakha Gambu was a Buddhist, the latter part of his name being a Tibetan word signifying 'the Wise'; later events showed him to be indeed wiser than Toghrul, though by a small margin.

They marched with their three *tumans* down the Onon. They were three days late in arriving at the rendezvous with Jamukha. The responsibility for this lay clearly with Temujin; Toghrul had been waiting for him on the Kimurkha when he got there. He was still inexperienced, and had waited as long as possible for more herdsmen to come in, so that his *tuman* would look more convincing. It was a breach of courtesy. The clansmen took little notice of time in their daily lives. Like any other upland farmers, they got up at dawn, worked with the beasts till sundown, ate and drank, and went to bed. But they were exact about time when they needed to be, and on this occasion the longer their armies delayed the more likely Tokhto'a was to get wind of what was coming, and take steps.

Jamukha indicated his disapproval by placing his forces in battle array, facing the newcomers. He knew perfectly well who they were, and riding out to greet them would have been the normal practice, but he was vexed, and showed it typically, with a gesture of frosty pride.

Toghrul and Temujin, finding this army drawn up against them, had no alternative but to arrange their forces in battle order too. They advanced cautiously down the valley until it was perfectly clear that the hostile force belonged to Jamukha, who was visible at the head of it. He rode a little way forward, and they rode to meet him.

He spoke to them coldly, when they met in between the drawn-up armies.

'Did we not agree that even in the snowstorm, even in torrential rain, we would be in time at the meeting-place? When a Mongol says "Yes" to something, is it not the same as if he had taken his oath? "Who fails to keep his agreement, we will cast him out of our ranks." Is not this what we said?'

Temujin might have reacted badly to this, but Toghrul was old and realistic, if not exactly wise. Moreover, he had dignity and the instincts of a ruler, and had a grasp of the principle that a ruler must on no account blame his subordinate.

'We were three days late at the place of meeting,' he said. 'It is right that our younger brother Jamukha should not only reprimand us, but also punish us. Let him decide what our punishment is to be.'

Jamukha had no idea of punishing them beyond getting

rid of some of his bad temper, and was immediately disarmed. Toghrul was a cunning old fox, and if he had not also been as devious as one it would have gone better with him. The confronting armies shed their menacing attitude and prepared for more serious business.

REVENGE ON THE MERKIT

They rode north and west and, coming down to the Kilkho, cut down saplings and tied them together into rafts. While they were doing so, a number of Tokhto'a's people, fishermen, sable-trappers and huntsmen, catching sight of this unusual activity, left all their gear and implements lying where they were, and fled to warn the Merkit. As a result, when Temujin and his companions fell on their tents during the night, Tokhto'a and a few of his people had fled down the Selenga; but they left most of their women and children behind. His tents were pillaged and his shrines overturned. The Merkit clansmen in their scattered encampments gathered themselves into bands and fought where they could; when they were defeated, the survivors were taken as captives. Toghrul and Jamukha took their share of the men for the most part as slaves; Temujin, shorter of men, liberated those among them who were willing to serve him as warriors.

The Mongols pursued the Merkit down the Selenga during the night. Temujin rode among his men in the forefront of the advance, shouting Berta's name whenever they came up with a group of fleeing Merkit. In one group that they overtook, there was a black covered wagon being whipped on through the woods. Its driver climbed down and ran off, pursued by the Mongol horsemen. Berta heard Temujin's voice and climbed down from it, followed by Khoakchin. In the bright moonlight they saw Temujin a little way off, looking anxiously round; they ran to him and clung to his bridle. Temujin dismounted and embraced Berta. Calling some of his men, he arranged for them to form a guard round the wagon; and, since the mood of the

82

Mongols was to deal with any women and children as the impulse of the moment suggested, and kill any Merkit clansman who was still armed and on his feet, he thought it best to stay with them for the rest of the night. He sent some of his men off with messages to Toghrul and Jamukha, saying: 'I have found that which I came to find. Let us ride no farther during the night, but dismount here.'

Toghrul and Jamukha called a halt to the pursuit. The Mongol war-bands, though they had not developed the organisation of their later years, were accustomed to operating in a disciplined fashion under the orders of their leaders; even in a rout like this, they were soon called back to regroup round the chieftains. The exhausted Merkit, finding themselves no longer pursued, for the most part lay down where they were, to rest for an hour or two.

Tokhto'a, the Merkit chieftain, rode on to the camp of Dair Usun of the Uwas. These two decided to put up no further resistance at that time. With a few of their followers, they fled onwards down the Selenga towards the Barkhujin country, by Lake Baikal, and so escaped. Khaghatai Darmala, the third chieftain, having had more warning than the other two, in his camp on the Kharaji steppes, gathered his warriors together and defended his tents. They were defeated and Khaghatai was captured. He was taken to the nearest *ail*, or group of tents, to be guarded there until he could be taken off in the direction of Burkhan Khaldun. A wooden k'ang was fastened round his neck. As this was being done, seeing the Mongols dragging the occupants out of the tents, and wishing to save them as far as he could from the extremes of molestation in the heat of the moment, he said: 'Belgutai's mother is in this *ail*.'

The news was taken to Belgutai, and the ransacking of this *ail* was held up for the time being. Belgutai came riding along from another part of the camp, but his mother, who had been cowering inside one of the tents, waiting for whatever might happen to her, heard the noises of shouting and screaming die away, and came to the door of the tent, wrapped up in an old sheepskin cloak. There were some

Mongol warriors waiting about outside, and she spoke to them.

'They say of my son that he will now become a great prince. But here I have been taken as his woman by a common man. How can I look on the face of my son?' She wandered off through the camp, and they let her go, having had the order not to molest the women of this *ail*. But when she came to the edge of the camp, seeing that the few people in sight were taking little notice of what she did, she ran off into the woods.

Belgutai came to the tent that had been pointed out to him, and found his mother gone. By questioning this one and that one, he learned how his mother, wrapped up in her old cloak, had gone off into the woods. He took a body of men and searched the woods all that day, but they could not find her; and she was never found, having determined to hide away from the sight of men. There is no doubt that she died there, within a short time, in the woods. She had never been Yesugei's wife, but as his woman she had been held in esteem; then her elder son Bektair had been killed by Temujin; and now the shame of her captivity was more than she could bear, though no man would have held it against her.

Belgutai was all his life an exceptionally genial and fore-bearing man, but now he was in an extremity of rage. He shot many of the Merkit captives with his bone-tipped arrows, holding them all responsible for the death of his mother; and the chieftains, recognising that he had particular cause for grief, did little to stop him. He sought out those of the Merkit who had been on the raid on Burkhan Khaldun, and their wives and children, and annihilated them, so that none of their line should remain. Of their other women and children, he took those that he thought fit for it into his tents for his personal service; and those that he did not think fit, he took as slaves and servants to attend about the door of his tent, and in his camp.

All the Mongols who had been on this expedition, except for those few who had been killed in the fighting, came back from it greatly enriched, since all the animals that had belonged to these Merkit were rounded up, as far as possible, and shared out fairly. Any small herdsman who had ridden off with Temujin on this expedition now had his increased flock of cattle and horses, sheep and goats; Merkit captives to act as his herdsmen, so that he had more time for war and hunting; and women and children to serve him in his bed and about his tents. There was no Mongol now with Temujin who was not in his way a small chieftain, with his own property and possessions, though he held them from Temujin;[47] and this gave them an excellent reason for looking to him for leadership and protection.

When Temujin went on that expedition against the Merkit, he was in a desperate position, a chieftain by name and line, but a man with no followers and without power. He came back as the leader of a large camp of his own, with an army of men whom he could train in the arts of war, since they now had leisure for it. They were not by any means a clan, though some of them were kinsmen of his who had been with Jamukha. But many of them, the herdsmen of his *tuman*, were no kin at all; and some of them were not even Mongols, but Merkit clansmen, those who chose to serve him and proved trustworthy. It was an army of men not necessarily of his own blood or of his own nation, who took personal service with him.

BERTA

As for Berta, she had been given by the Merkits to a man called Chilger, the younger brother of that Chileidu, from whom Yesugei had stolen Temujin's mother Hoelun long ago. Hence Chilger was also a younger brother of Tokhto'a. They gave her to him, to do as he wished with her; and he took her into his tent. It is said that during the time of her captivity he developed a great passion for her, not surprisingly, since she was extremely beautiful. What her feelings were towards him are less exactly known, and it was politic to assume that she treated him with extreme coldness. There is no doubt, though, that since he held absolute power over her she must have yielded to any demands of his, whatever mental reservations she may have maintained.

As a result of this, when Temujin's first child was born, some months later, no one, including Berta, could say with certainty whether he was Temujin's son or Chilger's. Despite this, Temujin treated Jochi always as his true son and firstborn heir. The only time his doubtful parentage caused any trouble was when the question of the succession arose; and then Chagatai used it as an excuse to dispute the rights of Jochi, whom he could never get on with, and in favour of Ogodai, the third son.

Chilger, the Merkit chieftain to whom Berta had been given, fled on the approach of the Mongol armies and was never found. It is said that he gave vent to various expressions of self-reproach, saying that, like a buzzard, whose fate it was to eat mice and voles, he had aspired to eat swans and cranes; and that, his life being of no more value than a few sheep-droppings, he would creep into a noisome cleft and there perish.[48]

If the suspicions about Jochi's parentage were justified, this Chilger, the brother of Chileidu of the beautiful hair, being the father of Jochi, was the grandfather of Batu, Khan of the Golden Horde, which would have been an agreeable revenge for Chileidu if he had lived to know of it.[49]

86

IX

The Rightful Khan

In the back of his mind, Temujin always sought power. He was like the man who mysteriously becomes rich when other men mysteriously do not; because whatever that man is doing, some part of his mind is always thinking about money. So some part of Temujin's mind was always thinking about power. Whether he set out with the intention of killing his half-brother for stealing a fish, or of getting his wife back from the Merkit, that tireless spirit in the back of his mind saw to it that he always ended up with more power over other men than he started out with.

Now, returning from the expedition against the Merkit, he expressed his gratitude to Toghrul and Jamukha in all sincerity.

'The Khan my father, and my *anda* Jamukha, have given me their aid. Heaven and Earth have strengthened my powers. I dedicate my forces to the service of almighty Heaven, and to our mother Earth. We have taken our vengeance on the Merkit, as men should; we have made an emptiness in their breasts; we have torn out their livers; we have annihilated the men of their line. Those that were left, we have enslaved. Having thus destroyed the Merkit, let us return to our own places.'

Toghrul then left them and went back to his *yurts* in the black forest of the Tula, hunting on the way. But Temujin did not return to his own place, the camp on the Burgi. He had formed a strong attachment to Jamukha, and desired to remain in his company. He went along with him to the banks of the Qorqonaq, with his men, and in due course the rest of his people from the upper reaches of the rivers joined him there. They had pastured their flocks in the mountain regions, because this was the place for small men, away from the great chiefs and other predators. Now they had a wider choice of pasture, and could graze their flocks in summer where they had formerly only ventured in the depths of winter. Targutai and his Taijiut were not so far away, but Temujin was too strong now for an attack on him to be lightly undertaken.

On the banks of the Qorqonaq, Temujin and Jamukha renewed their oath of blood-brotherhood.

Temujin took counsel with his advisers before forming this alliance, as was his custom before coming to any decision.[50] Previously Hoelun had been his only adviser of long experience; but he would ask the advice of Kasar and Belgutai as well, though they were of his own age. Now he had more of his kinsmen about him, among them men long in years and experience. They all agreed that the oath should be renewed, since the oath the two chieftains had taken in their childhood might be weakened by the passage of time. 'Men who are bound in blood-brotherhood,' the old men said, 'are like men who have only one life, common to both of them. Their oath forbids either of them to abandon the other in time of danger; they stand always to defend each other.'

The advice was good. Temujin needed, at least for the time being, the close companionship of Jamukha and his forces.

In renewing their oath, he and Jamukha exchanged presents, as the custom was. Temujin gave his *anda* a golden belt, the most valuable object he had found in Tokhto'a's camp; and the Merkit chieftain's best horse, with the exception of the one he had fled on. It was a bay mare, with a black mane and tail, that had not foaled for many years, and was swift and intelligent. Temujin's gifts were always the best he had. Jamukha was not to be outdone, and gave him in return a gold belt he had taken from Dair Usun's camp, and Dair Usun's horse, a grey which looked from a distance as if it had horns on its head, though on closer examination this proved illusory. So after this exchange of gifts neither of them was richer or poorer than before, and nobody could say that either of them had shown himself to be a lesser chieftain than the other. Temujin could afford to treat Toghrul with unfailing respect as a substitute father, and invariably did so, but towards Jamukha he had always to act as an equal, despite Jamukha's superior forces.

Nevertheless, the attachment between them was sincere. He and Jamukha were inseparable; they slept under the same blanket, and feasted together on the banks of the Onon, there at leafy Qorqonaq, in great and constant harmony. This attachment cannot have been altogether a source of joy to Berta. Having been rescued by Temujin from her captivity among the Merkit, she found herself coming second in his affections to his *anda* Jamukha. However, he discharged his duties towards her, and sons came along at the proper time; so that nobody else regarded this close friendship between the two young men as in any way exceptionable.

They remained in this state of close harmony for a year and a half. During this time, their camps moved together as one, from one grazing-ground to another.

During this time, too, messengers came to Temujin from many leading men,[51] even from some of those who, long ago, accepting the situation as it then was, had gone off with Targutai. The people needed a leader, and they had not found one entirely to their satisfaction in Targutai. His own clan, the Taijiut, was powerful, but naturally he would give his kinsmen precedence if his strength grew to such an extent that he had wealth to share or powers to delegate. These chieftains all had rivalries among themselves, and under Targutai they could not see things working out to their satisfaction. It was observed, though, that Temujin's followers were rewarded according to their talents and capacities, and their devotion to him, so that men such as Bo'orchu, the son of a small chieftain who happened to cleave to him, or even Jelmei, whose father was a wandering blacksmith, were becoming great men under him. Moreover, he rewarded his followers well; after the Merkit raid, the flocks and serfs had been shared out among his men with notable generosity.

The messengers had long talks in private with Temujin. The negotiations went well, but nothing could be done at the moment. Jamukha and Temujin were moving around as one camp, in close unity; if they came to Temujin, which of the two would be their chieftain?

Some men came to join Temujin, and his camp slowly grew in size, but they were small men, of no name. While this situation existed, no considerable chieftain could declare himself for Temujin, and it would have been outrageous for any of Jamukha's people to go so far as thinking of it, at least aloud.

At the same time, Jamukha, sincere though his feeling for Temujin was, had to bear in mind the possibility of Temujin's acquiring an unreasonable measure of influence. He maintained relations, though with caution, with those who might come to his aid if it should turn out that he needed it. Messengers came to his tent too, when he was alone, men from many clans, but notably from the Taijiut.

The advice of the old men who favoured this oath of blood-brotherhood had, nevertheless, been good. This was a time when Temujin needed a friend, an equal friend sworn to protect him as an equal. Without it he would not have had this invaluable breathing-space, this time when Prince Altan could talk quietly with Khuchar, and Sacha Beki with Taichu, and all of them could think how things were under

Targutai, and how they might be under someone else, and how the future might go, if they took the right decision at the right time.

THE BREAK WITH JAMUKHA

The gay young chieftains feasted and drank on the leafy banks of Qorqonaq, after that expedition against the Merkit. The winter came down, and they huddled in their tents while the snow whirled over the steppes. By the time the spring came the animals were thin; the ribs of the horses stuck out like the tent frameworks when the wind blows the felt against them. They moved to summer pastures and the flocks and herds grew fat; the love between Temujin and Jamukha was deep and strong, and the negotiations with other chieftains went on quietly at suitable times. Then the winter came sweeping down again from the north, but there were fires in the tents, meat to eat, and skins of fermented mare's milk to keep up the spirits.

When the spring came, the beasts were at first too weak to move far. But as the days lengthened, the pastures, exhausted by early grazing, became too poor to sustain them. On the sixteenth day of the first moon of summer, the Day of the Red Disc, they struck camp at dawn and moved off, Jamukha's people and Temujin's people, across the steppes, in search of the summer pastures.

Temujin and Jamukha rode at the head of the long line. Their way led them near a large camp of the Basut, a clan who were close adherents of the Taijiut; but the Basut had no reason to fear them. Temujin was no friend of theirs, but Jamukha was, and he had the power to restrain his *anda*, if his *anda* should take it into his head to acquire a few more flocks and serfs. All the same, this was not a moment that should be prolonged; nor was it likely that it should be. This large camp would need to go a long way to find enough fresh pasture, and the Basut themselves would be moving off soon enough to some distant part of the steppe.

Temujin and Jamukha were seen to be deep in conversation, as was common enough; but suddenly Temujin reined in his horse, and remained at a halt. Jamukha rode on.

Temujin turned and rode thoughtfully back towards his own people, slowly, because the wagon-train was moving in his direction, with the group of his own family at its head.

Nobody ever learned what were the actual words spoken between Temujin and Jamukha on this Day of the Red Disc. All that was known of it was what Temujin reported of it to Berta, and what Berta replied; but what a man tells his wife is not necessarily everything that has happened. He told her what he chose to tell, and the rest he kept to himself.

Having ridden back a little way, he waited there, still thinking deeply, until the wagon-train came up to him. Hoelun and Berta were riding at its head, with others, men and attendants, around them; neither of them had much use for huddling in covered wagons until much later years.

He spoke to Hoelun.

'My *anda* Jamukha has just said this to me. "Let us camp here; we are close to the mountain, where our horseherds and shepherds will find plenty of room for their tents. Let us camp here, where we are near to the torrent; our shepherds will find grazing for their sheep and lambs."[52] As I did not fully understand these words, I made no reply to him. Telling myself I should take counsel of my mother, I have come to you here.'

This suggestion of Jamukha's, if he made it, was clearly unreasonable. Both camps had just started out on their summer migration. It was absurd to suggest that they should stop after half a day's journey, when the grazing not far away had been exhausted in the first hunger of the animals, eating the young grass before it had fully grown.

What made it even less practicable was the presence of the Basut camp in the locality. To pass by was acceptable enough; to stop there would be clearly a hostile act. If the Basut stayed where they were there would inevitably be incidents, leading to trouble between Temujin and Jamukha, on the one hand, and Targutai, as overlord of the Basut, on the other. If the Basut moved away to avoid such trouble, they could legitimately claim that Temujin had driven them from their grazing-grounds.

The suggestion made by Jamukha, if he made it, was one which Temujin could not possibly accept. It is possible that Jamukha, feeling that the time had come to separate himself from Temujin, did in fact make this suggestion, knowing that Temujin could not accept it. But Jamukha, this cold, withdrawn man, had no close friends other than Temujin, and his feeling for Temujin was strong. Even if his interest demanded that he should separate from him, he would have delayed the separation; and it is by no means clear that he stood to gain by it. Temujin, on the other hand, had come to a time when it would profit him to part from Jamukha, and when further delay might lessen his growing influence among the clans. However deep his attachment was to Jamukha, no personal consideration ever stood up against that spirit in the back of his mind that worked always for power. Besides, he had plenty of other friends.

It is most likely that Temujin, judging that the time for parting had come, seized on some quite innocent remark of Jamukha's concerning the condition of the local grazing to give him an excuse for it. Jamukha may not even have realised until the following day that Temujin had quarrelled with him.

Whatever the truth of the matter, this is what Temujin said to Hoelun about it. And Hoelun would no doubt have replied, but before she could open her mouth Berta had leaped in to reply for her. This must have been a pleasant moment for Berta. No wife really appreciates it when her husband goes off to sleep under the same blanket with another chieftain for eighteen months.

'The *anda* Jamukha has always been known as a changeable man,' Berta said. 'The time has come when he has had enough of us. What he has said is in some way aimed at our disadvantage. We should not camp at all near here, but keep on riding through the night, since we are already in motion. That would be the best thing.'

Hoelun agreed with these words, and so did Temujin, as he might well, since he had almost certainly planned that this should happen. Jamukha's people, when night came, put up their tents, though the wagons were not otherwise unloaded, for a night's sleep. But Temujin's people rode grimly on, always looking straight ahead. It was a strange moment, this, the separation of two groups of people who had been together for so long. There were some difficult moments for individual persons, debts unsettled and love affairs suddenly broken off; but a man had to follow his chieftain, and there was nothing to be done about it.

There was no trouble between Jamukha's men and Temujin's on this day, but it was another matter with the Basut. Naturally they had had men on the hilltops, watching the slow progress of this vast army of people and sheep and horses, cattle and camels and goats and wagons, taking a course that would pass not very far from their own camp. They saw Temujin leave Jamukha to ride on alone; informants from the camp of Jamukha came to them during the day, hinting at trouble that nobody quite understood. Then Jamukha's people halted, and Temujin's people, moving on, drew away from them, until there was no more than a thinly drawn-out line of contact, and then no contact at all; that line of figures, making the last farewells, saying the last parting words, drew back, Jamukha's people to their own camp, and Temujin's to his moving army. And Temujin's people moved slowly on in the twilight, towards the camp of the Basut.

The Basut panicked. Temujin had no hostile intentions towards them, but he sent no message to say so, and if he had done they might have lacked confidence. They fled from their camp, and, making across the steppe one way or the other, came to Jamukha's camp, where they took refuge.

Their camp, deserted and unguarded, was not exactly pillaged, but it would have been unreasonable to expect a host of warriors, finding all these goods lying about as if abandoned, not to take anything that seemed useful, particularly since its owners belonged to a sub-clan of the

Taijiut, and were adherents of that same Targutai who had once chased their own chieftain into a bush and fastened a k'ang on him.

Temujin was in no mood to request his men not to pick up the Basuts' belongings, and there was no reason why he should. So his men's flocks and herds were increased by beasts of Basut origin. Somebody, too, looking into the Basut tents in case anything had been left behind, found a small boy who said his name was Kokochu. They took him to Temujin, who gave him to his mother as a present. This was not the first present of the kind he had given to Hoelun, who despite her experiences with her own sons liked small boys, and was always glad to have a few more about her. He had sent back a small Merkit boy called Kuchu as a present to Hoelun when they sacked Tokhto'a's camp. These two, Kuchu and Kokochu, were useful boys, but in no way exceptional. Temujin, finding that one of the best ways of pleasing his mother was to give her small boys, took particular care in selecting them after this, and picked some really outstanding ones.

THE COMING OF THE CLANSMEN

Temujin rode on at the head of his people, thinking. Jamukha was still a good deal stronger than he was. Temujin did not think he was in an aggressive mood, but there was nothing to be gained by relying on it, and the Basut affair would hardly soothe him. This was the moment to put those chieftains to the test who had sent their messengers to him. It was something of a gamble, because they might not come, thinking it better to wait; but the gamble had to be made some time, and there would never be a better moment than this.

Long before the sun set on that fateful Day of the Red Disc, he had sent his messengers galloping off across the steppes in every direction. The chieftains had shown some inclination to join him; they must make up their minds now. If they were going to come, let them come. They could wait, of course, but his true friends would be those who came now.

The response was gratifying; it was more than Temujin had hoped for. He had picked, with infallible instinct, that one moment when, all over the steppes, the hesitant chieftains had decided that they needed a leader, and concluded that this was the leader they needed.

He rode all night at the head of his people. As the day whitened towards dawn, they could see, far off, groups of clansmen coming towards them. The first to arrive were the three brothers Tokhu'arun of the Jalair; they had ridden all night after receiving Temujin's message. Khada'an Daldurkhan came with his brothers, the five brothers of the Tarkhut. Onggur, Temujin's cousin, the son of Menggetu Kiyan and grandson of Bartan Bahadur, came with a large group of his kinsmen. Khubilai[53] came from the Barulas, and Dokholkhu from the Mangqut, with many of their clansmen. All these leaders rose to be great captains under Genghis Khan.

There came also, among the first to arrive, Bo'orchu's kinsman Ogolai, and Jelmei's two younger brothers, abandoning their clans, the Arulat and the Uriangqadai. One of these brothers of Jelmei was Subetai, now grown old enough to leave his father. This was that Subetai Bahadur who brought Korea to submission, chased the Shah Mohammed from Samarkand, conquered the Georgians and the Kumans, and rode round the Caspian with Jebe; and, in later years, under Ogodai, overthrew the armies of Russia, Poland, Hungary, Serbia and Bulgaria, and advanced to the gates of Vienna. Subetai was a lean youth when he came to join Temujin; later he was not only a great prince, but grew remarkably fat.

The clansmen who came at this time to join Temujin are too numerous to name. They came from many clans; from the Basut, the Suldus, the Jalair,[54] the Qongqotan, the Olkunut, the Qorolas, the Durben and the Ikireis; from the Noyakin and the Oronar.

Many of the first arrivals were groups of clansmen who

had left their clans in small groups of warriors. As the days went on, those who arrived brought with them wagons, flocks and herds; and after some time there came in sight an entire moving camp of the Baarin clan, led by Khorchi and the old man Kokochos, and others. These Baarin were descended from Bodonchar, from that woman he had stolen, who had previously conceived the ancestor of the Jadaran. So they were kinsmen of Jamukha, and their negotiations with Temujin had of necessity been cautious and tentative.

Their principal chieftain, Khorchi, came riding out ahead of the main body, and approached Temujin, who received him courteously. The people of Temujin were moving slowly on, like a vast snowball rolling across the steppes, gathering up new adherents on its flanks and growing always in size. Temujin rode slowly along with Khorchi, a little apart, at its head.

Khorchi said to him: 'We of the Baarin were born of that woman who was captured by the august Bodonchar, long ago. We come from the same womb as Jamukha, though we are not of the same seed. We would not have wished to separate ourselves from him, but a heavenly sign came to us, which I saw with my own eyes.'

Temujin listened attentively to the tidings of this timely vision.

'A white cow came,' Khorchi went on, 'and circled round Jamukha. It struck with its horns Jamukha's wagon, in which his tents were carried; then it struck Jamukha himself. In doing so, one of its horns was broken; it had only one crooked horn left. It stood there stamping the earth, bellowing repeatedly: "Bring me back my horn!"

'Then there came a hornless ox, a white ox, and rooted up one of the great poles of Jamukha's tent. It was as if the tent-pole lay along its back like a harness. So, dragging this tent-pole along, it followed the spoor of your camp, Temujin, bellowing: "Heaven and Earth have agreed together, that Temujin shall be the ruler of the people. Now I am bringing the lordship of the people to him."

'This vision my own eyes have showed to me. Now,

Temujin, if you become the ruler of the people, how will you reward me for the truth of my vision?'

Temujin reflected on this. He was not disposed to quarrel with the truth of Khorchi's vision; defection from Jamukha, by a kinsman of his, demanded some supernatural justification.

'If Heaven does indeed grant me the leadership, I will make you the leader of a *tuman*.'

'What reward is that to me, a man who has brought you tidings of such importance, to be made leader of a *tuman*? Besides making me chief of a *tuman*, let me have thirty wives; let me choose them from the finest and best girls of your people. And, furthermore: listen favourably to my words, whatever they may be.'

Temujin agreed to these stipulations with ease. From the way things were going, it looked as if there would be plenty of maidens for Khorchi to choose his thirty wives from. As for Khorchi's words, Temujin was always ready to listen to advice, whether he took it or not.

More clansmen came to him: from the Ganigas, the Unjin and the Sakhayit. The prince Daritai came too, Temujin's uncle, he who had ridden beside Hoelun when Yesugei stole her from Chileidu, and tried unavailingly to quieten her.

There came also a chieftain not only kin to Jamukha, but of the same clan, the Jadaran, a man called Mukhalkhu. He, too, drove a good bargain, and was rewarded with a command over the horseherds.

THE CHOOSING OF THE KHAN

The people moved on, and after several days' journey they established their summer camp on the river Kimurkha. Here, within the next week or two, they were joined one after the other by three great camps, all of which had left Jamukha to come to him.[55] One was a camp of the Jurkin, led by the two brothers Sacha Beki and Taichu, who were grandsons of Okin Barkak and great-grandsons of Kabul

Khan. These proved half-hearted in their adherence and came to a bad end, but at this time they were a strong addition to Temujin's people. Then there was a group led by Khuchar Beki, another cousin of Temujin's, the son of his uncle Neikun Taiji, Yesugei's elder brother; and the third group was led by none other than Prince Altan, the third son of Kutula Khan. Prince Altan had no great power under his command, but he was naturally regarded with great respect, and his adherence to one party or the other was a sign that many men might consider carefully. In the former days, when Yesugei died, he had cast his lot with the Taijiut, and allied himself with Targutai; now he came with his men to Temujin.

As the season advanced they broke camp again and moved farther up into the mountains to encamp where the stream called Sanggur broadened out into a blue lake, in a hollow of the massif of Guralgu. The flocks and herds ate the good sweet grass of the mountains, and the chieftains talked together. None of these great men who had lately arrived among them, Daritai, Prince Altan, Khuchar and Sacha Beki, could serve under each other, nor would Temujin's own men have served under any of them; but none of them had any basic objection to serving Temujin. They had had no one to lead them since Kutula died, and a leader was badly needed.

They approached Temujin. He made a decent pretence of unwillingness, offering each of them in turn his submission, if they should be chosen as Khan. It was safe for him to do so, since he knew that none of them was in a position to accept it.

A general council of all the chieftains was called, and the three most notable men among them, Prince Altan, Khuchar and Sacha Beki, came forward. They addressed Temujin formally, in the following manner:

We will make you Khan; you shall ride at our head, against our foes.
We will throw ourselves like lightning on your enemies;

We will bring you their finest women and girls, their rich tents like palaces.

From all the peoples and nations we will bring you the fair girls and the high-stepping horses;

When you hunt wild beasts, we will drive them towards you; we will encircle them, pressing hard at their heels.

If on the day of battle we disobey you,

Take our flocks from us, our women and children, and cast our worthless heads on the steppe.

If in times of peace we disobey you,

Part us from our men and our servants, our wives and our sons;

Abandon us and cast us out, masterless, on the forsaken earth.

In the days to come, all these great chiefs disobeyed the Khan. In the days of his greatest defeat, when he retired to Baljuna, none of them kept their promises, except Daritai, who thought better of it at the last moment. It was only his own men who obeyed him in the days of defeat.

Having elected him Khan, they wished to find some suitable title which would show the regard in which they held him. He could not be called the Khan of the Mongols, as Kutula had been, since he was not Khan of all the Mongols, or even of the greater part of them. They wished to show that the Khan they had chosen was their rightful ruler.

The steppe peoples were accustomed to the titles and official ranks conferred on them by the Chinese, their nominal overlords. So the title they now chose for Temujin was taken from a Chinese word *jeng*, meaning right, correct or chief. They added to it the '-s' which the Mongol language demanded; and so they named him Jenggis Khan, the true, rightful or chief ruler. But in the speech of the Mongols this sounded more like Jinggis, or Chinggis; and the Uighur scribes, when they came to write it down, wrote it as Chinggis.[56]

This was an important event, the choosing of Temujin

as Khan, but none of those present realised quite how important it was. The outer world beyond the steppes did not hear of it at all. Not so much as a single Chinese official expert on barbarian affairs noted it down. As for the Mongols, they took no notes, but trusted in their memories, and they had good memories for battles and conversations, but took little interest in dates. The result was that fifty years or so later, when these things were written down, nobody could decide exactly when the election took place. Some said that since it took place two years after the expedition against the Merkit the date of it must have been the Year of the Sheep, 1187. At that time Temujin was twenty. But others pointed out that the date of the Merkit raid was not known either, and maintained that it must have been two or three years later.

X

The First Years of the Khan

Because the name of Genghis Khan became great in later times, it is natural to assume that when he acquired it he was already a great Khan, and recognised as such by those about him. This is far from the truth. His father Yesugei, who was never called Khan, had a far greater following, and was obeyed by such chieftains as Targutai. And Yesugei had no power comparable with that of Kutula Khan, his grandfather. Temujin, this new Khan, was a very small Khan. He ruled over a miscellaneous collection of herdsmen, grazing their flocks in a small area of the upper Onon and Kerulen rivers, a territory occupied at the same time by several other independent rulers.

His position was precarious, but less precarious than it had been a couple of years previously in the Guralgu massif, when a small band of raiders could chase him into the recesses of Burkhan Khaldun and take everything he had. He now had authority over certain chieftains who had yielded it to him of their own will, and might be expected to withdraw it again if things turned out badly. But he also had men of his own.

What he needed most was an effective army, and he began to organise and train one. He was fortunate in having about him a small nucleus of men who were wholly devoted to him, and stood to gain or lose everything under his leadership, having no following of their own. Some of them were his early companions, whose worth had been proved. Others he selected from the new men who had come to him. He made these men captains, giving them command over groups of horsemen in his new army, and appointed others to take charge of his commissariat, to control his herdsmen and their flocks, and to see to the supply of his troops with horses and remounts.[57] They were all young, and responded with enthusiasm. Ogolai, the young kinsman of Bo'orchu, was immediately made a captain, as was Jelmei's brother Subetai. Subetai expressed himself with typical fervour.

'I shall seize everything out there that belongs to you, like a rat or a black crow; I shall guard you against your enemies as the felt of your tents protects you from the wind.'

Nobody saw anything ludicrous in this eager devotion. Temujin was one of those dangerous men who have the power to arouse exaltation in their followers, so that they are no longer moved entirely by thoughts of self-preservation and the desire for a quiet life, but become slightly mad. Such men may bring empire, like Caesar, or faith, like Mohammed, or terror, like Attila, but whenever they appear, certain changes occur in the world, which may or may not be beneficial in the long run, but always cause considerable discomfort to many.[58]

The new Khan created an army which was more disciplined than any previously known among the Mongols. His bodies of horsemen, drilled in mock battles by their enthusiastic young captains, became accustomed to obeying words of command; they wheeled and retreated, shooting arrows over their cruppers, and turned to attack again, in tight and well-ordered formations. On a campaign, none of them would stop to eat whenever he felt hungry, or turn aside to sack a small camp, rejoining the army later. The other steppe people were good fighters, and accustomed to obeying their own chiefs in battle, but they did not have this long, rigorous training that would make them act as one man. They might still defeat Temujin's army in battle, and did so on several occasions, but his men always fell back in good order, and remained with him to fight again.

DEFEAT AT DALAN BALJUT

On his election as Khan, Temujin sent messengers with the news to Toghrul, Khan of the Keraits.

'It is well that my son Temujin has been made Khan,' Toghrul told the messengers. 'How could you live without a Khan, you Mongols? Do not break faith; do not untie this knot; do not once again rip off the collar of your coats.'

Temujin also sent messengers to Jamukha. Jamukha's first thoughts were of Prince Altan and Khuchar, who had left him and gone over to Temujin. He sent back this message to them:

'You two, why have you created this division between Temujin and me? Why have you pierced the flank of your *anda*, stabbing him in the ribs? Why did you not make Temujin Khan while we were still together? What was in your thoughts when you made him Khan?

'Altan, Khuchar: keep this oath you have sworn. Let my *anda* have peace in his heart; having sworn companionship with him, at least serve him well.'

He did not, though, recognise Temujin as the rightful Khan. Neither of these two men could regard the other as a superior. Nevertheless, he expressed no hostility towards the new Khan. It may have been in his mind that some time they might be friends again. Even in the first open warfare between them, when the breach was still recent, and his anger was aroused, he showed some reluctance to inflict the greatest harm. The occasion of it was a typical neighbourly quarrel, such as was bound to occur sooner or later. Jamukha's grazing-grounds lay too close to Temujin's for such clashes to be avoided.

One of Temujin's people, Jochi Darmala, was grazing his

horses on the Saari steppes. Jamukha's younger brother Taichar was encamped near by, in front of the mountain called Jalama. Taichar considered that Jochi Darmala was trespassing on his own grazing-grounds. He rode down with a few of his men and drove off Jochi's horses to his own camp.

Jochi Darmala tried to persuade his companions to follow him and recover his horses, but they refused, lacking the heart for it. He thereupon decided to go after them himself. He followed in the trail of his horses, keeping at a reasonable distance.

When night came, and Taichar and his men had pitched camp, Jochi Darmala came galloping out of the darkness, stretched out along his horse's back; lying, as it were, on his liver, so that he could discharge his arrows while offering as small a target as possible. He rode in a circle round the camp, drawing and loosing rapidly. One arrow struck Taichar in the spine and killed him on the spot. Jochi Darmala disappeared into the darkness, rounded up his horses, and started driving them home. Taichar's men did not even pursue him. The onslaught had been so ferocious that they believed they had been attacked by a large body of horsemen; and they saw no profit in riding off into the night to be shot at by these phantom marksmen. Their chieftain had stolen the horses in the first place, and now, being dead, he had no need of them.

Jamukha, when the news was brought to him, fell into a cold fury. He had helped Temujin to recover his wife Berta from the Merkit, and sworn companionship with him; they had lived together in love and trust. As a return for this, Temujin had left him on a specious excuse, tempted some of his important followers to leave him, and had himself declared rightful Khan. Now one of Temujin's men had killed his own brother.

He sent around among the neighbouring clans, offshoots and dependents of the Jadaran, and raised an army. Everybody was glad of a good excuse like this for a fight, where reputation could be gained, along with serfs and cattle.

Two men of the Ikireis came to Temujin and told him that Jamukha's army was on its way through the passes of the Ala'ut. Temujin gathered his army together and set out to meet him. Their armies were about equal in size on this occasion. Temujin's training programme had hardly got under way and affected the outcome little; Jamukha was a far better general. Temujin's men were defeated and fell back in confusion. The devotion of his army to its leader had not helped much towards victory, but it was useful in defeat. Most Mongol armies would have melted away, groups of men going off to defend their own people and make what arrangements with the victors that they could, while the chieftain and the hard core who had nowhere else to go were hunted down or chased out of the country. Temujin's men stayed with him. They took refuge in the gorges of Jerena on the Onon.

Jamukha's army might have followed them there and finished them off, but the outcome of such an action was far from certain. It was difficult terrain, and a great many lives would be lost; the clansmen lacked enthusiasm for the project. Jamukha took the wiser course and retired. 'We have driven them into the gorges of the Jerena,' he said to his counsellors, deriving what satisfaction he could from the partial victory.

His anger was still not appeased. On the way home he passed by the camp of the Chinos, a clan that had failed to support him in this venture. He sacked and pillaged their camp, and seventy of their leading men were brought to him as prisoners.

Jamukha's men, at his command, set up seventy large cauldrons in the forest, filled them with water, and lit fires underneath them. The seventy leading men of the Chinos were then put into these cauldrons and boiled alive, as an example to others.

The example was not unnoticed. As soon as Jamukha got home his army dispersed, the clansmen of the thirteen offshoots and dependent clans going off to their own different *yurts*; and two of these clans immediately deserted him.

Jurchadai of the Uru'ut and Khuyildar of the Mangqut took counsel with their people and, being of one mind, marched away and joined Temujin. In any future battle, Jamukha having proved himself to be the better general, they might find themselves on the losing side. But death in battle was a matter to which they had no deep-rooted objection; whereas under a chieftain whose outbreaks of bad temper took such a bizarre form as Jamukha's they felt neither secure nor happy.

The loss to Jamukha was greater than he knew, since these Uru'ut and Mangqut clansmen proved as faithful as they were ferocious, and without them Temujin would hardly have survived.[59]

This affair in which Jamukha boiled the Chino chieftains alive created a deep impression. In later days men in distant lands, knowing Genghis Khan to have been a great and terrible chieftain, believed that it was he who committed this outrageous deed.[60] But the truth was that Jamukha boiled these chiefs. Genghis Khan would never have perpetrated such a stupidity. He destroyed people who stood in his way, but he took no great interest in the way they died, and was on one or two occasions so considerate as to take account of their own preference in the matter. If he had acted with needless cruelty his men would not have served him so well, and his power would have been less. Jamukha was not so single-minded. He wanted power, but he sometimes wanted even more to gratify his own peculiar impulses.

After boiling these Chinos, he cut off the head of their principal chieftain and rode home dragging it at his horse's tail. His own chieftains looked at it with mixed feelings, appreciating Jamukha's ruthlessness, but each one recognising how easily that head might have been his own.

THE RETURN OF MUNGLIK

Another of those who left Jamukha and came to Temujin was Munglik the Qongqotadai. It was he who had brought

Temujin back to the camp of Yesugei when Yesugei was poisoned by the Tatars. Later he had gone off with Targutai, and now he was serving Jamukha; but the sight of those cauldrons was too much for him, and he came back to Yesugei's son.

He brought with him his seven sons, one of whom was Teb Tenggeri, the shaman. As every man knew, the spirits of the gods resided in all things, in the rocks and trees, the mountains and the rivers. They greatly loved the rivers, and Genghis Khan never approved of the practice of bathing in running water, in case this should offend them. This caused much trouble between him and the Sarta'ul, the people of Mohammed, who made more of this business of washing than the Christians or the Buddhists. Teb Tenggeri was already famous as a wizard and a priest, one who could placate the spirits of the earth, and intercede with the greater spirit in the sky.

Hoelun was glad to see Munglik again. He had deserted her in those difficult days, when everybody went off to join Targutai, but at least he had been one of the last to leave. He was a man about her own age who had no wife, the mother of his seven sons having died. Hoelun was still of an age when the society of innumerable small boys was less than completely satisfying. Munglik was often in attendance in her tent. It was rumoured, among those who knew nothing of the matter, that she married him. Nothing could be more absurd. Hoelun, like Temujin, did not demand that a man must be of noble birth. A man made his own nobility, like Subetai, the blacksmith's son. But Munglik was no Subetai. He was a steady, thoughtful man, and a good servant. What use Hoelun made of this faithful servant was her own affair—many a queen has done the same—but as for marriage, she would as soon have married Genghis Khan's horse.

Temujin's defeated army emerged cautiously from the gorges of Jerena. They had lost few men, and a defeat or two does no harm to an army, if it preserves its morale. Then the clans came to him, the Uru'ut and the Mangqut, great fighters of the line of Bodonchar, and lesser leaders and individuals like Munglik. The defeat took on some of the aspects of a victory.

The first crisis of Temujin's reign had been satisfactorily surmounted. It had looked like disaster, but the solid devotion of his army had been confirmed, and more adherents were coming in.

'These people have come over to me from Jamukha,' he said to Hoelun and Kasar. 'The country is coming over to me. Let us feast here in the forest, by the Onon.'

THE FIGHT WITH THE JURKIN

The chieftains of the Jurkin, Sacha Beki and Taichu, were camped near him with their people. Temujin invited them to join him in this feast.

It was a feast held on the spur of the moment, in a sudden access of high spirits, and the formalities of protocol were neglected. Everything was harmonious at the beginning, but the Jurkin were a proud and independent people. They had acknowledged Temujin as their rightful Khan, to enhance their own position, but they had no idea of serving him with selfless devotion, like his own men. They were descended from the eldest son of Kabul Khan, Okin Barkak, that chieftain who had the misfortune to be impaled by the Chin Emperor. Okin Barkak had been given a great start in life by his father the Khan, who chose for him all his most capable men, the strong fighters, those whose livers were filled with fierce thoughts, who had a vice-like grip in their thumbs, and big lungs full of the free air. These massive men went off with Okin Barkak to form his clan. After his lamentable end they were inherited by his son, Kutuktu Yurki. They and their mighty sons became known as the Jurkin clan. They were an élite of warriors, and strong men came willingly to join them. There were other such bands on the steppes, clans for whom fighting was the reason for their existence rather than the means of defending themselves. It is said that those Juyin Tatars who poisoned

Yesugei were another of these warrior bands, but of Tatar affairs there is no speaking with certainty. Sacha Beki and his brother Taichu were now the chieftains of the Jurkin, and all of them were proud men, looking out for insults wherever they might find them. Everything started off well. A skin of mare's milk was brought and poured out, starting with Temujin, and going on to Hoelun and Kasar, mother and brother of the Khan. Then Sacha Beki and Taichu were served. This was correct. But then the cook Shiki'ur, who had been drinking, went off to a group of Jurkin ladies with the next wineskin, and began pouring out their drinks, not caring much who was served first now that the important people had been seen to. Cooks were highly regarded among the Mongols. A man who was skilled at the art was a prized acquisition of any chieftain, and had a great deal of personal freedom, besides possessing more artistic temperament than was usual among these down-to-earth folk.

Shiki'ur made the mistake of pouring out the first drink into the beaker of Abagai, Sacha Beki's third woman. The chieftain's first and second women, the ladies Khorijin and Khu'urchin, were immediately incensed. 'Why do they serve Abagai first, instead of us?' they demanded. Leaping up, they seized the cook Shiki'ur and began to pummel him, in the most ladylike way.

Shiki'ur, in the grip of the two ladies, shrieked and wept. 'Why do you beat me like this? Because Yesugei Bahadur is dead. Because Neikun Taiji is dead. That is why.'

Shiki'ur was confused in mind. Neikun Taiji, for one, could have done little to protect him from the Jurkin, even before he was dead. But there is often a substratum of truth in the hasty utterances of half-drunk cooks. Shiki'ur gave vent to a belief that was general in the camp, whether justified or not: that Temujin had less control over his associated allies than Yesugei had had.

Shiki'ur went off to weep on the steppes, drinks were poured for Sacha Beki's principal ladies, and peace seemed to be restored, but the initial harmony had gone, and the chieftains went on drinking in an atmosphere where any incident was likely to arouse bad feeling.

Belgutai took no part in this feast. Somebody had to stay sober, to make sure that order was kept in the camp. He was some little distance away, keeping watch over the horses. It was no duty for a man of his rank, but the procedure was realistic. It cannot be expected that all the common men will stay sober when all the princes are drunk. It is best to have one prince stay sober to do the work of those common men who are incapable of it.

Belgutai was standing there watching over the horses when they brought up to him a man of the Khadagin clan, a dependent of the Jurkin. This man, they said, had been found in the saddle-enclosure, stealing a bridle. It was not improbable in the circumstances. Belgutai would have taken a light view of the matter, but unfortunately there was a sober prince of the Jurkin standing near by. This was Buri Boko, a man of great strength and impermeable self-esteem. He was a grandson of Kabul Khan and a cousin of Yesugei, a man barely in his middle age. His principal claim to fame was that he was a mighty wrestler, who could overcome any man between the Onon and Kerulen rivers in single combat.

It was this Buri Boko who had been chosen to oversee the affairs of the Jurkin camp while everyone else got drunk. It was his privilege and duty to defend his men. He came up to Belgutai and insisted that the man should be released.

Belgutai could not agree to this proposition, made, as it was, in a hostile and overbearing fashion. Words passed between them; and Buri Boko, confident in his strength and princely status, at last took it upon himself to release his man personally. He started setting about the men guarding him. Belgutai thereupon rolled up his right sleeve and grasped Buri Boko's clothing, intending to pull him away from the prisoner. Buri Boko shook himself free, drew his sword and struck at Belgutai's shoulder, cutting it so that the blood ran down.

Belgutai was all his life a remarkably good-humoured man, except when stirred by some unusual event such as the death of his mother. It suddenly struck him that this quarrel was quite absurd. This was a feast, it was a fine day, and nobody really cared whether one of the Jurkin stole a bridle or not. He commanded his men to let the prisoner go and wandered off, letting Buri Boko take the man away.

Temujin, who was sitting in the shade under a tree, saw Belgutai cross his field of vision. He was slightly intoxicated, but he knew blood when he saw it. He rose and went over to Belgutai, and asked him what had happened. Belgutai told him.

'They must not be allowed to do this to us,' the Khan said.

'The wound is nothing,' Belgutai said. 'There is no need for you to quarrel with your kinsmen on my account. The wound is healing already. If you want to have peace with your kinsmen, Brother, forget the whole thing. Just stay here a few moments, and leave things alone.'

Temujin could not take this attitude. If there were more people like Belgutai, willing to drop a pointless quarrel, the world would be a more peaceful place, but there have never been many, and Genghis Khan was not one of them.

According to custom, people had come unarmed to this feast. Everybody's weapons were hidden away in their tents, except for those of Buri Boko and Belgutai, who were standing guard. It was an excellent custom. Even in the drunken anger of the moment, Temujin did not send for weapons. Instead, he and his men started pulling down and breaking off the branches of trees, and snatching up paddles from the milk churns, in order to attack the Jurkin. The Jurkin did the same, and fought back. The feast ended in a general brawl. Some of Temujin's men had seized the two troublesome women, Khorijin and Khu'urchin, and they were detained.

Sacha Beki, sobering up in his tent, began to think that the whole affair had been regrettable. He sent messengers to Temujin, saying that he wished to be at peace, and asking for his two women back. Temujin sent the women back, saying that he too wished for peace, and suggesting that they should forget the whole thing.[61]

Relations were never the same after this between Temujin and the Jurkin. He always sensed a lack of willing co-operation. If they had kept faith with him this feast would have been forgotten. But the Jurkin could not forget it. It is often so with people who make trouble; they are more angry with the people they have annoyed than the people they have annoyed are with them.

THE RESTORATION OF TOGHRUL

There was little change now among the Mongols for some years. The situation was stable. There were several large groups of clansmen, all much of a size, following one leader or another. The Chin Emperor in Peking heard nothing but good reports from his spies and agents beyond the Wall. The steppe peoples were quiet, and apart from little local troubles, nothing disturbed the peace.

One of these small local troubles occurred in the Kerait country. In Temujin's thirtieth year, news came to him, as to the Chin Emperor, that his patron, Toghrul Khan, had been deposed.[62] This was the doing of that Black Erke who had fled to the Naiman after Toghrul's accession, and had refused to be reconciled with his brother when Yesugei brought Toghrul's uncles to order and put him back on the throne. Erke raised an army from among the Naiman, by permission of the Khan, Inancha Bilgei, and rode against his brother. Toghrul fled with only a few men, and took refuge with the Khan of the Kara Kitay, beyond the Altai, in Turkestan.

He was not happy there. Less than a year later he fled with his few attendants from the country of the Sarta'ul, the Mohammedan lands, and, passing through the country of the Uighurs and that of the Tangut, came into the country of the Mongols, from the south-west. This was a hard journey for Toghrul, who was ill-equipped for it. They had some camels, but little food. His attendants succeeded at one point in stealing five goats; but for this they would not have survived the crossing of the western Gobi. Short of water-skins, as of everything else, they survived the longer stretches between water-holes by drinking the blood of their camels, tapping it from the veins on their necks. They had only one horse between them, a bay which was half blind.

They came to the Mongol country in a state of almost total exhaustion. At that time Temujin was at his summer pasture on the banks of the Burgi, on the upper Kerulen, that same place in front of Burkhan Khaldun where the Merkit had swooped down on him years ago. Hearing of the arrival of Toghrul, he sent messengers to him, and requested the people of those parts to treat the Khan his father with hospitality. He himself set off behind the messengers, and met with Toghrul at the Lake Gusa'ur Nor. He greeted the Khan with respectful devotion, made him sit on the seat of honour in his tent, gave him lavish presents, and collected servants from his own people to serve in Toghrul's retinue.

He then rode with him to the black forest on the Tula, with his army. Erke Kara fled, and Genghis Khan restored Toghrul to his Khanate. They took a vow there in the black forest, on the banks of the Tula, a vow similar to that which men took on declaring themselves *anda*; but with this vow Toghrul and Temujin swore themselves to be as father and son.

Having so sworn, they went off on a joint expedition against the Merkit. Tokhto'a had returned long ago and reassembled his people; the two Khans rode against him and pillaged them once again. Tokhto'a fled, taking refuge as before with the Barkhujin, on the shores of Baikal. It is said that Temujin, as a dutiful son of Toghrul, took no profit from this enterprise, but gave everything his men captured from the Merkit, men and animals, to the Kerait Khan.

Jamukha was still an ally of Toghrul, and Toghrul played him and Temujin off against each other. All these alliances shifted and changed like the sands of the Gobi. Temujin served Toghrul Khan faithfully; he needed to have a strong and friendly ruler behind him, when he had so many rivals in the Mongol country. It did not seem to him that he could stand alone.

This joint expedition against the Merkit was the first of several, which brought them great profit, and made many men apprehensive of Temujin's growing power.

XI

The Steppe Wars

In 1198, when Temujin was thirty-one, a breath from the outer world came blowing into this steppe country.

The Chin Emperor, the Golden Khan of the Kitay, was having trouble with the Tatars. Those people, after all the battles they had had with the Mongols in Kutula's time, had not gone on to achieve much power themselves. They fell into disunion, just as the Mongols did, and had no single Khan to rule them.

The Chinese naturally encouraged this disunity by setting one local ruler against another, since times were best for them when the steppe peoples were quarrelling among themselves.

The Tatar chieftain Megujin, who ruled over many Tatar clans in a large tract of country around the lakes Dalai Nor and Buir Nor, fell into disfavour with the Chinese. They claimed that he had disobeyed certain requests they had made of him; but besides this he was growing too powerful for their comfort. Accordingly the Chin Emperor ordered his minister, Wanyen Siang,[63] to lead his armies north and subdue this people.

The Chin Emperor's armies came into the eastern steppes

and won certain battles against Megujin, the Tatar; but Megujin's power was by no means destroyed. It is often difficult for the powerful armies of a rich nation to subjugate a poor and undeveloped country, whose people know the land they live on and fight for their right to live there in their own way.

Megujin and his people fell back across the steppes, retreating from the country of the big lakes, till they came to the river Ulja, which runs eastwards between the Kerulen and the Onon, in the lower part of their courses. It was a long way for Wanyen Siang to go, and far from his base. His advanced troops went forward and fought the Tatars, and the Tatars fell slowly back, westwards up the Ulja, harassing their attackers all the way.

EXPEDITION AGAINST THE TATARS

Wanyen Siang sent messengers to the Mongol tribes, who were nominally tributary to the Chin Emperor, demanding their aid against the Tatars. Temujin received the emissaries of the Emperor courteously, and listened to their demands. They were on their way to the camp of Toghrul on the Tula, Toghrul being a notable leader of long though precarious standing, and well known to them. Of Genghis Khan they had heard little or nothing; his name was still unknown, except perhaps to some expert in tribal affairs at the court of the Emperor, who may have had a report mentioning the name of this petty tribal chieftain hidden away somewhere in his files.

Temujin called his council to discuss this matter. 'Since ancient days,' he said, 'these Tatar people have been our enemies. They have slain our fathers and our forefathers. This is an excellent opportunity to crush them between two opposing forces.'

The council raised no objection to this plan. Temujin, sending the emissaries of the Chin Emperor on to Toghrul, despatched with them messengers of his own.

'Wanyen Siang, the chancellor of the Golden Emperor'

(Temujin called him Ongging Chingsang, in the Mongol speech), 'has driven Megujin and his Tatars back up the Ulja. His forces are following them. We have them in a pair of pincers, these Tatars who caused our fathers and forefathers to perish. Let the Khan my father come quickly.'

Toghrul agreed whole-heartedly with Temujin's views, and accepted the Emperor's demands. He gathered together his warriors and set out to join Temujin.

Temujin summoned his own men and his allied princes from their outlying camps. The Jurkin were included in the summons, but those mighty warriors did not come. After waiting for them for six days, the two Khans set out without them. They rode down the Ulja, where the Tatars with Megujin at their head were occupying an entrenched camp. The advanced troops of Wanyen Siang were occupying the river valley and the hills beyond.

The Mongol and Kerait armies drove the Tatars out of their encampment. Megujin was slain and large numbers of the Tatars with him.

Wanyen Siang, hearing that Toghrul had acceded to his demands and was sending an army against the Tatars, had moved forward with reinforcements to join his advanced troops. After the battle, Toghrul and Temujin came to his camp and were received honourably by him. He conferred on Toghrul, in recognition of his services, the title Wang, or Prince. Henceforth Toghrul was known always as Wang Khan, or, as the Mongols pronounced it, Ong Khan.

Wanyen Siang was graciously pleased to recognise that valuable assistance had been given to the new prince by his vassal Temujin, also known as Genghis Khan, this small Mongol chieftain of whom he could not recall having previously heard. It was clearly desirable to reward him by some title too, but he did not merit so grand a designation as the Kerait chieftain. Wanyen cast about in his mind for a suitable title. *Chao t'ao shi*, Commissioner for Peace in the Border Regions, would do very well; but it would be as well not to puff up the self-esteem of this insignificant man by imposing such grandeur on him in a single step.[64] He decided to designate him Vice-Commissioner for the time being; or, as the title went in Mongolian, *ja'utkhuri*.[65]

The two Khans attended formally in audience on Wanyen Siang.

'By attacking Megujin in the rear, and destroying him,' he told them, 'you have rendered a great service to the Golden Emperor. I shall make a report to the Emperor on this service rendered by you. As for giving Genghis Khan the greater title of *Chao t'ao shi*, a full Commissioner of the Peace, it is the Emperor who must decide.'

So, greatly satisfied, the chancellor Wanyen Siang returned home. Ong Khan and Genghis Khan shared out the booty that they had taken from the Tatar camp, and set off back to their homelands. Temujin secured among his personal share of this plunder a golden cradle and a coverlet embroidered with pearls, objects of immense rarity and value; also, a matter that seemed of less note at the time, he took along a small boy, who had been found in the camp, as a present to Hoelun. This boy had a golden ring in his nose and wore a fine shirt trimmed with sable fur, which was a sign of rare wealth and luxury at the time. Nobody knew who his people were, and he was too young to give any account of himself, or even tell them what his name was. However, on the clear evidence of his nose-ring and his shirt, Hoelun said: 'This must be the son of a good man, the descendant of a man of good standing and impeccable ancestry.' Nobody was inclined to contradict this. She gave him the name Shikikan-kutuku, which was later shortened to Shigikutuku, for the greater convenience of those addressing him, and brought him up to be an attendant on her own sons.

Shigikutuku grew up to be not only a valiant fighter but wise and learned beyond all the Khan's other companions. He laid down all the laws by which the lands of the Mongols came to be governed. Naturally it was Genghis Khan who told him what the laws were to be, but it was Shigikutuku who collected them into a proper system, administered them, and made them known to the people, so that everybody understood and obeyed them.[66]

THE ABOLITION OF THE JURKIN

Temujin's *auruq*, his headquarters camp, was at this time at the lake called Hariltu Nor. His people were too numerous now to move about the country in a body, as they had done in the old and simpler days, when he separated from Jamukha, and the clansmen first came to join him. Now the camps of his dependent clansmen covered a wide area, pasturing on the steppes the animals they lived on. Temujin's swift messengers, headed by those leaders, Arkhai Kasar, Takhai, Sukagai and others, whom he had appointed when he was first made Khan, delivered his commands among the camps, and brought him the news from them. His army, too, lived in camps scattered about the steppes, each with its own horseherds and means of sustenance, exercising under his appointed captains. At the Khan's own camp the only troops were his own personal bodyguards, the day-guards and the night-guards, picked and trusted men; and his commissariat, his cooks and servants, besides his own immediate family with their retinues.

Naturally these people from his headquarters were not all to be taken with him on a campaign. When he rode on this expedition against the Tatars, many of them stayed behind, in the *auruq* by Hariltu Nor, looking after things while he was away.

He returned from his campaign to hear bad news from the people there. While he was away, they had had trouble with the Jurkin. A body of these quarrelsome men had come to the camp on some errand or other. A fight had started, as tended to happen when the Jurkin visited anywhere, and ten of Temujin's men had been killed. The cause of the fight was of no importance to the Khan; the outcome of it infuriated him.

'Are we to put up with this from the Jurkin?' he stormed and raged. 'When we were feasting by the Onon, first of all they beat my cook Shiki'ur. Then they wounded Belgutai in the shoulder. They said they wanted to make peace, so we gave those two women, Khorijin and Khu'urchin, back to them. Then when we rode against our old enemies, the Tatar, who murdered our fathers and our forefathers, we waited for those same Jurkin, and they did not come. Since they act as enemies, let them be treated as enemies.'

His army being still assembled, he mounted and rode against the Jurkin. They were encamped at the Seven Hills on the Kerulen, near the island Kode'e.[67] The people scattered and fled when the Khan and his army came down on them; the camp was pillaged. Sacha Beki and Taichu, with a few of their men, escaped to the gorges of Teletu. Temujin's warriors pursued them and captured them. They were brought before him.

He looked at them with distaste.

'What were the words that passed between us in former days?' he asked them.

They were sullen. 'We do not remember our words,' they said. 'Remind us of our words.'

Temujin reminded them of their words, when they had elected him Khan: 'If on the day of battle we disobey you, take our flocks from us, our women and children, and cast our worthless heads on the steppe.'

They made no reply, but, as the chronicle says, stretched out their necks. They were taken away, and their heads were lopped off. Their remains were thrown out on to the steppes, as they themselves had once requested.

Having dealt with Sacha Beki and Taichu, Temujin turned his attention to the Jurkin clansmen. The clan was dangerous, and he decided to abolish it entirely. Its members were dispersed so that they no longer had any life in common; they became servants, concubines or warriors, according to their aptitudes.

The three sons of Telegetu, a chieftain of the Jalair, came before the Khan. These three men had been with the Jurkin. But men were to be used for what they were worth; Temujin did not care if a man was a Jalair or a Jadaran, a

Taijiut or a Tatar, if he was prepared to serve him. The eldest of the three brothers, Gu'unua, presented his two sons to the Khan, saying: 'Let them be slaves in your household. If they desert your threshold, cut out their livers and throw them away.'

One of these two sons was Mukhali, who later became the greatest of all those who served under Genghis Khan. He was raised to the rank of Go-ong, or, as the Chinese say, Kuo-Wang, Prince of the Ruling House. The Khan in his last years left him to complete the conquest of northern China while he himself went off to conquer the West.

The second brother also gave his two sons to the Khan. The third, Jebke, had no sons; but he brought with him from the Jurkin camp a youth called Borokhul.[68] Mukhali and Borokhul were soon singled out by Temujin for their exceptional talents, and rose in his service with such remarkable rapidity that within a few years Ong Khan, in one of those recurrent crises that beset him, specially requested that Temujin should send to his aid those Four Coursers of his, Bo'orchu, Chila'un, Mukhali and Borokhul, whose swiftness in action was already famous in all the steppes.

One man of the Jurkin whose future seemed doubtful was the princely wrestler, Buri Boko. His pride and bad temper rendered him impossible to live with, and there was continual bad feeling between him and Belgutai. He was too great a man to serve under anyone else, and Temujin could find no legal justification for executing him. One day, seeing Belgutai and Buri Boko among those around him, he suddenly commanded that they should wrestle together. In the first hold Buri Boko allowed himself to fall, knowing that he could throw Belgutai off without difficulty. Belgutai, sitting on top of him, was unable to press him to the earth. He glanced at the Khan, who bit his lower lip. Belgutai, understanding the signal, held his knee against Buri Boko's back, crossed his arms behind his neck and jerked it upward, so that Buri Boko's back was broken. He rose from the fallen wrestler and wandered off moodily, leaving the grandson of Kabul Khan lying on the earth. This was not the kind of mission that Belgutai relished, but even the most amiable of men had sometimes to act against his better nature in the Khan's service. The device would have been regarded with as little enthusiasm by anyone else, but for the one circumstance which Temujin had reckoned on: Buri Boko had no friends.

JAMUKHA IS PROCLAIMED KHAN

The power of Genghis Khan had made little impression on the chancellor Wanyen, but it was great enough to appear a dangerous menace to those of the steppe people who were not his friends. During the next two or three years, messages passed between the chieftains in many parts of the steppe, as far east as the land of the Tatars, and as far west as those of the Naiman, beyond the Kerait country, towards the Altai Mountains. They needed to find some Mongol leader that they could set up in opposition to Temujin, before his power grew too great. Targutai was growing old, and had no firm hold over his people; the natural choice was Jamukha. In the Year of the Hen, 1201, they met together on the Arguna, the continuation of the Kerulen north of Khulun Nor, before it flows into the Amur, and there they elected him Khan.

They were a strange collection of people, including men not only of many different Mongol clans, but also of distant nations. There was a group of Alchi Tatars; a group of the Naiman, the Turkish people from the west, under their Khan, Buyiruk;[69] and from the Merkit came Kutu, the son of Tokhto'a. The chieftain Kuduka Beki came with his forest people from the north, the Oirat. The Mongols were of many clans, the Salji'ut, the Ikireis, the Qorolas, the Durben and others. These Durben were descended directly from Borjigidai,[70] the remote ancestor of the Borjigin, and his queen Mongqoljin the Fair. There was great bitterness between them and the Alchi Tatars. Then there was a group of the Onggirat, the clan from among whom Temujin had

123

acquired his wife Berta. And there was naturally a large assembly of the Taijiut, the irreconcilable enemies of Temujin. They were led by several chieftains, Targutai among them, another being the very strong fighter A'uchu Bahadur.

Between so many different people all kinds of accommodations and adjustments had to be made and old quarrels patched up, such as that between the Durben and the Alchi Tatars. These matters had been discussed for three years, since the negotiations started, and even now when they met together there was still some peacemaking to be done. But at last all these things were settled. Under the supervision of the shamans, who were numerous in this assemblage, oaths were taken between the agreeing parties, and a stallion and a mare were ritually hacked into pieces, to ensure the approval of the gods. The whole party moved off along the river, and on a suitable promontory, where the Kan flows into the Arguna, Jamukha was proclaimed Gur Khan. This meant Sole Ruler; the title had been used by many other chieftains in the past, but it was regarded as the most suitable counterblast to Temujin's title of Rightful Ruler. The formal preliminaries being concluded, the whole army moved off under its new Khan to attack Genghis Khan.

Temujin was at that time in the Guralgu massif. The news of what was happening was brought to him by various sympathisers among those concerned, and at last a man of the Qorolas rode into the camp with the tidings that the army had assembled, Jamukha had been proclaimed Khan, and they had set off against him.

Temujin sent messages to Ong Khan, and put his own army in readiness. Ong Khan joined him, and they rode off down the Kerulen. Jamukha was nominally a vassal of Ong Khan, like Temujin, but the army he had assembled was too powerful a combination for Ong Khan's liking.

THE BATTLE OF KOYITAN

The advance parties of the two armies met one evening.[71] Prince Altan, Khuchar and Daritai were riding ahead of

Temujin's people, and Sanggum, Jakha Gambu and Bilgei Beki led the advance guard of Ong Khan. On the side of Jamukha came A'uchu Bahadur the Taijiut, Kutu of the Merkit, Buyiruk Khan of the Naiman, and Kuduka Beki[72] of the Oirat. The opposing advance guards held a parley, keeping a suitable distance and shouting at the tops of their voices. The outcome of the parley was brief:

'It is late: we will fight tomorrow.'

In the morning, the main armies moved up and began to deploy, flinging out their wings right and left among the wooded valleys of Koyitan.

This would have been a memorable battle if it had taken place, but the gods decided against it. Usually they flung their weight into a battle on one side or the other, as is evidenced by the fact that one side or the other usually won; but on this occasion it appears that Heaven thought it best to have no battle at all.

It may be that the shamans among Jamukha's newly acquired people had rendered the gods weary by their repeated importunities when the oaths were taken along the Arguna. Now, on this fateful morning, instead of leaving well alone and preparing their horses and weapons for battle, they made more sacrifices, appealing to the gods to send down a thunderstorm to strike down their enemies. Buyiruk Khan and Kuduka Beki of the Oirat were especially skilled at this kind of rain-magic.

The thunderstorm duly appeared, but instead of falling on the armies of Temujin and Ong Khan, it fell on those of Jamukha. Torrential rain fell, and in between the fearful flashes of lightning there was almost total darkness. The armies of Jamukha, striving to deploy into battle positions, found themselves struggling through marshes, as floodwater swept down into the low ground, and falling into quagmires.

Saying to each other: 'We are not beloved of Heaven', they dispersed in confusion.

Considering the noted skill of Buyiruk Khan and Kuduka in producing magic thunderstorms, the misdirection of this one was thought by many to be inexplicable. It has to be borne in mind, though, that among this miscellaneous assembly of people led by Jamukha, enthusiasm for a full-scale battle of this kind was lacking. If it had been a matter of riding down on Temujin's unprepared camp, as they had been led to believe, they would have been happy enough. Instead of this, they found themselves confronted by a large army, led by two redoubtable chieftains who were accustomed to fighting together.

Buyiruk Khan and Kuduka saw no profit in fighting such a battle, in a cause in which they were not greatly concerned, in a distant land. If the thunderstorm had fallen on Temujin, he would merely have waited until it stopped and given battle as soon as conditions improved. It cannot be denied that the shamans appealed for a thunderstorm; the gods in their wisdom sent one where it would do most good, by giving Jamukha's reluctant allies an excuse to desert him.

Buyiruk Khan collected his men together and marched back to his own country, in the foothills of the Altai. Kutu of the Merkit, son of Tokhto'a, went back to his lands along the Selenga. Kuduka the Oirat set off for his forests beyond Lake Baikal. A'uchu Bahadur and Targutai, with the Taijiut, hastened back towards the Onon. Jamukha, abandoned by his allies, moved off with his own people back towards the Arguna, and, in a fury of bad temper, pillaged along the way the clansmen who had recently joined in electing him Khan.

Temujin and Ong Khan, having won this victory without striking a blow, took counsel together about their next best course. The allied forces from distant lands might well be allowed to make their way home; they came from too far away to be an immediate menace. Those leaders whose forces were nearest home must be dealt with while they were in a state of disarray.

Ong Khan set off in pursuit of Jamukha, following him down the Arguna. On the way, however, he decided that a serious punitive expedition would be misguided. The large force of many nations assembled by Jamukha no longer existed. It suited his own interests better to have two chieftains, rivals to each other, in the adjacent territory, rather than one who was too powerful. Once he was well clear of his ally, he broke off the pursuit, wheeled left towards the west, and rode back to his own Kerait country.[73]

THE DESTRUCTION OF THE TAIJIUT

Temujin, according to his own part of the agreement, pursued the Taijiut towards the Onon. They were his primary enemies and the target he had chosen.

A'uchu Bahadur rode fast until he reached the Onon. Having crossed it, he arranged his men on the farther bank in a posture of defence, with their shields to the water. They had suffered negligible losses, having lost no one but stragglers. The Taijiut people from whom his warriors came also assembled here for protection, and arranged their wagons in circles in the forest, sheltering behind them. They came in from all their outlying camps during this day or two, since they could hope for nothing from Temujin but to be pillaged and killed or enslaved.

Temujin and his army came down to the Onon, and deployed for battle. In the morning they struggled across the river and hammered at the Taijiut shield-wall. The battle was desperate. Here and there they gained a foothold; sometimes they were driven back again into the river, but sometimes they kept possession of a part of the bank. When night came, the battle was still undecided; the warriors lay down to sleep where they were, fully armed, waiting for the morning.

Temujin and his guards were among those who fought their way across the river and remained to sleep on the northern side, on a stretch of the river bank surrounded on three sides by the Taijiut. He had been wounded in the neck in the fighting. In the night he went here and there among his men, organising the defence of the bridgehead. Then he lay down to sleep. He had lost a great deal of blood and was in a weakened condition.

Jelmei was in attendance on him. He insisted on tending the Khan alone, through the night. Those learned in medicine among the Mongols insisted that a wound like this should be sucked continually while the blood was still flowing; it was regarded as highly dangerous that it should be allowed to clot prematurely.[74]

Jelmei attached his lips to the neck of the unconscious Khan and sucked throughout the remainder of the night, taking his lips away only when his mouth was full of blood, so that he could spit it out.

In the middle of the night Temujin regained consciousness and said: 'The blood has completely dried up. I am thirsty.'

The nearest water was the river, but it was muddy and bloody after the battle, and there was no nourishment in it. To ford the Onon in the darkness would take too much time, even if it were possible. Jelmei took off his cap and his boots, his cloak and his shirt, so that he had nothing left on but a pair of breeches. He slipped through their own defences and those of the enemy, moving silently in the darkness, and came to a circle of wagons. He climbed into a few of these, looking for mare's milk, but could find none; in their hasty march to assemble here, the people had let their mares go free without milking them. Since there was no fresh milk, he took from one of the wagons a big skin of curdled milk,[75] and slipped back through both lines of defence with it. Heaven, as the chronicle says, protected him; but his extreme skill and agility of movement must also have contributed to his preservation.

He went in search of the best water he could find, brought it back, mixed it with the curdled milk, and gave this to the Khan to drink. Temujin was still half-conscious, sunk back on his cloak. Jelmei helped him to raise himself; three times he took breath and drank.

'Within me, I feel my eyes are brightening,' he said.

He sat up, raised his head higher, and looked around him. The day was coming, and an uncertain light lay on the thinly-wooded steppe. By it he could see all around him a little bloody marsh, where Jelmei had spat out the blood from his mouth.

Temujin looked at it and said: 'Would it not have been better if you had spat a little farther away?'

Jelmei replied: 'As you were in a desperate condition, I was afraid to go farther away from you. I was in haste; what I happened to swallow, I swallowed, and as much as I could spit out, I spat out. In my agitation, a great deal of it went into my stomach.'

The Khan considered this for a little, and then said: 'Why did you run naked in among my enemies, when I was in this situation? If they had captured you, would you not have told them where I was, and how matters were with me?'

Jelmei replied: 'This is what I thought. If I was captured, I was going to say to them: "I was going to give myself up to you, but they guessed my intention, and seized me. They were going to kill me, and took off all my clothes; but when I had nothing left on but my breeches, I managed to escape and so I came to you." That was what I was going to say. If they had believed me, they would have given me clothing and taken care of me. Then at the right moment I would have seized a horse and come back to you. That is what I thought, when I went to find refreshment for the Khan, who is the apple of my eye.'

Temujin thought a little more. 'What shall I say now?' he said at last. 'When the three Merkit came against me on Burkhan Khaldun, you were the first to go down from the mountain and make sure they were gone. Now you have saved my life by sucking the blood with your mouth. Then, when I was tormented by thirst, you went naked among my enemies, without thinking of your own safety, to bring me drink and put fresh life into me. These three services you have done me will always remain in my thoughts.'

He struggled to his feet. All around, the Mongols were taking up their weapons and preparing for battle. But there was silence from the side of the enemy; and when they went forward from their defences, they found that the Taijiut warriors had gone off during the night, deciding that the battle was lost and there was nothing more to be done.

Some of the Taijiut people had also fled, and others were seen making their way off from the camp. Most of them, though, had stayed within their wagon-circles, thinking that they could not flee very far and were bound to be overtaken; they would bring less trouble on themselves by staying where they were and submitting to whatever fate brought them.

SORKHAN SHIRA

Temujin had horses brought across the river, and sent his men in pursuit of the Taijiut. He himself was riding with a party in the hills beyond, rounding up the fleeing people and killing or capturing the warriors, when he heard a shrill voice crying from a hilltop rising from the side of the pass over which they were riding. It was a woman dressed in red, who cried repeatedly: 'Temujin! Temujin!'

'Whose woman is that, shrieking up there?' Temujin asked.

He sent some of his men up to interrogate her. She said to them: 'I am Sorkhan Shira's daughter, Khada'an. The warriors seized my husband and were going to kill him. So I cried out to Temujin, thinking he might rescue him.'

Temujin had not seen or heard of Khada'an since the distant day when, as an escaped captive in the camp of the Taijiut, he entered the tent of Sorkhan Shira. Sorkhan had warned her, then a small girl, to keep silent. When her words were brought to Temujin, he galloped up to the top of the hill, dismounted, and took Sorkhan Shira's daughter in his arms, to comfort her. But her husband, it was found, had already been killed.

After they had rounded up the people in this locality, they camped for the night. The Khan sent for Khada'an and made her sit by his side, in the seat of honour.

Among the people who were brought in the next day were Sorkhan Shira and his sons; and with them a young man called Jirkho'adai of the same clan, subjects of the Taijiut.

Temujin said to Sorkhan Shira and his sons: 'It was you who threw to the ground the heavy wood that was on my neck; you took the shameful collar from me. That was a great service you did me, father and sons. But why have you come to me so late?'

Sorkhan Shira replied: 'I looked on you always as my true Khan. But what reason was there to hurry? If I had come sooner, the Taijiut, my lords and masters, would have scattered to the winds like ashes everything I left behind, my wife and sons, my herds and all my goods. Knowing this, I was in no haste. But now we have come to join ourselves to you.'

'It is well,' the Khan said. There was no denying the truth of Sorkhan Shira's words. A small man could not transfer his allegiance in the way a chieftain could.

Temujin examined with curiosity the face of the young man who had been brought in with them. Men were the material he worked with, and he did not forget a face, even one seen briefly and in unfavourable circumstances.

'When we were at Koyitan,' he said, 'manoeuvring here and there, in the face of the enemy, getting ready for the battle, someone shot an arrow from the top of the hill and struck my horse in the shoulder, the brown war-horse with the white mouth. Who shot that arrow from the mountain?'

'I shot it,' the young man admitted. 'If the Khan puts me to death, there will be nothing left of me but a little piece of earth. But if I am pardoned, I shall ride in front of the Khan against his enemies, cleaving the bright water, and shattering the hardest stone.'

The Khan studied the young man and considered his words. 'A man who has acted as an enemy,' he said, 'usually hides himself, or at least keeps quiet about what he has done. This man does not try to hide anything. He is a man worthy of companionship. His name is Jirkho'adai; but since he shot my horse with an arrow, I shall call him Jebe, the arrow. He shall ride with me.'

In later years this same Jebe, the Taijiut, conquered Kara Kitay, and, with Subetai, led the armies that marched round the Caspian, defeating all the peoples it met on the way: a feat of arms that had never been performed before.

In this way Temujin made use of such of the Taijiut who were fortunate enough to draw their capabilities to his attention. Others were enslaved in enormous numbers and distributed among his followers. As for the leaders, A'uchu Bahadur and others, they were slain and scattered to the winds like ashes, even to the children of their children.

TARGUTAI

Targutai, the old Taijiut chieftain, hiding in the forest, was seized by some men of the Baarin clan, Shirgu'etu and his sons Alakh and Naya'a. Targutai was too old and fat by now to ride a horse, so they put him in a wagon.

Some of his kinsmen, getting word of this, came along to release him. Shirgu'etu knew that they would kill him, whether Targutai was alive or dead. He climbed on the wagon and sat astride Targutai, waving a sharp knife. He could at least take a chieftain along with him as a cushion to rest his head on in the underworld.

Targutai shrieked out to his kinsmen: 'Shirgu'etu is going to kill me. What good will it do you to take away my lifeless body? Go away quickly, before he kills me.'

He went on babbling to Shirgu'etu, sitting astride him: 'Temujin will not kill me. When he was still little, because there was fire in his eyes and spirit in his face, and he was left in a masterless camp, I had him with me, to teach him. I taught him as I would have brought up a two- or three-year-old colt. If I had wished to kill him, I could not have brought myself to do it. He will remember this now. Temujin will not kill me.'

His kinsmen said to each other: 'We came here to save our father's life. But if Shirgu'etu kills him, what will be the use of his lifeless body to us?' So they rode away.

After they had gone, Naya'a said to his father and brother: 'If we go to Genghis Khan, taking Targutai with us as a captive, he will say: "These are men who have raised their hands against their lawful master. How can they be worthy of trust? How can they be our companions? The best thing to do with such men is to cut their heads off."

'It would be better to let Targutai go, and then go ourselves to Genghis Khan and say: "We have come to offer you our strength. We captured Targutai, and were on our way to you, but then we said to each other: We cannot betray our rightful lord. How can we bring him to his death? So we let him go, and now we come to offer our strength to you in an upright fashion." '

The others agreed with these words of Naya'a. They let Targutai go and went to Temujin without him. The Khan listened to their story attentively.

'If you had come here, having laid your hands on your lawful ruler, I should have had your heads cut off, you and your sons and your sons' sons. Your feeling that you should not betray your lawful master was correct.'

Temujin had strict standards in these matters. A man like Jebe, an enemy, who loosed off an arrow at him, could be pardoned, but there was no pardon for a man who raised his hand against his own lord. Temujin had a highly developed instinct, not only for acquiring power, but for preserving it. He knew, as all rulers must learn, that another ruler might be dangerous to him, but the people they both ruled were more dangerous still.

He rewarded Naya'a with a commission in his army, making him captain of a hundred. Naya'a was one of those men of high principles who have little hesitation in voicing them; men find them useful, if they can subdue their irritation. Naya'a's principles served him well on another occasion, when the Khan suspected him of unauthorised dealings with the lady Hulan. He rose to command ten thousand men, and it is certain that but for his high principles he would have died young.

XII

The Year of the Dog

No man can view clearly the crisis of his own life while he is passing through it. These six years from the Year of the Hen to the Year of the Tiger, 1201 to 1206, were the vital period of Temujin's rise to power. In the first of those years he was a small vassal of Ong Khan; in the sixth he was Khan of all the steppe peoples. In the middle of that period he fell to his lowest ebb, retiring in defeat to Baljuna, with all his adherents fallen away. Yet he still struggled to preserve his alliance with Ong Khan, seeing in it his one hope of survival. He struggled desperately against his own fate, and only found his own way when fate forced it on him.

The great alliance against him in the Year of the Hen was no great success, but this is not to say that Jamukha was finished as a rival leader. He remained as a rallying-point for any Mongols who were unwilling to recognise Temujin as their rightful ruler. They were a people accustomed to independence, not to say anarchy; and anarchy has its solid advantages as against authoritarian rule. Two Khans, in fact, were better than one, for any chieftain, large or small, who liked to regulate his own affairs.

So Jamukha still had plenty of supporters, and Temujin was not yet strong enough to finish him off. He was still a small Khan, though he was stronger than he had been.

Ong Khan had troubles of his own. Not long after the battle of the magic thunderstorm, at Koyitan, a number of his brothers and uncles once more plotted against him. One of them, suddenly uncertain what advantages would accrue to him from it, betrayed the plot to Ong Khan. The conspirators were arrested, and, as the chroniclers recalled, they were laden with fetters and spat upon by all. One of them who got warning in time was Jakha Gambu, that younger brother who had fought with Ong Khan at Koyitan. He had subsequently tried to lead some of the Kerait people over to Genghis Khan, and now, finding his manoeuvres had brought him to a state of hopeless confusion, he fled to the Naiman.

DALAN NAMURGAS

In the Year of the Dog, 1202, Temujin took his armies eastwards on another expedition against the Tatars. He decided that the time had come for the tightening up of discipline among his followers. He issued an order that nobody should stop to plunder. When the enemy were defeated in battle, the victory was to be followed up, the leaders pursued and captured, and the armies destroyed. The booty would then be collected and shared out.[76]

The order was more far-reaching than it seemed. One major trouble with these steppe wars, as Temujin clearly saw, was that they had little permanent result. The defeated enemies merely ran away, taking with them as many of their women, children, serfs and flocks as could keep up with them. They needed only a short time for reassembly to be ready to fight again. The power of the victor would be more effectively increased if the defeated were more severely dealt with before anything they had left behind was picked up.

135

It was unfortunate for the world that the inconclusive nature of these wars made so strong an impression on Genghis Khan in his early years. He learned that any enemy he left alive would within a short space of time be an enemy again. The only man he could trust was one who submitted to him without reservation on the first encounter. Such a man he could get on with. Others were only safe if they were dead.

His own immediate followers obeyed the decree which forbade premature looting. They had come to him intending to obey him, and they set no limit to their obedience. It was not to be expected that such semi-independent princes as Altan, Khuchar and Daritai, the Khan's own uncles and cousins, should heed such unreasonable demands.

Temujin came up against the Tatars at Dalan Namurgas, on the Khalkha, east of Buir Nor, and defeated them in battle. They fell back; the Mongol armies pursued them, slaying and capturing them in large numbers.

The princes, Altan, Khuchar and Daritai, were less assiduous in the pursuit. Finding a great number of animals roaming the steppes in the absence of their Tatar owners, they followed the usual custom of rounding them up, and collecting anything that took their fancy in the abandoned Tatar camps.

Temujin, having issued a clear order, could not tolerate their disobedience. He detached portions of his army, placed them under the command of Jebe and Khubilai, and sent them off after the disobedient princes, with orders to take away from them everything they had captured. The outcome was what might have been expected. Prince Altan and Khuchar, retiring in haste with as much of their booty as they could take with them, departed from their allegiance to him. They re-established themselves as independent chieftains, entering into such arrangements with Ong Khan, Jamukha and other rulers as seemed desirable.

Daritai, however, seeing a little more clearly than the others, submitted to having his booty taken away from him.

Owing to his determined pursuit of the Tatars, Temujin found that he had a very considerable number of Tatar prisoners. They were kept under guard in the Mongol camp, and for the most part they were not greatly perturbed by their situation. Some of the chieftains might expect to be executed, but the lesser men had a reasonable hope of surviving. Some might have to serve as warriors under the Mongols, or even be enslaved, but a slave of talents could always hope to become a warrior again.

Temujin held a council to decide what to do with them. It was a great matter, and nobody was present at this council but his own family. The Khan's intention to wipe out his enemies on a large scale came as a shock to them, since it went beyond anything to which they were accustomed; but they could do nothing to dissuade him.

Belgutai had naturally made friends among the Tatar prisoners. One of these was Yeke Charan, the principal Tatar leader. Belgutai wandered sadly across to talk to him. When Yeke Charan asked him what decision the family council had come to, Belgutai did not hesitate to tell him.

'We agreed to measure you against the linchpin,' he said.

This was a not unknown procedure, though it had never been applied on quite such a vast scale. Prisoners were led past the wheel of a wagon. Those who were taller than the linchpin were beheaded; the children, who were smaller, survived to be taken into the Mongol armies when they grew up.[77]

The outcome of this conversation was natural enough, though Belgutai, in his garrulous goodwill, had never thought of it. Yeke Charan told his fellow-prisoners of the Khan's decision. Having nothing to lose, they rose up against their guards and fought their way out of the camp, taking with them what weapons they could seize. They gathered themselves together on a hilltop in a tight formation of fierce warriors. Men who are going to be killed whatever happens, and know it, fight well. The destruction of the

Tatars, which was in due course accomplished, cost many Mongol lives.

Temujin was remarkably lenient towards Belgutai.

'Because Belgutai revealed the decision of the family council,' he said, 'our army suffered great losses. From now on, Belgutai will take no part in the council. While it is being held, he will remain outside, keeping order in the camp, and he will sit in judgment during that time over the quarrelsome, the thieves and the liars. When the council is finished and the wine is all drunk, then Belgutai can come in.'

He ordered at the same time that Daritai should be banned from the family councils, for disobeying his *yasakh*.

YESUGEN AND YESUI

The Khan acquired a new woman from among these Tatars. She was Yesugen, the daughter of the chieftain Yeke Charan. He found her pleasing, and treated her with favour. Yesugen was wise enough not to quarrel unduly with fate, which had urgently disposed of her father, but provided her with some measure of fortune herself.

While they were still in the Tatar country, she said to Temujin: 'The Khan, showing favour towards me, takes care of me well and provides me with goods and servants. But I have an elder sister, Yesui, who would please the Khan even more than I. She is married; Yeke Charan acquired a son-in-law, who came to live with her. But at present, in this dispersion of the people, I do not know where they have gone.'

Temujin was a little taken aback by this unwomanly generosity.

'If your elder sister is even more beautiful than you are, I will send men in search of her. But if she comes, will you give up your place to her?'

'If the Khan pleases, as soon as I see my elder sister, I will give up my place to her.'

Temujin gave the order that Yesui must be searched for; and the warriors found her hiding in the forest, with the son-in-law who had been given to her. The husband fled, but the lady Yesui was brought in.

Yesugen, as soon as she saw her elder sister, rose, made her sit on the seat she had lately occupied, and herself took a seat lower down. The Khan found Yesui as agreeable to look on as Yesugen had said; she rose rapidly in his favour, and remained all his life one of his favourite women.

One day the Khan was sitting outside the tent, drinking with some friends. He sat between the lady Yesui and the lady Yesugen; and he heard the lady Yesui suddenly catch her breath. Temujin said nothing to her; but after reflecting for a time he called the princes Bo'orchu and Mukhali to him and said: 'Have all the people here divide themselves up into their clans. If any find a man with them who is not of their clan, let them set him aside.'

When the people were arranged, clan by clan, a young man, good-looking and alert, was standing apart from all the clansmen. When they asked him who he was, he replied: 'I am the son-in-law of Yeke Charan the Tatar, to whom was given his daughter Yesui. When we were surprised by the enemy, I was frightened, and escaped; then I came here, telling myself that it would be safe here. In the middle of so many people, how should I be recognised as a stranger?'

When these words were reported to the Khan, he said: 'He was already an enemy; he is now a masterless man. What has he come to spy on us for? We have measured people of his kind against the linchpin of a wagon wheel. There is no need for any further investigation. Take him out of my sight.'

They cut the young man's head off immediately. It is not recorded that Yesui mourned him; like Hoelun years before, she had done better for herself.

EXPEDITION AGAINST THE NAIMAN

In this same Year of the Dog, when Genghis Khan went against the Tatars, his old friend Ong Khan rode against the Merkit. The expedition was reasonably successful.

139

Tokhto'a Beki got away again, but Ong Khan captured his two sons Kutu and Chila'un, and took possession of a couple of his daughters, along with a lot of women and other people. Some held that he should have given some of this booty to Temujin, in return for providing him with men and cattle after his eviction of Erke Kara; but it is too much to expect of princes that one should pay his debts to another if there is no special reason for it.

Temujin appears to have borne no grudge against Ong Khan in this matter. Both Khans were in a high good humour, this early summer of the Year of the Dog, after their two expeditions had gone so well. Last year they had seen the assorted allies of Jamukha melt away before them; the Taijiut had been pillaged and were no longer a danger; shrewd blows had been dealt at the Tatars and the Merkit. It was a good time to extend their power further.

They set off against Buyiruk Khan of the Naiman, that same chieftain who had come from the foothills of the distant Altai to set up Jamukha as Gur Khan. Ong Khan had reconciled himself with Jamukha, whom he needed as a foil to Temujin, but he suspected that Jamukha was still maintaining relations with Buyiruk.

The powerful Khan of all the Naiman people, Inancha Bilgei, had died about the time when Ong Khan and Temujin joined with Wanyan Siang to attack the Tatars. His kingdom had been divided by his two sons, Bai Bukha and Buyiruk. Bai Bukha, better known by his Chinese title of Tayang Khan, ruled the northern part, and Buyiruk Khan the southern.

These Mongol and Kerait armies coming up against him were more than Buyiruk Khan could face. He retreated with his armies to the extremity of the Naiman country, and crossed the Altai into the borderlands of the Uighurs. The two Khans followed him across that range. For a time they lost track of him, but by good fortune captured one of his scouts who had broken his saddle-girth while escaping up the mountain from the river Urunggu. Having ascertained which way Buyiruk Khan was going, they followed him down the Urunggu and caught him up at the lake called Kishil-Bashi. Here his army was defeated, but Buyiruk Khan himself escaped and survived for some years, being finally slain while hunting in the Altai after the defeat of Tayang Khan. His name meant the Commander; other rulers had held it, such as Ong Khan's father Khurchakhus Buyiruk Khan. As for his brother, Tayang Khan, his name signified that the Chinese considered him the principal ruler north of the Gobi. But neither of these brothers was worthy of their father, Inancha Bilgei.

Temujin and Ong Khan were returning towards the crossing of the mountains when they came up against an army of the Naiman from the northern part of the kingdom, the realm of Tayang, led by a pugnacious warrior called Kokse'u Sabrakh. Kokse'u Sabrakh was a better man than either of those brothers. It was late in the day when the two armies deployed face to face with each other, the one fresh and the other travel-worn. They prepared to sleep where they were, ready to give battle on the following day.

Ong Khan had begun to tire of this expedition. There had been little profit from it, his armies were half-hearted and he was a long way from home. He was disturbed by the increasing strength of his vassal Temujin, and confused by messages he received from his other vassal Jamukha, insinuating that Temujin was carrying on secret negotiations with the Naiman, and intended to betray him.[78] The old Khan was grown so devious by now that he thought everyone as devious as himself. Since Jamukha was negotiating with the Naiman he must surely have good grounds for stating that Temujin was doing the same. Ong Khan decided to betray Temujin before he was betrayed himself. He had fires lit along his battle-front, as a blind, and under cover of darkness he assembled his men and marched off into the mountains, making for home.

Temujin woke in the first light of day and, looking towards the battle-front of his ally, saw that he was no longer there.

'These people have left us to cook in the pot,' he observed.

141

Attacking Kokse'u Sabrakh single-handed was beyond his strength. He commanded his army to mount, and with swift discipline they rode off, fading away into the mountains. The years of training were beginning to tell. It was an orderly body of troops that made its way back through the passes and across the Naiman country to encamp on the Saari steppes.

This expedition had a considerable effect on him. It was the first time he had ridden beyond the borders of the lands of people he knew; and the first people he encountered, the Naiman, could not stand up against well-trained Mongol warriors. It might well be that no one else could.

The expedition made a different impression on Ong Khan. His army, anything but united, straggled home through the passes and across the steppes, dispirited and disillusioned with its leader.

Kokse'u Sabrakh, the pugnacious Naiman, observed on the morning of what should have been the battle that one of the armies confronting him had disappeared during the night; the other made off as one man at first light. Pursuit would be profitable. On the one hand, there was a disciplined body of Mongols, making its way back through the passes by which it had come; on the other, there was a straggling mob. He followed Ong Khan's army, and came up with them when they had begun to disperse to their camps in the Kerait country. Kokse'u Sabrakh fell on the nearest Kerait people, who were the people of Ong Khan's son Sanggum. He pillaged a number of camps, capturing, among others, Sanggum's women and sons; and seized half the people and flocks of Ong Khan, who had by that time retired into the gorges of Telegetu.

In this confusion the two captive sons of Tokhto'a the Merkit, Kutu and Chila'un, escaped, and set off down the Selenga to rejoin Tokhto'a.

Ong Khan, in his distress, sent Temujin a message. 'My people and my tents, my women and my children, have been taken by the Naiman. I send to ask of you, my son, to send me your Four Coursers. Help me to regain my people!'

Temujin believed the support of Ong Khan was essential to his survival; moreover, a man owed his ruler unquestioning obedience, and he had vowed to regard Ong Khan as his father. Ong Khan had betrayed him; it was not sufficient justification to betray Ong Khan.

He sent his Four Coursers, Bo'orchu, Mukhali, Borokhul and Chila'un, later called Bahadur. These four were already famed for their swiftness and the tight discipline of their men. When they arrived on the scene, Sanggum was still trying to organise a defence to beat off the Naiman attacks. There was a series of scattered local engagements; in one of these, Sanggum's horse was wounded in the haunch by an arrow, and he was in imminent danger of capture, when the Mongol forces arrived and rescued him. The Naiman, by now somewhat dispersed, were in no condition to withstand these fresh attacks. The Mongols followed them up and recovered the flocks and people who were being slowly driven off westwards. Kokse'u Sabrakh gave up the fight and retired to his own country.

Ong Khan sent fulsome messages of gratitude to Temujin. 'In former days,' he said, 'the father rescued and gave back to me my people. Now the son has sent his Four Coursers to save me and my lost people. Let the guardian spirits of Heaven and Earth witness that I shall be grateful for ever.

'As for me,' he said further, 'I am now old. When I go aloft, to the Heavenly Kingdom, who will govern all my people? My younger brothers are worthless; my son, Sanggum, is good for nothing, and he is the only son I have. If I make Temujin the elder brother of Sanggum, I shall have two sons; I shall be at peace.'

Ong Khan was unjust to his son Sanggum, who was a courageous warrior and a notable general; but he was also vain, moody and petulant, and these faults of character often rendered him intolerable both to his father and to others.

When everything had settled down, the two Khans met in the black forest of the Tula, and there renewed their oaths, declaring themselves once more to be father and son. The oaths were large and binding. 'When we fall on our enemies, we will fall on them together; when we hunt wild beasts, we will hunt them together. If, like fanged serpents, people try to poison our minds against each other, we will not let our minds be poisoned; we will believe only that which we say to each other with our own mouths, through our own teeth.'

It was an admirable oath, and Ong Khan would have done well to keep it. It was taken in the autumn of the Year of the Dog, 1202, and it lasted as long as the spring of the Year of the Pig, which, by ancient Chinese custom, was the year immediately following.

XIII

The Tide Turns Against Genghis Khan

Temujin's position was less secure than it looked. The expedition against the Tatars had been successful, and so had that against the Naiman. His nucleus of immediate followers was solidly loyal. But in the shifting struggle for power among the tribal leaders, all his other associates might fall away at any time if it seemed convenient to them to do so.

The alliance with Ong Khan was a frail prop, which needed strengthening. Temujin sought an answer in a family alliance. He suggested to Ong Khan that a younger sister of Sanggum's, Cha'ur Beki, should be given in marriage to his own eldest son Jochi. Temujin was thirty-five, and Jochi was a grown man. In return, he offered a princess of his own house to Sanggum's son Tusakha.

Ong Khan could not persuade his son to agree to this arrangement. Sanggum was a touchy middle-aged man, aware of his own weakness. He knew that he was a brave and skilful general, and found it intolerable that despite this his reputation did not stand high among other men. He was bitterly jealous of Temujin. He expressed his antagonism to the idea of the betrothals in trivial terms; there was something always a little womanish about Sanggum.

'If one of our family goes to them,' he said, 'he stands at the door, looking into the tent. If one of their family comes to us, he sits in the depths of the tent, looking towards the door.' The door-corner was the place for servants; the seats of honour were deep in the tent, looking towards the entrance.

Such were the terms in which Sanggum refused to give away his younger sister. When this reply was brought to Temujin he knew he had no friends in that quarter. As the chroniclers say, he let his inner heart withdraw itself from Ong Khan and Sanggum.

THE ENEMIES OF TEMUJIN

Jamukha, hearing of the rejection of Temujin's proposal, knew that the tide was turning against his old *anda*. In the spring of the Year of the Pig, 1203, the principal opponents of Genghis Khan met with Sanggum in the shadow of the height of Jeje'er, in the western part of the Mongol country. Jamukha was there, Prince Altan and Khuchar, the chieftain Abugajin of the Khadagin, Sugatai of the Noyakin, the young chieftain To'oril[79] and Khaji'un Beki. Jamukha repeated his assertions that Temujin was exchanging messages with the Naiman, and urged the others to attack him openly while there was time. Prince Altan and Khuchar expressed their willingness to wipe out the house of Hoelun; Abugajin, To'oril and Khaji'un Beki spoke with great ferocity.

'My *anda* Temujin exchanges messages with his friend Tayang Khan of the Naiman,' Jamukha said. 'His mouth speaks of "father" and "son", but his heart seeks friends elsewhere. If you do not act before he does, what will become of you? If you ride against him, I will take him on the flank.'

Prince Altan said, on behalf of himself and Khuchar: 'As far as these sons of Hoelun are concerned, we will kill the eldest, and we will give you the younger ones to finish off yourselves.'

'I will bind his hands,' Abugajin said. 'I will bind his hands and feet, and give him over to you.'

'We will take away the people of Temujin,' To'oril said. 'When his people are taken away, what will become of him then?'

'Sanggum, my son,' Khaji'un Beki said, 'whatever your thoughts may be, I will go with you up to the uttermost heights, or down to the depths of the abyss.'

They worked themselves into a state of fury and determination, these plotters in the shadow of the height of Jeje'er. They were right to do so; this was the critical moment at which the advance of Temujin to power over them and all other men might be stopped, if it was ever to be stopped at all.

It was necessary to obtain the agreement of Ong Khan. They sent a messenger to him in his camp not far away, to ask for his support.

His reply was: 'How can you have such thoughts towards my son Temujin? We have for a long time leaned on him. If we now harbour such evil designs, Heaven will not look on us with favour. Jamukha has a supple tongue; he speaks well, but is what he says always as true as it sounds?'

Sanggum was stung by this reference to Jamukha's unreliability. 'When a man speaks to you with his mouth and his tongue, why should he not be believed?' he replied tartly. The messages went backwards and forwards from camp to camp; Ong Khan remained obdurate, and at last Sanggum went to see him himself.

'As long as you go on living,' he said, 'we are Temujin's subjects. You are old. Suppose you, his father and Khan, are stabbed to death in full daylight, or stifled in the black night, do you think he will give the government over to anyone else? This people, brought together with such care by your father Khurchakhus Buyiruk Khan—is it I who will then govern them? Or by whom do you wish them to be governed?'

Ong Khan was grief-stricken. Clear duty pulled two ways; whatever he did, he did wrong to someone.

'How can I harm my child, my son?' he pleaded. He meant Temujin; it was not the attitude most calculated to soothe his real son, Sanggum. 'Can it be right to plot against him, when he has for so long been a support to us? Heaven would not look on us with favour.'

Sanggum could not govern his fury. He had no reply to make; he rushed from the tent, letting the door-curtain drop behind him. It was too much for Ong Khan; he called him back.

'Even if Heaven looks on us with disfavour,' he said, 'how can I abandon my own son? Act as you will; it is you who must decide.'

The decision was ultimately fatal to Ong Khan. Sanggum was in the wrong, and Ong Khan knew it. He was old, and had had great troubles in his life.

Sanggum went back to his colleagues. He had conceived of a plan for disposing of Temujin without actually fighting him.

'Those others asked my sister Cha'ur Beki of us,' he said. 'Now, let us fix a day, and invite them here, to eat the betrothal feast. Then we can seize them.'

They agreed to this plan. A message was sent to Temujin, acceding to his demand for Sanggum's sister, and inviting him to a feast.

There was nothing to be gained, as Temujin saw it, by refusing. It was an unexpected change of heart, but a welcome one. No news had come to him of a meeting of the leaders; his need for allies clouded his judgment. He set off to the betrothal feast, with his son Jochi, and a force of ten men. There was no need for more; many of his own men, including Kasar, his brother, were still with Ong Khan.

On the way, he called in at the tent of Munglik. Hoelun was at the *auruq*, but Munglik's tents were in the west. A great lady's friends are not always to be found at the tent door.

148

Munglik, less obsessed with the political situation than Temujin, was immediately suspicions.

'When we asked for Cha'ur Beki,' he said, 'they would not give her to us, out of their distrust for us. Why do they summon us now, to eat the betrothal feast? This may be all very good and fine, but it is as well to find out. My son, we must act carefully. Let us excuse ourselves, saying: "It is spring. Our herds of horses are lean; we must fatten up our herds."'

Temujin was quickly persuaded. He sent messengers to Sanggum, excusing himself from attending, and asking them to eat the betrothal feast, with his messengers acting as his substitutes.

As soon as the message was delivered to them, Sanggum and the others knew that Temujin had guessed their intentions. He had stayed the previous night with Munglik; he could not have got very far on his return journey. They decided to set out in pursuit of him the next morning, at first light.

THE PURSUIT OF GENGHIS KHAN

Prince Altan's son, Charan the Tall, went back to his tents after this meeting and spoke to his wife about what had happened. 'We have decided that tomorrow morning we will seize Temujin,' he said. 'Can you imagine how Temujin would reward a man who took a warning message to him!'

His wife was horrified by this careless talk. 'How can you say such words?' she asked. 'What would happen if one of our people, hearing them, thought you were speaking in earnest?'

The woman's fears were well founded. One of their horseherds, Badai, who had been bringing some mare's milk to the tent, overheard the conversation. He did not, however, go and report it to Prince Altan. Instead, he went and told his friend, another horseherd by the name of Kishilik.

Kishilik decided to go himself and find out what was happening.

He went up to the tent, where he found Charan's son sitting outside, sharpening his arrows. The family argument was still going on inside. When the young prince saw Kishilik approaching he called out to those inside the tent: 'If anyone hears what you are talking about, our tongues will be cut out and our mouths stopped up.' The argument inside the tent abruptly ceased. The young prince spoke to Kishilik. 'Go and catch my grey Merkidai horse and the brown with the white mouth; saddle and bridle them. We shall be riding off early in the morning.'

Kishilik obediently went away, back to his friend Badai. 'It is indeed true, what you have just said,' he said, having heard enough to confirm it. 'Now let us go and warn Temujin.' The leaders thought they might still stop the rise of Temujin; some of their followers saw ahead more clearly.

The two horseherds went and caught the young prince's grey horse, and the white-mouthed brown his father was to ride. They saddled them and left them in a convenient place, tethered near their own tents. This was a matter that would cost them their lives if their plan was discovered; they had to move with extreme caution. They needed food for the journey, but could not be seen preparing it. They took a lamb into their tent, killed it there, and cooked it over the fire. It was not safe to be seen collecting an unusual quantity of firewood so late in the evening. To cook the meat, they burned up the planks of their beds; whatever might happen, it was certain that they would not need these beds again.

As soon as it was dark they stole out, mounted the two horses, and rode off. The theft would be discovered in a few hours, when Prince Altan's son and grandson went to mount their horses before dawn.

They rode hard over the steppes during the night, and came to the tents of Genghis Khan, where he was sleeping on his homeward journey. They reported to the night-guard the words they had heard. Since their message seemed one to be taken seriously, they were led in to the Khan, who was aroused to hear it. Badai told his story, and Kishilik added the words he had overheard.

'May it please the Khan,' he ended by saying, 'there can be no doubt about this. They have decided to surround and capture you.'

Temujin had little difficulty in believing them. As for their action in coming to him, if they had been the subjects of some other ruler, the Khan might well have had them beheaded; but fortunately for them they were the men of Prince Altan, and hence, in Temujin's estimation, his own men, so their action was wholly praiseworthy. These two horseherds did well for themselves that night; three years later they were both made commanders of a thousand, with the privilege of sharing the emperor's cup; besides this, they were granted immunity from criminal proceedings for the first nine offences they committed, which even for a Mongol was a generous allowance.

At this moment, though, there was no time to think of rewarding anybody, and the foreseeable future shrank to a very small space. Sanggum, Prince Altan and the others would by now have set off; there were many of them, and Temujin with his ten men was far from home. They mounted and rode within a few minutes, leaving everything, tents, bedding and other belongings, behind.

Riding eastwards, they came to some people of Temujin's on whom he could rely, men of the Uriangqadai. He sent out messengers to summon his forces, left Jelmei there to organise a rearguard defence, and rode on in the shadow of the mountain called Mao Undur. Late in the afternoon of the following day he dismounted by the sands of Khala-khaljit,[80] to eat and rest.

THE BATTLE OF KHALAKHALJIT

As the evening shadows lengthened his men began to come in. Many of his people, though, were still far away. Those who came included the Uru'ut, under Jurchadai, and the Mangqut, under Khuyildar. These were some of his finest warriors, these Uru'ut and Mangqut clansmen who had come to him at the beginning, after he separated from

Jamukha. But it was a small army that assembled, and it had come in haste. Some of his advisers pressed the Khan to retreat further, but he chose to make his stand here.

The pursuit was swift. Temujin's people had hardly dismounted when two horseherds rode into the camp from the west, coming round the side of Mao Undur. 'While we were pasturing our horses on the fresh grass,' they reported, 'we saw the dust of the enemy there behind us, in front of Mount Mao, skirting the red sands, the Hula'un Burakhat. Since we saw that the enemy was coming, we came to you, driving our horses before us.'

Temujin commanded his forces to mount again. The Uru'ut and Mangqut were drawn up in the forward positions, facing the enemy's line of advance.

The forces of Jamukha and Ong Khan came in sight round the corner of the hill. There was only an hour or two of daylight left. Their forces were not as large as they would have wished, but they were still considerably larger than those that had been hastily assembled by Genghis Khan. They saw the small army deploying in the sandy valley below.

'Who are those people with my son Temujin?' Ong Khan asked. 'Are they good fighters?'

'Those are the Uru'ut and the Mangqut,' Jamukha said, studying them. 'They fight very well. They keep order when they manoeuvre, turning like one man. They are brought up to the use of the sword and the lance from the earliest age. Look, you can see their black and spotted yaks'-tail standards. They are people it is as well to be on guard against.'

'Is that so?' Ong Khan asked. Having gone into this battle, though it was against his will, he had to do so wholeheartedly, and he was an old craftsman in the art of war. 'We will send Kadakh and the Jurkin against him, in the van.' These were some of those Jurkin who had been with Jamukha when Temujin destroyed their clansmen. 'Behind the Jurkin we will throw in Achikh Shirun, with the Tuman Tubegen. Then the Olon Dongqayit. Then Prince Khori

Shilemun, with the guards. Then ourselves with the main army.' He thought for a few moments. 'Brother Jamukha: take command of the army.'

Jamukha could hardly refuse, but he was not at all happy. There was always in the depths of this strange man a lingering regard for his former *anda*. He went aside from the Kerait Khan and spoke to his own companions.

'Ong Khan gives me command of this army, which is really his,' he said. 'I have never been able to fight against my old *anda*. If Ong Khan tells me to command this army, it is because he knows he is less capable of commanding it than I am. He takes the opportunity of leaving the burden to me. We will have news of it taken to my *anda*; it is as well that he should be warned.'

Jamukha despatched a messenger to ride round about to Temujin's forces, to disclose the order of battle to him, and the fact that he, Jamukha, would be commanding.

Temujin received the message with total lack of concern.

'What do you make of that, Uncle Jurchadai?' he said to the Uru'ut chieftain. He did not wait for a reply. 'Take command of the van,' he said briefly. The enemy were advancing down the hill.

Khuyildar of the Mangqut was with them. Before Jurchadai could acknowledge the command, he said: 'I shall fight in front of the Khan, my *anda*. O Khan, my friend: you may decide who will provide for my orphaned children.'

'We will both fight at the head of our clansmen, Uru'ut and Mangqut together,' Jurchadai said equably. He was older than Khuyildar, and less hot-headed. The two chieftains went forward to command their clansmen; the front lines clashed.

In this first engagement, the onrush of the Jurkin was held and turned back; but the chieftain of the Tuman Tubegen, Achikh Shirun, making through the press to Khuyildar, struck him from his horse. The Mangqut chieftain's men surrounded their leader, fought off the Jurkin, and carried him back to the camp.

The Jurkin were thrown back on the Tuman Tubegen

153

by Jurchadai. The superior discipline of Genghis Khan's army told heavily in this otherwise unequal struggle. Jurchadai and some of his clansmen forced their way so far through the ranks of the Tuman Tubegen that they came within close range of Sanggum, commanding the van of the main force. Sanggum had advanced far forward; war was his favourite occupation, and this battle was vital to him. He viewed with fury and impatience the disarray into which the allied armies had been thrown by this small and disciplined force. The day was darkening fast; there was little time to achieve a victory. Spurring forward, he was struck in the cheek by a Mangqut arrow. The Kerait clansmen surrounded him and carried him back to Ong Khan's command post.

With the coming of darkness it was clear that neither side had won this battle of Khalakhaljit Elet. For Temujin the miracle was that he had not lost it, considering the size of his army. There was no possibility of regrouping where they stood; in a whole day of battle, defeat would be certain. Temujin's army, falling back from its contact with the enemy on the dark steppe, continued its orderly retreat without dismounting. There was no pursuit: Ong Khan's people had been thrown into some confusion, and had to reorganise.

THE DESERTION OF THE CLANS

After marching for a few hours, Temujin's army turned and regrouped in battle order; they slept during the few hours of darkness that remained, lying by their horses.

At first light, the Khan said: 'If they come up with us, we shall fight.'

When the roll was called, it was found that, of the chieftains, Ogodai, Borokhul and Bo'orchu were missing.

The Khan said: 'Bo'orchu and Borokhul, who are both trustworthy men, have stayed behind with Ogodai. They would not abandon each other, living or dead.'

The day gradually brightened; the small army, drawn up

in battle order, watched the west for signs of the enemy. A single horseman came in sight, far away. As he drew nearer, it was seen to be Bo'orchu. 'Heaven be thanked!' the Khan said. He turned to make obeisances to the sun, beating his breast.

Bo'orchu rode up to him. 'My horse was struck by an arrow in the charge,' he said. 'I fled on foot. The Kerait had just fallen back to form a circle round Sanggum. Luckily I came across a packhorse; its load had fallen to one side, and it was standing there, not moving. I cut the load off and mounted the packsaddle. So I got away from the battlefield. I found the track our people had taken; and here I am.'

Just then another horseman was seen in the distance. There seemed to be a single rider, but as he came nearer it could be seen that there was another pair of legs dangling down, one on each side. As they approached, the horseman was seen to be Borokhul, riding on the crupper, and supporting Ogodai, who was sitting on the saddle in front of him. There was blood on Borokhul's face, running from the corner of his mouth. Ogodai had been struck by an arrow in the vein of the neck; Borokhul had been following the Mongol practice of sucking the blood from the wound, so that it would not coagulate prematurely.

Temujin wept; his heart was heavy at this lamentable sight. He ordered a fire to be lit with all haste; Ogodai's wound was cauterised, and his thirst slaked with drink.

Temujin was still prepared to fight if the enemy should come up, but Borokhul reported that they appeared to be falling back. 'The dust of the enemy is moving away,' he said. 'I saw it rising in a long cloud in front of the height of Mao, towards the red sands of Hula'un Burakhat. They are going off in that direction.'

'If they had come up we should have fought them,' Temujin said. 'Since they have shirked the battle and stolen away, we will re-form the army and fight them again later.'

They turned and marched off, up the rivers Alqui and Shilugeljit; and went far off to the eastward, to Dalan Namurgas, beyond Buir Nor, in the Tatar country.

155

Messages were sent to the clans, those who had taken the oath to serve Genghis Khan, but none came to join him. Many thought that Ong Khan and Jamukha together were too strong for him. After his recent triumphs, he came suddenly to the nadir of his fortunes. If Ong Khan and Jamukha had followed him up they might have destroyed him. But they lacked resolution, and Ong Khan was distraught by the wounding of Sanggum.

At Dalan Namurgas, someone came in with news of Ong Khan. This was Khada'an Daldurkhan, who had been appointed to the commissariat by Temujin on his election as Khan; he had lately been among Temujin's men serving with Ong Khan. Now he had slipped away to rejoin Temujin, leaving behind him his wives and children and all his possessions. He was able to report on what had happened at Khalakhaljit.

'When Sanggum was struck by an arrow in his painted cheek and fell,' he said, 'he was carried back to Ong Khan. Ong Khan said: "We have stirred up trouble where we should not have stirred up trouble; where we should not have fought, we fought. So, alas, they have driven a nail[81] into the cheek of my son. But since we have saved his life, let us attack them again."

'But Achikh Shirun, of the Tuman Tubegen, said: "Khan, Khan, let things be. When you wished for a son, not yet having one, you made prayers and invocations, with magic spells, praying with all those 'abais' and 'babais' of yours.[82] Now that at last you have a son, let us take care of him. The greater part of the Mongols has gone over to Jamukha; Prince Altan and Khuchar are with us. The Mongols who came up against us in revolt, under Temujin, where will they go now? They have nothing but the single horse that each man rides; the trees of the forest are their roofs. If they do not come to us of their own accord, we will go and gather them in, these people, as one gathers up horse-dung for the fires."

'On these words of Achikh Shirun, Ong Khan said: "It is well. Let it be so, but my son shall have no part in it. Do not disturb him; take good care of him." So saying, he turned away from the field of battle.'

It was still not safe to linger here, where all the clans were hostile or uncertain in their allegiance. Temujin moved off northwards, down the river Khalkha. A count of his people was made; there were two thousand six hundred of them, all that remained loyal to the Khan. They marched down the river, thirteen hundred of them, Temujin's own warriors, on the western bank, and the Uru'ut and Mangqut on the eastern bank. They had flocks and herds with them, but these were insufficient, and they had to reinforce their food supplies by hunting.

Khuyildar, who had been wounded by Achikh Shirun at the battle at Khalakhaljit, had never fully recovered from his wound, but he insisted on taking part in the hunts, despite Temujin's warnings that he was not yet fit to do so. His half-healed wounds reopened; carried back to the camp, he died. Temujin was deeply affected by the death of this faithful Mangqut warrior. He had his body carried up to a high place on the mountain Ornu'u, burial in a high place being a singular mark of honour. He often afterwards paid tribute to the memory of Khuyildar, and made special provision for his descendants.

THE RETREAT TO BALJUNA

The Khalkha river flows into Buir Nor. Here the clan of the Onggirat was encamped, the old clan of Dai Sechen. Temujin sent them a message: 'If the Onggirat remember the bonds of blood between us, let them submit. But if they want war, we will fight.' The Onggirat submitted to him; their warriors joined him, and the Khan touched nothing that belonged to them.

He camped for a time on the east side of the river Tungga, and from there he sent messages to all his old associates and rivals. He thought there was still a possibility of reconciliation with his patron.

He sent Arkhai Kasar and Sukagai to Ong Khan. 'O

Khan my father,' his message ran, 'we have dismounted to the east of the Tungga. The grass is good here, and my horses have rebuilt their muscles.

'O Khan my father, what bitterness do you have against me? The stool on which I sat has been overthrown; the smoke that rose from my tents has been dispersed. Why have you done this to me? Have you been stirred up against me by someone at your side? Have you been goaded on by someone coming between us?

'O Khan my father, what did we agree upon, on the red hills of Jorkhalkhun? Did we not agree on this: "If a fanged serpent tries to stir us up, one against the other, we shall not let ourselves be stirred up; we shall believe only that which we say to each other with our own mouths?" Now, Khan my father, have you parted from me after something you heard me say with my own mouth?

'Though I am weak, there is strength to be found in me. Though I am poor, there is wealth to be found in me. When one of the two shafts of a wagon breaks, the ox cannot draw it. Am I not like a second shaft to you? When one of the wheels of a wagon breaks, it cannot move. Am I not even as your second wheel?'

This was the preamble to Temujin's message. He went on to recount the whole history of Ong Khan and of the association between them.

He concluded: 'And now, O Khan my father, what grievances do you have against me? Send me your messengers to tell me why you are bitter against me. Send Khulbari and Iturgen. If you do not send them both, send one of them.'

When he heard these words, Ong Khan said: 'Alas! in separating myself from my son Temujin, I broke the rules of good conduct; I turned from an oath from which no man should turn.' His heart was full of sorrow. Finally he said: 'If I harbour evil thoughts against my son, may my blood run as it runs now!' Pronouncing this oath, he pricked the end of his little finger with the knife he used for sharpening arrows, let the blood run into a little cup of birch-bark, and sent it back to Temujin.

Temujin also sent a brief message to Jamukha.

'Not being able to bear the sight of me, you have made the Khan my father separate himself from me. In former days, the first one of us who got up was privileged to drink from the blue cup of the Khan our father.[83] When it was I who drank from it, having got up first, you were jealous. But now you can drink from the blue cup of the Khan our father as often as you like.'

No answer came to this, or to the message he sent to Altan and Khuchar.

'Khuchar, when I said to you: "You are the son of Neikun Taiji: be our Khan", you did not wish to be Khan. Altan, when I said to you: "Kutula Khan, your father, ruled us: be our Khan", you also did not wish to be Khan.

'When, going back to a line senior to Bartan Bahadur's sons, I said to Sacha Beki and Taichu: "Be Khan", they also did not wish to be Khan.

'If one of you others had been Khan, I should have thrown myself in the vanguard against your enemies; I should have brought you the fair-cheeked girls, the fine-shanked geldings. When we went out to drive game, I should have driven towards you such a multitude of wild animals that their legs would have been tightly pressed together.

'Having now bound yourselves in companionship with the Khan my father, be faithful. Do not let it be said that you are neglectful of him. I, the *ja'utkhuri*, served him well; do not let people say of you that you did less.

'And let nobody else, whoever they may be, camp at the sources of the three rivers.'[84]

He also sent a message to Sanggum.

'I am the son who was born with a coat on; you, Sanggum, are the son who was born naked. The Khan our father has taken care of both of us equally; you have vented your hate on me because, Sanggum, you feared I might rise above you. Now, do not let the heart of the Khan our father be troubled, but bring him peace. Do not dwell on the idea of being ruler while the Khan our father is still living.'

Temujin specifically requested that all those he addressed should send him two messengers with their reply; it was the courtesy due to his rank. No messengers came. Even Sukagai, who had been one of the messengers to Ong Khan, did not come back; his wife and children were with Ong Khan, and he did not dare to leave them. Arkhai Kasar returned alone, with the little cup of birch-bark containing Ong Khan's blood. He told Temujin how Sanggum had received his message. The prince had remarked:

'Why does he go on saying "the Khan our father"? Does he not really mean "that murderous old man"? Why does he go on speaking of me as his *anda*? Does he not really mean "the friend of Tokhto'a, the dupe of the shamans"? It is quite clear what lies behind his words. Raise the standard of war; let the horses graze till they are fat and strong. Let there be no more delay.'

There was no doubt that Ong Khan was allowing himself to be overridden in everything by Sanggum, however much blood he sent around in birch-bark cups. The lack of support for Temujin appeared to be general. The clans that could do so were waiting to see how things would go; those that were forced to move would move against him.

He retired still farther east, and came down to pasture his flocks by the shores of the Lake Baljuna, at the head-waters of the Tura, beyond Tarei Nor.[85] Here he met some people of the Qorolas, who, being close at hand, readily submitted to him.

At Baljuna, with his small army, his faithful Uru'ut and Mangqut, and such people as had come to him from the Onggirat and the Qorolas, he waited for the moment when he could recover his fortunes. He might have continued for years to be a vassal of the Kerait; after the defeat at Khal-khaljit Elet he was alone.

XIV

The Return from Baljuna

One day, while he was at Baljuna, his brother Kasar rode into the camp. Like others of Temujin's people, he had been with Ong Khan. He had slipped away with a few followers, leaving behind him his wife and three of his sons. He was in an exhausted condition. Unable for a long time to find any trace of Temujin, he had sought for him among the ridges and valleys of this wild eastern country; his supplies had run out, and he had nourished himself and his few men by hunting the small steppe animals and eating them raw, including the skin and tendons.

Temujin was delighted to see him, and his arrival suggested a plan. He sent two of Kasar's men, Khali'udar of the Jaurat and Chakhurkhan of the Uriangqadai, to Ong Khan, with a message purporting to come from Kasar.

'You will tell the Khan my father that Kasar has sent you, saying: "I have sought everywhere for my elder brother, but I have lost sight of him. I followed in his track, but I could not find the way he had gone. I have called after him, but my voice has not been heard. Now I sleep below the stars, with a turf for pillow. My wives and sons are with the Khan my father. If I obtain a guarantee of my safety, I will return." Say that you have been sent with these words. We shall follow after you, and will wait for you at Arkhai Geogi on the Kerulen. Come back to meet us there.'

Having sent Khali'udar and Chakhurkhan off, he broke camp, sending Jurchadai and Arkhai ahead as vanguard. Leaving Baljuna, he followed them, riding westwards with all his men, up the Kerulen to Arkhai Geogi.

Khali'udar and Chakhurkhan, arriving at Ong Khan's camp, delivered the words purporting to come from Kasar. Ong Khan had raised up his golden palace-tent and was feasting. He suspected nothing. The two men who had been on that terrible journey with Kasar were plainly exhausted and travel-worn; Temujin must have fled far beyond the Mongol lands, taking refuge with the forest peoples or the Jurchen.

He said: 'Very well, let Kasar come. As a guarantee of his safety, I shall send Iturgen to him.'

Iturgen rode off with Kasar's men. As they approached the meeting-place on the Kerulen, he saw from a distance that he had been brought to a strong camp with many warriors. He turned immediately and fled.

Khali'udar's horse was swift; he caught up with Iturgen easily, but did not dare to attack him. Passing him on one side, he rode across his path, to cut him off. Iturgen hesitated, uncertain whether to fight his way past Khali'udar. Chakhurkhan's horse was slow, but, coming within range as Iturgen hesitated, he shot an arrow which struck the crupper of Iturgen's black horse. The horse, rearing violently, threw Iturgen; Kasar's two men seized him and brought him to Temujin. The Khan, without saying a word to Iturgen, said: 'Take him to Kasar. Let Kasar decide what to do with him.' Kasar also had nothing to say to Iturgen; he struck off his head on the spot with a blow of his sword.

Khali'udar and Chakhurkhan said to Temujin: 'Ong Khan suspects nothing. He has had his great golden tent set up and is feasting. If we set off immediately, marching night and day, and encircle them, we shall be able to take them by surprise.'

Temujin set his forces in motion, sending Jurchadai and Arkhai on in advance, and riding night and day. No news of their coming went ahead of them; the clansmen melted away into the hills as they came by, judging that this was the last of all moments that they would choose to take sides.

THE BATTLE OF MOUNT JEJE'ER

Ong Khan's camp was at the entrance of the gorge of Jer, near the height of Jeje'er. The old Khan was, as Khali'udar and Chakhurkhan had said, feasting; he was free from care. Temujin had been a useful and faithful vassal, but he had never really trusted him. He did not trust Jamukha either; but Jamukha did not have that dangerous gift that Temujin had, of attracting men to serve him. And the last he had heard of Temujin was that respectful though reproachful message from far away; not even Temujin's brother Kasar could find where he had now gone.

Temujin's army rode down on them out of the steppes like one of those sudden summer storms, and encircled the camp. There was hardly any time to organise the defences, but Ong Khan's men fought desperately. Most of these battles were won or lost in a single day. The night might intervene, as at the battle against the Taijiut at the crossing of the Onon, or the virtual defeat of Temujin at Khalakhaljit, but by morning one side or the other had made its decision that it was best to abandon the fight. Here at Jeje'er there was no question of a retreat.

This was the decisive battle of Genghis Khan's career. If he was defeated here, it was the end of him. His forces were already small, and no more support would come to him if he lost.

Ong Khan's supporters knew that, even if they could fight their way out through the encircling warriors, they would be pursued and cut down with utter ruthlessness. There was no room in the world any more for Genghis Khan on the one side and Ong Khan and his allies on the other.

At Jeje'er, the fighting went on for three days and

three nights: on the third day the encircled forces, exhausted, submitted. It was found that somehow Ong Khan and Sanggum had slipped through the encircling forces and made their escape. The valiant commander, Kadakh Bahadur, was brought before Temujin. He said:

'We have fought for three days and three nights. I said to myself: "How can I seize and deliver up to his death the man I have looked on as my lawful ruler?" I could not deliver him up; I kept up the fight for three days, in order to give him time to get far away and save his life. If I am to die for it, then I will die. But if Genghis Khan grants me his mercy, I will fight for him with all my strength.'

Temujin said: 'Is not this a worthy man, who will not deliver up his lawful ruler to death, but fights on, so that his master shall get far away, and save his life? This is a man who is worthy of companionship.'

He granted Kadakh Bahadur his life, saying: 'Khuyildar gave his life for me; now Kadakh Bahadur and a hundred of his Jurkin shall enter into the service of Khuyildar's widow and his sons. Their sons and daughters shall serve the descendants of Khuyildar for ever.'

With this victory everything on the steppes was changed. Jamukha was helpless without Ong Khan. The Mongol clans submitted to Temujin; they would not disobey him again. The power of the Merkit and the Tatars was already broken.

The Kerait found no leader under whom they could combine. Temujin dealt with them piecemeal, in a series of incursions into the Kerait country. Jakha Gambu, Ong Khan's younger brother, was pardoned; he had rendered Temujin certain services in the past, and besides this he had two attractive daughters. One of these Temujin took for himself, the other he gave to his youngest son, Tuli.

He gave the palace-tent of Ong Khan, with all the wealth it contained, not only the golden wine vessels, bowls and drinking-beakers, but also the household staff who looked after these things, to the two horseherds, Badai and Kishilik, who had warned him of the surprise attack; and appointed men of the Dongqayit and Kerait to be their bodyguards.

The ten thousand Tubegen were divided up; the Dongqayit were enslaved; the powerful Jurkin warriors were divided up into small groups among the different clans. Only one powerful enemy remained in all this world of the eastern steppes: this was Tayang Khan of the Naiman.

THE END OF ONG KHAN

Ong Khan and Sanggum fled westwards to the border of the Naiman lands. They came one day to the Neikun watercourse. Ong Khan, tormented by thirst, went down to the stream to drink. Sanggum, more wary, lingered in the forest, watching. A scout of the Naiman, Khorisu, saw the old man, and went to find out who he was. 'I am Ong Khan,' the stranger said. Khorisu cut him down on the spot, and went home to recount this peculiar incident to his family and friends.

Sanggum, lurking in the woods, left that place and came after further wanderings to the arid region of Chol. Here, while he was searching for food and water, he came across some wild horses standing about, tormented by flies. Sanggum dismounted and gave his horse-boy Kokochu his horse to hold while he stalked them with bow and arrows. There were only the three of them, Sanggum, Kokochu and Kokochu's wife. Kokochu decided it was time to abandon Sanggum. He mounted and began to trot away. His wife ran after him, and he halted.

'In former days,' she said, clinging on to his bridle, 'in the days when there were still gold-embroidered clothes to wear and savoury foods to eat, the prince used to call you "My Kokochu". How can you abandon him now, and ride away from him?'

'Do you want to be Sanggum's woman, then?' he asked her.

'I am as ashamed as if I had the face of a dog,' his wife said. 'At least give him the golden drinking-cup, so that he can scoop up water with it.'

Kokochu threw the golden drinking-cup behind him, with the brief words: 'Let him take it.' His wife mounted behind him, and they rode till they came to the camp of Genghis Khan on the borders of the Kerait and Mongol countries.

'I have left Sanggum in the desert, in Chol,' Kokochu said. Anyone who knew Temujin would have warned Kokochu that his conduct was unwise. An account of this affair was taken to the Khan.

'I will reward his wife,' Temujin said. 'He himself, though, Kokochu the horse-boy, who comes here having betrayed his rightful lord, who could now have trust in him, when he offers himself as a companion?' He had Kokochu beheaded and his body thrown out on the steppe.

Sanggum travelled on to the land of the Uighurs, and there, having taken up banditry for lack of a better way of making a living, he was ultimately captured and executed.

TAYANG KHAN OF THE NAIMAN

When news was brought to Tayang Khan that someone claiming to be Ong Khan had been slain at the Neikun watercourse, his mother, Gurbesu, said: 'Ong Khan was the great Khan of former days. Bring his head here! If it is really he, we will sacrifice to him.'

She sent a message to Khorisu, commanding him to cut the head off and bring it in. When it was brought to her, she recognised it as that of Ong Khan. She placed it on a white cloth, and her daughter-in-law carried out the appropriate rites, daughters-in-law being especially qualified in this regard. A wine-feast was held and stringed instruments were played. Gurbesu, taking up a drinking-bowl, made an offering to the head of Ong Khan.

When the sacrifice was made to it, the head grinned.

'He laughs!' Tayang Khan cried. Overcome by religious awe, he flung the head on the floor and trampled on it until it was mangled beyond recognition.

The great general Kokse'u Sabrakh was present at these

ceremonies, and observed them without enthusiasm. It was he who had been the only Naiman general to offer resistance to Temujin and Ong Khan on their expedition against Tayang Khan's brother Buyiruk.

'First of all,' he remarked, 'you cut off the head of a dead ruler, and then you trample it into the dust. What kind of behaviour is this? Listen to the baying of those dogs: it has an evil sound. The Khan your father, Inancha Bilgei, once said: "My wife is young, and I, her husband, am old. Only the power of prayer has enabled me to beget my son, this same Tayang. But will my son, born a weakling, be able to guard and hold fast my common and evil-minded people?"

'Now the baying of the dogs seems to announce that some disaster is at hand. The rule of our queen, Gurbesu, is firm; but you, my Khan, Torlukh Tayang, are weak. It is truly said of you that you have no thought for anything but the two activities of hawking and driving game, and no capacity for anything but these.'

Tayang Khan was accustomed to the disrespect of his powerful general, but he was stung into making a rash decision.

'There are a few Mongols in the east. From the earliest days this old and great Ong Khan feared them, with their quivers; now they have made war on him and driven him to death. No doubt they would like to be rulers themselves. There are indeed in Heaven two shining lights, the sun and the moon, and both can exist there; but how can there be two rulers here on earth? Let us go and gather those Mongols in.'

His mother Gurbesu said: 'Why should we start making trouble with them? The Mongols have a bad smell; they wear black clothes. They are far away, out there; let them stay there. Though it is true,' she added, 'that we could have the daughters of their chieftains brought here; when we had washed their hands and feet, they could milk our cows and sheep for us.'

Tayang Khan said: 'What is there so terrible about them? Let us go to these Mongols and take away their quivers.'

'What big words you are speaking,' Kokse'u Sabrakh said. 'Is Tayang Khan the right man for it? Let us keep the peace.'

Despite these warnings, Tayang Khan decided to attack the Mongols. It was a justifiable decision; his armies were stronger, but time was on Temujin's side. Tayang sought allies, sending a messenger to Alakhu Shidigichuri of the Onggut, in the south, the guardians of the ramparts between Qashin and the Khingan. 'I am told that there are a few Mongols in the east,' he said. 'Be my right hand! I will ride against them from here, and we will take their quivers away from them.'

The Onggut chieftain took orders from the Chinese when he had to, but he took none from the Naiman. His reply was brief: 'I cannot be your right hand.' He in his turn sent a message to Temujin. 'Tayang Khan of the Naiman wants to come and take away your quivers. He sent to me and asked me to be his right hand. I refused. I make you aware of this, so that when he comes your quivers will not be taken away.'

Temujin, grateful for this warning, sent him five hundred horses and a thousand sheep. His friendship with Alakhu was valuable to him at a later time.

WAR AGAINST THE NAIMAN

When he received Alakhu's message Temujin, having wintered near Guralgu, was holding one of his immense round-ups of game on the camel-steppes of Tulkinche'ut, in the east. The beasts had been encircled by the clansmen and warriors; the chieftains were gathered together, about to begin the great hunt.

'What shall we do now?' some of them said to each other. 'Our horses are lean at this season.'

It was the spring of the Year of the Rat, 1204. The snow had only lately left the steppe; the horses had found nothing to graze on during these recent months. Their ribs stuck out and they lacked strength.

The Khan's youngest brother, Temuga, spoke up. Temuga

was a capable young man, wholly lacking in Temujin's genius, but a man of spirit, whose loyalty was never in any doubt. From long custom he was called Otchigin, the Hearth-prince; he was six years younger than Temujin, and in this Year of the Rat he was thirty-one.

'How can that serve as an excuse,' he said, 'that the horses are lean? My horses are quite fat enough. How can we stay sitting here, when we receive a message like that?'

Prince Belgutai spoke. His words were respected by all, even though by reason of his excessive good-nature he was barred from the family councils of the Khan.

'If a man allows his quivers to be taken away during his lifetime, what kind of an existence does he have? For a man who is born a man, it is a good enough end to be slain by another man, and lie on the steppe with his quiver and bow beside him. The Naiman make fine speeches, with their many men and their great kingdom. But suppose, having heard their fine speeches, we ride against them, would it be so difficult to take their quivers away from them? We must mount and ride; it is the only thing to do.'

Temujin was wholly disposed to agree with these sentiments. He broke off the hunt, set the army in motion, and camped near Ornu'u on the Khalkha. Here he paused for a time while he carried out a swift reorganisation of the army. A count was held of the people; they were divided up into thousands, hundreds and tens, and commanders of these units were appointed. Also at this time he chose his personal bodyguards, the seventy day-guards and eighty night-guards. These guards of his were very important to the Khan; apart from his family and intimate associates they were the people closest to him, in whom he reposed most confidence.

Having reorganised the army, he marched away from the mountainside of Ornu'u on the Khalkha, and took the way of war against the Naiman.

The spring of the Year of the Rat was by now well advanced. During this westward march came the Day of the Red Disc, the sixteenth day of the first moon of summer.

On this day, the moon being at the full, the Khan caused the great yak's-tail banner to be consecrated, letting it be sprinkled with fermented mare's milk, with the proper observances.

They continued the march up the Kerulen, with Jebe and Khubilai in the van. When they came on to the Saari steppes, they met with the first scouts of the Naiman. There were a few skirmishes between the Naiman and Mongol scouts; in one of these, a Mongol scout was captured, a man riding a grey horse with a worn saddle. The Naiman studied this horse with critical eyes, and thought little of it. 'The Mongols' horses are inordinately lean,' they said to each other.

The Mongol army rode out on to the Saari steppes, and began to deploy themselves for the forthcoming battle. This was the biggest battle in these parts for many generations; it was a war of nations rather than of clans. Dodai Cherbi, one of the newly appointed captains, put a proposal before the Khan.

'We are short in numbers compared to the enemy; besides this, we are exhausted after the long march, our horses in particular. It would be a good idea to settle in this camp, so that our horses can graze on the steppe, until they have had as much to eat as they need. Meanwhile, we can deceive the enemy by making puppets and lighting innumerable fires. For every man, we will make at least one puppet, and we will burn fires in five places. It is said that the Naiman people are very numerous, but it is rumoured also that their king is a weakling, who has never left his tents. If we keep them in a state of uncertainty about our numbers, with our puppets and our fires, our geldings can stuff themselves till they are fat.'

The suggestion pleased Temujin, who had the order passed on to the soldiers to light fires immediately. Puppets were constructed and placed all over the steppe, some sitting or lying by the fires, some of them even mounted on horses.

At night, the watchers of the Naiman saw, from the flanks of the mountain, fires twinkling all over the steppe.

They said to each other: 'Did they not say that the Mongols were very few? Yet they have more fires than there are stars in Heaven.'

Having previously sent to Tayang Khan news of the lean grey horse with the shabby saddle, they now sent him the message: 'The warriors of the Mongols are camped out all over the Saari steppes. They seem to grow more numerous every day; their fires outnumber the stars.'

When this news was brought to him from the scouts, Tayang Khan was at the watercourse of Khachir. He sent a message to his son Guchuluk.

'I am told that the geldings of the Mongols are lean, but the Mongols are, it seems, numerous. Once we start fighting them, it will be difficult to draw back. They are such hard warriors that when several men at once come up against one of them, he does not move an eyelid; even if he is wounded, so that the black blood flows out, he does not flinch. I do not know whether it is a good thing to come up against such men.

'I suggest that we should assemble our people and lead them back to the west, across the Altai; and all the time, during this retreat, we will fight off the Mongols as dogs do, by running in on them from either side as they advance. Our geldings are too fat; in this march we shall make them lean and fit. But the Mongols' lean geldings will be brought to such a state of exhaustion they will vomit in the Mongols' faces.'

On receiving this message, Guchuluk Khan, who was more warlike than his father, said: 'That woman Tayang has lost all his courage, to speak such words. Where does this great multitude of Mongols come from? Most of the Mongols are with Jamukha, who is here with us. Tayang speaks like this because fear has overcome him. He has never been farther from his tent than his pregnant wife goes to urinate. He has never dared to go so far as the inner pastures where the knee-high calves are kept.' So he expressed himself on the subject of his father, in the most injurious and wounding terms.

When he heard these words, Tayang Khan said: 'I hope

the pride of this powerful Guchuluk will not weaken on the day when the clash of arms is heard and the slaughter begins. Because once we are committed to battle against the foe, it will be hard to disengage again.'

Khorisu Beki,[86] a general who commanded under Tayang Khan, said: 'Your father, Inancha Bilgei, never showed the back of a man or the haunch of a horse to opponents who were just as worthy as these. How can you lose your courage so early in the day? We would have done better to summon your mother Gurbesu to command over us. It is a pity that Kokse'u Sabrakh has grown too old to lead us. Our army's discipline has become lax. For the Mongols, their hour has come. It is finished! Tayang, you have failed us.' He belted on his quiver and galloped off.

Tayang Khan grew angry. 'All men must die,' he said. 'Their bodies must suffer. It is the same for all men. Let us fight, then.'

So, having created doubt and dismay, and lost the support of some of his best leaders, he decided to give battle. He broke away from the watercourse of Khachir, marched down the Tamir, crossed the Orkhon and skirted the eastern flanks of the mountain Nakhu. When they came to Chakirma'ut, Temujin's scouts caught sight of them and brought back the message: 'The Naiman are coming!'

THE BATTLE OF CHAKIRMA'UT

When the news was brought to Temujin he said: 'Sometimes too many men are just as big a handicap as too few.'

Then he issued his general battle orders. 'We will march in the order "thick grass", take up positions in the "lake" battle order and fight in the manner called "gimlet".' These were the names of various tactical disciplines in which he had drilled his army. He gave Kasar the command of the main army, and appointed Prince Otchigin to the command of the reserve horses, a special formation of great importance in Mongol warfare.

The Naiman, having advanced as far as Chakirma'ut,

drew themselves up in a defensive position on the foothills of Nakhu, with the mountain behind them. It was an error. They might have overwhelmed this smaller army in a general attack. As it was, the Mongols forced their scouts back on to the forward lines, and then their forward lines back on to the main army, and drove tightly-knit formations of horsemen again and again into the Naiman ranks. The Naiman, pressed back on themselves, could do nothing but retreat gradually up the mountain. Many of their men, fierce and courageous warriors, hardly had the chance to fight at all, but were cut down in an immobile mass of men as soon as the Mongols reached them.

Tayang Khan, with his advisers, also retreated up the mountain as the day advanced. From the successive spurs to which they climbed, each one higher than the last, they could see the whole of this dreadful disaster as it took place below them.

Jamukha was with Tayang Khan. He took a malicious pleasure in pointing out to his ally the principal personages on the Mongol side.

'Who are those people over there,' Tayang Khan asked him, 'who throw my warriors back as if they were sheep frightened by a wolf, who come huddling back to the sheepfold?'

Jamukha said: 'My *anda* Temujin has four hounds whom he brought up on human flesh, and kept in chains. They have brows of copper, snouts like chisels, tongues like bradawls, hearts of iron and tails that cut like swords. They can live on dew, and ride like the wind. On the day of battle they eat the flesh of men. You see how, being set loose, they come forward slavering for joy. Those two are Jebe and Khubilai; those two are Jelmei and Subetai. That is who those four hounds are.'

He pointed out to him also the Uru'ut and the Mangqut, who, as Tayang Khan remarked, seemed to bound like foals set loose in the morning, when, after their dams have suckled them, they frisk around her on the steppe. 'They hunt down men who carry lances and swords,' he said.

'Having struck them down, they slay them, and rob them of all they possess. How joyful and boisterous they look, as they ride forward!'

'Who is it coming up there in the rear,' Tayang Khan asked him, 'who swoops down on our troops like a ravening falcon?'

'That is my *anda* Temujin. His entire body is made of sounding copper; there is no gap through which even a bodkin could penetrate. There he is, you see him? He advances like an eagle about to seize his prey. You said formerly that if you once set eyes on the Mongols you would not leave so much of them as the skin of a lamb's foot. What do you think of them now?'

By this time the chieftains were standing on a high spur. Below them, the great army of the Naiman, Jamukha's men with them, were retreating in confusion, fighting desperately as the Mongols hemmed them in.

'Who is that other chieftain,' Tayang asked Jamukha, 'who draws ever nearer us, in a dense crowd of men?'

'Mother Hoelun brought up one of her own sons on human flesh. He is nine feet tall; he eats a three-year-old cow every day. If he swallows an armed man whole, it makes no difference to his appetite. When he is roused to anger, and lets fly with one of his *angqu'a* arrows, it will go through ten or twenty men. His normal range is a thousand yards; when he draws his bow to its fullest extent, he shoots over eighteen hundred yards. He is mortal, but he is not like other mortals; he is more than a match for the serpents of Guralgu. He is called Kasar.'

They were climbing high up the mountain now, to regroup below its summit. Tayang Khan saw a new figure among the Mongols.

'Who is that coming up from the rear?' he asked Jamukha.

'That is the youngest son of Mother Hoelun. He is called Otchigin the Phlegmatic. He is one of those people who go to bed early and get up late. But when he is behind the army, with the reserves, he does not linger; he never comes too late to the battle-lines.'

174

'We will climb to the peak of the mountain,' Tayang Khan said.

Jamukha, seeing that the battle was lost, slipped away to the rear and descended the mountain, with a small body of men. One of these he sent to Temujin with a message. 'Say this to my *anda*. Tayang Khan, terrified by what I have told him, has completely lost his senses. He has retreated up the mountain as far as he can. He could be killed by one harsh word. Let my *anda* take note of this: they have climbed to the top of the mountain, and are in no state to defend themselves any more. I myself have left the Naiman.'

Since the evening was drawing on, Temujin commanded his troops in the forefront of the attack to draw back. Bodies of men were sent forward on the wings, east and west, to encircle the summit of Mount Nakhu. There they stood to arms during the night. During the night, the Naiman army tried to break out of the encircling ring. Bodies of horsemen plunged down the mountainside in desperate charges; many fell and were trampled to death, the others were slain. In the first light they were seen lying about the mountain in droves, like fallen trees. Few were left defending the peak; they put up little resistance to the force sent up against them.

It is said that Tayang Khan, suddenly gaining courage when it was too late to be of any use to him, tried to fight his way out through the encircling army. When captured he was gravely wounded, and he died not long afterwards. His son Guchuluk Khan, though, was still at liberty; he tried to dig himself in on the Tamir, but was driven out of his entrenchments and took to flight with his attendants. He took refuge with the Gur Khan of the Kara Kitay. The Gur Khan was ill rewarded for his hospitality; Guchuluk rose to such power under him that he finally overthrew his host and took possession of his kingdom, though it is true that he maintained the Gur Khan in the state of a monarch until he died. Guchuluk was originally a Christian, but became a Buddhist when he married the Gur Khan's daughter, and treated his Moslem subjects in Kashgar and Yarkand with great harshness. When, fourteen years after the great victory of Chakirma'ut, Jebe led the Mongol armies in a brilliant campaign against the Kara Kitay, the Moslems, learning that Jebe had ordered that all men should be allowed to worship in whatever manner they chose, rose up against Guchuluk, who fled to the Pamirs and was there slain by Ismail, the governor of Kasan.

After the battle of Chakirma'ut the Mongol clansmen who had been with Jamukha came over to Temujin. There were men of the Khadagin, the Salji'ut, the Durben, the Taijiut and the Onggirat amongst them.

The mother of Tayang Khan, Gurbesu, was brought to him.

'Did you not say that the Mongols smelt badly?' he asked her. 'If that is so, why have you come here?' He took her into his tents to serve him.

Among those captured on the mountain top, the Mongols found an attendant of Tayang Khan who was no warrior, but in the absence of weapons carried at his belt a peculiar device whose purpose no one could readily understand. He was brought before the Khan, who questioned him at length. It appeared that he was an Uighur, by the name of Tatatonga, and what he carried was the seal of Tayang Khan, which he had hoped to deliver over to Guchuluk. Temujin approved of the Uighur's loyal attitude to his late rulers, and took both the man and the seal into his service.

It was this same Tatatonga who, by the command of the Khan, devised a form of letters which could be used for writing down the Mongol speech; the letters which were used thirty-six years later, under the great Khan Ogodai, to write down the history of the Mongols, at the seven domed hills on the Kerulen.

XV

The Last Steps to Power

Tokhto'a was back at the head of his people, the Merkit. Of all Temujin's old enemies, these proved the most difficult to crush, and held out the longest. In the autumn of the Year of the Rat, 1204, following his victory over the Naiman, he rode against them again, and defeated them in a battle on the Saari steppes. Tokhto'a escaped once more, with his sons Kutu and Chila'un, and a small body of his people.

HULAN

Dair Usun of the Uwas, whose clansmen were known as the Fair Merkit on account of their remarkable good looks, decided to make his submission to the Khan. His most valuable propitiatory gift was his daughter Hulan, a beautiful and spirited girl. Travelling towards the Khan's headquarters, they were apprehended by some of the Khan's warriors under the command of Naya'a, the young captain of high principles who had wisely refused to deliver up his former chieftain Targutai.

Dair Usun, when he was brought before Naya'a, said:

'I am on my way to offer this, my daughter, to Genghis Khan.'

Naya'a decided to detain them for a few days. The country was swarming with Mongol troops, pursuing the scattered Merkit clansmen. 'If you go alone, in these unsettled times, the warriors will take your life,' Naya'a said, 'and anything may happen to your daughter. We will go together to present your daughter to the Khan.'

When he judged that the country was quieter, some days having passed since the Merkit chief and his daughter fell into his hands, Naya'a set out with them, and brought them to Genghis Khan. He, hearing Naya'a's account of the matter, was extremely angry, believing that Naya'a had detained Hulan not for her safety, but for his own enjoyment.

The lady Hulan spoke up boldly. 'Naya'a explained to us that he was a high officer of Genghis Khan. He told us that the way was unsafe, and said he would escort us to you. If we had first met with warriors other than those commanded by Naya'a, the situation might have been much more difficult for us. Our meeting with him was most fortunate. May it please the Khan: if Naya'a is to be tried, let me provide evidence in his favour by allowing myself to be examined in the closest detail. It will be found that I am, by the will of Heaven, in the same state of innocence as that in which I was born.'

Naya'a said: 'My face is one which would never be turned from the Khan. When I have found fair-cheeked girls and women, and strong horses, among the defeated peoples, my view has always been that these are for the Khan to dispose of as his own property. If I have ever had any thoughts but this, let me die.'

Temujin had Hulan examined by his women, as she proposed, and it proved to be as she had said, that she was an untouched virgin. She became the Khan's favourite among all his women; it is said that, inspired by her beauty and courage, he immediately possessed her, scandalously defying convention, on a tiger-skin rug, in full audience.

Afterwards he fell into a state of terror, thinking that this impulsive act might give offence to his wife, Berta. He sent Prince Mukhali to her with the delicate mission of informing her of the event, and waited for Mukhali's return with a message of forgiveness before he dared to confront her.[87]

He released Naya'a with honour, saying: 'He is a man true to his word. I will raise him to a high position.'

Many of the Merkit people, fleeing from the battlefield, shut themselves up in an entrenched camp with palisades, on the heights of Taikhal. Temujin sent Chimbai, the son of Sorkhan Shira, with the army of the left wing, to attack the entrenched Merkit.

THE PURSUIT OF TOKHTO'A

He himself pursued Tokhto'a and his sons. The pursuit was long; as he followed them westwards, the winter came down. The Khan with his army went into winter quarters in the Arai foothills of the Altai. By the time he crossed the mountains, in the spring of the Year of the Ox, 1205, Guchuluk, the son of Tayang Khan, had joined Tokhto'a, with such of the Naiman people as he could bring together. Neither of them had any considerable forces, but they determined to make a stand on the Bukhduna river in the region of the Irtish.

When Temujin's men came up with them, and the battle commenced, Tokhto'a Beki was struck by a stray arrow, and fell. As his sons had no leisure to bury the body and could not carry it with them, they cut off the head and took that. The small body of Naiman and Merkit, whose courage in standing to fight was regarded by all as doing them great credit, were put to flight; the retreat was in the nature of a rout. Many of them were swept away and drowned in the crossing of the Irtish. Those who reached the farther bank fled wherever they could. Guchuluk, the most determined of all, travelled on to his distant destiny in the land of the Kara Kitay.

Such as were left of the Merkit, with Tokhto'a's sons at

their head, retreated through the countries of the Khanglin and the Kipchak. Temujin did not at this time pursue them farther, but turned back, recrossed the Altai, and travelled back to his headquarters camp on the Tula.

Chimbai had forced the Merkit to capitulate, in their Taikhal fortress; some were slain, others taken as soldiers. But those of the Merkit who had already submitted now rose up in revolt. They were stationed at the *auruq*, the head-quarters camp, under insufficient guard, or what they thought was insufficient; so that when they broke out they had to be overpowered by a miscellaneous body of serving-men, domestics, attendants, horse-boys, cooks and herdsmen. It had been Temujin's intention to treat them as a clan, under their own leaders, as was the custom; but finding them so irrepressible, he separated them from each other and divided them up in small groups among other clans.

Temujin, whose presence was needed in his own country, now sent Subetai in pursuit of Tokhto'a's distant sons. Subetai had swiftly grown to enormous stature and bulk; none of the steppe horses could carry him far, and he customarily travelled in an iron wagon.

Temujin gave Subetai detailed instructions on the conduct of his mission. He was strong enough by now to detach portions of his army and send them off on such errands under the command of his trusted companions. But he liked his companions to feel that everything they did was done by his own direct orders, and so he left as little as possible to chance.

'Tokhto'a's sons have been startled into flight after a skirmish. If they rose up like birds and flew to Heaven, would you not, Subetai, seize them in flight like a hawk? If they burrowed into the earth like marmots, would you not dig after them as if you were a spade? If they dived into the Tenggiz-sea like fishes, would you not scoop them out like a drag-net?

'I send you to climb over high passes and cross broad rivers. You must take good care of the horses and remounts, and be sparing with their provisions. It serves little to begin thinking of the horses when they are already lean, and to economise with the victuals only when they are already running short.

'On your way you will encounter wild animals in enormous numbers. In regard to these you must use wisdom and foresight, not allowing the soldiers on the march to gallop off in pursuit of them or hold unregulated game-drives. When you have to arrange such game-drives, to assure supplementary stores for the men of the army, you must hunt in a correct and orderly fashion. The men must not be allowed to ride in a careless or undisciplined manner. You must not allow them to tighten the girths too much when hunting. They must not tug on the bit when on the march, but give the horse a free mouth. Those who depart from proper discipline must be given a thorough cudgelling.

'As for those who violate orders, if they are people who are known to Us, you shall send them back to Us for punishment; but all others, who are not known to Us, you shall have beheaded on the spot.

'You shall think of your mission, and of no other thing. If eternal Heaven grants that the sons of Tokhto'a fall into your hand, what would be the use of sending them to me? Execute them on the spot.

'Go hence. Remember that, though We stay behind, We are always near you. And Heaven protect you.'

Subetai returned home in the Year of the Tiger, 1206, having pursued Kutu and Chila'un as far as the Chui river, where he killed them.

THE END OF JAMUKHA

In the battle of Chakirma'ut, Jamukha, who had allied himself with the Naiman, had lost many of his men, and the rest had deserted him, seeing that his cause was lost. He went away, a fugitive, with five men, and climbed the Tanglu mountains, which separate the lands of the Uriang-qadai from those of the Mongols, in the south. It was a hard life they led in the mountains; they stole beasts from all men's herds, and were friends of none.

One day they killed a sheep and, having roasted it, sat eating it.

'I wonder whose sons raised up this sheep that we are eating now?' Jamukha mused.

As he sat before the fire, intent on the sheep, his followers laid hands on him, bound him, and brought him before Genghis Khan.

When Jamukha was brought before the Khan, he said: 'As a carrion crow will sometimes seize a Mandarin duck, so from time to time a common slave will lay hands on his rightful lord. My august friend, is it possible that you should take such people into your service?'

It was clearly not possible.

'How can a man who has laid his hands on his rightful lord be allowed to live?' Temujin said. He had the five men beheaded immediately, before Jamukha's own eyes. After the bodies had been carried out, he said to Jamukha:

'Now we two are together again. Let us be companions! Once we lived in unity, each being to the other as the second shaft of a wagon; but then you decided to separate yourself and go aside. Now, let us be together again, and stay together. If one of us forgets something, the other will remind him of it; if one slumbers, the other will wake him up.

'Though you kept yourself apart from me, you were still to me a friend I respected; you even brought me good fortune. Although you sundered yourself from me, when the day came on which we had to fight against each other, you suffered in heart and soul for it. How do I know this? On the sands of Khalakhaljit, when I fought against the Kerait people, you sent me a message telling me of the words spoken by the Khan my father, Ong Khan; this was a service from you. At Chakirma'ut, you sent me a message telling me how you had put fear into the hearts of the Naiman with your menacing words. This was a further service.'

Jamukha replied: 'In former days, in our days of youth, by the forest stream of Qorqonaq, I swore friendship with my master and *anda*; we ate together, spoke unforgettable words to each other, and in our beds kept ourselves apart from all others. But we were stirred up against each other by persons of evil will, provoked against each other by crooked tongues. When we finally separated, we spoke insulting words.

'Thinking of these things, I am often overcome by remorse. I have lived in the hope, though I knew it was impossible, of drawing near to you again, and of seeing the warm countenance of my ruler and *anda*. Often, thinking of those old days when we spoke unforgettable words to each other, I have been cast down with sorrow, and I have lived in the patient hope, though I knew it could hardly be, of seeing again the faithful countenance of my ruler and friend.

'Now my *anda* says, in his kindness, that he would take me as a companion. At the time when I might have been a companion to you, I was none. Now, my friend, you have subdued the people all round about, and seized hold of the lands beyond. Heaven has given you a glimpse of the imperial throne. When the whole world is waiting for you, what kind of prize would I be to you as a companion?

'I would appear to you in your dreams, my friend, in the black night, and make your thoughts sorrowful in the bright day. I would be like a louse in your neckband, a biting gnat in your leggings. I have been a man who has had many women; even in that I feel I have been untrue to my friend, I have fallen into error.

'Now, during both our lifetimes, my reputation has suffered greatly, in all the land, from the rising sun to the setting sun. You, friend, were born of a wise mother. You have capable brothers; you have valiant companions; you have innumerable horses.

'I am inferior to you in all these things. I was abandoned by my father and mother as a small child; I have no brothers. My wife is a babbler, my friends are untrustworthy. Therefore I am inferior to my *anda*, who has been favoured by Heaven.

'If you would be so gracious, my friend, as to put me to death with all possible speed, you would find that this act would bestow the gift of peace on my soul. If you condescend to kill me, pray do so without spilling any blood. When I am dead, bury my body on some high place. I shall be a guardian in Heaven for the grandsons of your grandsons, as long as time shall last; I shall pray for you eternally.

'I am of noble birth, and an only son. My *anda* is of even nobler birth, and through his great majesty and power he has overcome me. Do not forget the words I have spoken. Think of them in the evening and in the morning; talk of them with your companions. And now, make away with me, quickly.'

Temujin, having considered these words, replied: 'My friend set himself apart from us, and spoke against us. He has been a man from whom much could be learned. Now he wishes to live no more. But I cannot kill him merely at his request, without proper justification; the oracle has not decreed that it should be so. He is a man of great importance. Let this be the reason for his execution: at the time when those horses of Jochi Darmala's were stolen, you, Jamukha, for that reason came up against me, and, when we fought at Dalan Baljut, drove me into the defiles of Jerena, causing me great anxiety. Is this not so?

'Now, when I wish to take you as a companion, you refuse. When I wish to spare your life, you do not wish it.

'I will, according to your request, cause you to be slain without the shedding of blood.'

In this way the Khan acceded to the request of Jamukha in the most considerate fashion available to him. Jamukha was wrapped in a carpet and crushed to death; in this way his spirit, which according to the belief of the shamans resides in the blood, was not lost, but was preserved to intercede for the Khan and his descendants in the courts of Heaven.

The oracle had been consulted, and had given no sign

that Jamukha deserved to be slain. The bones of sheep had been heated in the prescribed manner, and the marks on them read by the most skilled shamans. It was therefore necessary to find some justification for it. This had been done, since in the eyes of the Khan it was an unpardonable sin to cause him any fear or anxiety; which was the reason for his particular anger against the Taijiut and the Merkit.

So all that could be done to make the execution of Jamukha both just and merciful had been done. The manner of his end did much to restore his reputation among men.

THE EMPEROR OF THE STEPPES

In the year after the death of Jamukha, the Year of the Tiger, 1206, the people of the felt tents, all the clans of the steppes, came to the source of the Onon to affirm their adherence to Genghis Khan. The nine-tailed white banner was raised on the river bank; the clansmen took the oath of allegiance. Before this, Temujin had been Khan of only a few of the Mongols, a true Khan, but a small one. Now he was proclaimed Khan of all the people of the felt tents, Emperor of the Steppes.

He was in the thirty-ninth year of his age.

XVI

The Emperor of the Steppes

Ogodai was called Khan of Khans, but this title was never used by Temujin. Ogodai's brothers and nephews were powerful princes, ruling vast territories, though they recognised him as Khan over them all. Temujin, too, had Khans and princes under him, but they ruled for him, and he ruled through them; there was only one rightful ruler, one Genghis Khan.

In this assembly at the source of the Onon the Khan took the first steps necessary to transform his little Khanate into the nucleus of a great empire. Ninety-five of his trusted companions were made the principal commanders of his army, each commanding a thousand men.[88] This is not to say that they had always a thousand men serving in arms under them, but in time of war, or at the Khan's command, they were each to bring a thousand properly trained warriors to serve on his expeditions.

SHIGIKUTUKU

Temujin wished to give special evidence of his favour to Mukhali, Bo'orchu and his other closest companions. When he had decided upon the nature of these favours, he called on Shigikutuku, who attended on him in the palace *yurt* for such purposes, to summon the princes to him so that these honours, titles and commands could be ceremonially conferred on them.

Shigikutuku said: 'Before whom have Bo'orchu, Mukhali and the rest made themselves especially deserving? Above whom have they distinguished themselves by rendering special service? If it is a matter of conferring favours, have I rendered any less service? Have I given less of my strength? From the time when I lay in the cradle, and grew up by your august threshold, until this little beard sprouted on my chin, I have never given a thought to anyone but you. From the time when they held the chamber-pot between my thighs, I have sojourned at your golden threshold, and grown up there, and all that time I have never taken a step to one side. You have let me sleep at your feet; you have kept me safe and sound like a little child till I woke up. What sign of favour will you give me now?'

Genghis Khan was not at all displeased by this singular outburst.

'Are you not my latest-born younger brother?' he said. 'I give you as a sign of my favour this decree: you shall receive the same share of booty as my other brothers.

'When, under the protection of eternal Heaven, I brought the entire people under my dominion, you were like an eye that saw for me, an ear that heard for me. I further decree this: it will be you who shall decide how the people shall be shared out between us, between our mother Hoelun, ourselves, our brothers and our sons. You shall name those of the people of the felt tents who shall serve each of us, and those of the people of the plank doors.[89] And no one, whoever he may be, shall dispute your ruling in this.'

He empowered Shigikutuku with the supreme charge of all law business among the Mongols. 'Punish thefts and robberies among the whole people; resolve cases of fraud. Those who deserve death, have them killed; those who have done damage, let them pay compensation.

187

'These matters of the division of the people,' he went on, 'and the legal matters of the whole people, these you shall set down in writing, binding the pages in a volume. And what Shigikutuku has set down and established in deliberation with me, and recorded in this book in blue writing on white paper, this none may alter, down to the furthest posterity.'

If Shigikutuku was surprised at this swift response to his plea, he was too much of a lawyer to show it. Clearly the Khan had settled in his own mind long ago what he was going to use Shigikutuku for; and indeed in the delicate matter of the apportionment of the bondsmen he was the only possible person, since no other man would have been regarded by the Mongols as sufficiently honest and unprejudiced to undertake it. Since he was also just and intelligent he was naturally most fitted to become the leading judge and at the same time the compiler of the legal code. That he was infinitely devoted to Genghis Khan was fortunate, since these numerous duties would leave him with little time of his own.

He replied: 'How can I, a last-born brother, claim an equal share of booty with the others? But if it pleases the ruler: grant me people from the cities walled round with earth.'

Genghis Khan said: 'I see you have considered this already. It is for you to decide.' An appointment was an appointment, and if Shigikutuku thought he needed people from the walled cities, he had only to grant them to himself. That he needed them cannot be denied; not a nomad on the steppes could hold a pen, the scribes dwelt in the cities, and Shigikutuku's urgent need was for secretaries.

Having at last settled Shigikutuku's affairs, the Khan proceeded to call his other companions before him. Above all the others he honoured Mukhali, who, as a youth, long ago, when the Jurkin clan was destroyed, had been made to do homage to Genghis Khan by his father. The Khan conferred on him now the Chinese title of Kuo-Wang, Prince of the Ruling House. The Mongols pronounced it Go-ong.

Later the Khan left his trusted lieutenant, Prince Mukhali, to complete the conquest of north China while he himself returned from that country to see to his other affairs.

Even at this time the Khan could no longer command all his army at once, in all the border regions of his realm. Bo'orchu, his first companion, who had ridden off with him years ago on a sudden impulse, to help him to recover his stolen horses, was appointed to command all the forces in the west, in the foothills of the Altai. Khorchi, the stout commander who had come to him with his Baarin clansmen when the Khan first separated from Jamukha, was given command of the border guards in the north, against the forest tribes.

Naya'a, the young officer of high principles whose life had been saved by the courage and presence of mind of the lady Hulan, when he was falsely accused of detaining her for his own pleasure, was appointed to command ten thousand men in the centre.

Many others of his old companions he honoured by his praises, and gave them high commands in his armies.

The old guard, the eighty night-guards and the seventy day-guards, received special honours, and their numbers were increased to a thousand of each. These bodyguards were subsequently strengthened to ten thousand, and became the main nucleus of the army. As headquarters troops, they supervised the staff of the palace tents, the serving-women and boys, the camel-herds and ox-herds; they had charge of the palace wagons, the yaks'-tail flags, the kettledrums and lances, the drinking-bowls and the dishes. They aided Shigikutuku in carrying out the law, and undertook the storage and issue of quivers, bows, armour and all other weapons. They kept the horses in order, and saw to the loading and unloading of the palace tents, and the issue of silk.

SUBMISSION OF THE STEPPE NATIONS

The Khan wished to be at peace with the nations around his borders. There was, in his opinion, only one way of

189

making this peace secure: they must acknowledge him as their ruler. He sent his armies against them, and for the most part they wisely submitted without putting up any resistance.[90]

Some did not even wait for a force to be sent against them. One of these wise rulers was Idu'ut, the Khan of the Uighurs. He sent envoys to Genghis Khan with a message. 'It is as if the ice has melted from the river. With joy I have heard of the name and fame of Genghis Khan. If the Khan is favourably disposed towards me, granting me some trifle, the buckle of his golden belt, or the patch on his dark red coat, I will be his son, placing all my strength at his disposal.'

Temujin insisted that the Uighur Khan should visit him in person. 'Idu'ut shall come here, bringing with him gold and silver, pearls both great and small, brocade, damask and woven silk.'

Idu'ut came, bearing all these things. He was received with favour, and took away with him one of the Khan's many daughters, the lady Al.

THE DEATH OF BOROKHUL

Other peoples and rulers were not so wise, thinking themselves stronger than they were. The Khan sent Borokhul on an expedition against the Khori Tumat, the twenty times ten thousand tribesmen of the forest beyond Lake Baikal. They were ruled by a fierce, warlike woman, the widow of the late Khan. Her tribesmen fell on the Mongol vanguard as it struggled through the dense forest in the darkening evening. Borokhul, riding with the van, was struck down and killed.

When the news was brought to Temujin, he fell into a terrible rage. Dissuaded by Bo'orchu and Mukhali from leading a punitive expedition himself, he sent instead the brutal Dorbai Dokhshin, a man of iron will. Dorbai, to avoid being ambushed like Borokhul, went round about the mountains by a difficult route. He made his men fell saplings along the way and lay them down to form a road for the army to march over. His army obeyed him with the discipline born of terror. Each man was ordered to carry ten rods over his shoulder, so that if he disobeyed an order the means of whipping him were ready to hand. Dorbai fell on the Khori Tumat in a surprise attack and subdued them with great savagery.[91]

TEB TENGGERI THE SHAMAN

During these years many of the Mongols fell under the influence of Teb Tenggeri, the shaman, Munglik's youngest son. The people were richer now, and had more leisure time to think of spirits and such things, instead of placating them as far as custom demands and then forgetting them, as wiser men do. Teb Tenggeri was famous for his supernatural powers. He was believed to ride a horse into the skies to talk with spirits. Neither hunger nor cold had any effect on him; he could fast as long as he wished to, and he could sit naked in the snow until it turned into steam with the heat of his body.

The seven sons of the thoughtful Father Munglik, the seven young princes of the Qongqotadai, lacked their father's wisdom. They were restless and ambitious. One day, having had some argument with Kasar, they surrounded him and not only treated him with disrespect, but handled him roughly.

Kasar, astonished and aggrieved, went to complain to Temujin, expecting to be granted permission to take his revenge on the Qongqotadai; but Temujin had grown suspicious of his powerful brother, and heard him without sympathy. Kasar went away to sulk in his own tents.

Temujin himself stood in awe of Teb Tenggeri. Having fulfilled so many earthly ambitions, he was greatly concerned at this time, and during his later years, with the meaning of life, and the relation between men and the higher powers of Heaven.

Teb Tenggeri sought an audience with the Khan, and

said to him: 'The ruler of Heaven has sent me a prophecy, saying: "At one time, Temujin shall have the realm in his hand; at another time, Kasar." Who can say what will happen if you do not forestall Kasar in his ambition?'

Temujin went with a bodyguard that night to ride to Kasar's tents. Kuchu and Kokochu, the first two boys, now men, that he had given to Hoelun, went to her and told her that the Khan had ridden to arrest Kasar.

Though it was night time, Hoelun had a white camel harnessed to a black covered wagon, and drove after the Khan to Kasar's tents.

She arrived there at sunrise. Temujin had had Kasar bound, and had taken away his cap and girdle, as a sign of his disgrace; he was about to try him. When Hoelun came storming into the camp, he trembled before her. She herself, in her rage, got down from the wagon, loosed Kasar's bonds and gave him back his cap and belt.

She sat down with her legs folded under her, pulled out her ample breasts from her dress, spread them out on her knees and said: 'Do you see these? They are the breasts from which you sucked. You, who, as the proverb says, gnawed your own afterbirth, tore your own umbilical cord![92]

'What has Kasar done? When I nursed you, Temujin, you drained one of my breasts. Khaji'un and Otchigin together could only drain one of them. Kasar, though, drained them both, and gave me peace. He emptied my breasts, and I was free!

'My cunning Temujin received the gift of the spirit. Kasar received strength, and skill in shooting with the bow. He brought under your dominion those who sought to escape from it; he shot down those who sought to flee. Now, when your enemies have been brought to their end, you wish to look on Kasar no more.'

Temujin said: 'When my mother is angered against me, I am terrified. I am ashamed of myself. Let us go back to the camp.'

They returned to the tents, and peace was made. But the Khan was still full of mistrust. Without letting Hoelun know of it, he took away many of Kasar's men, leaving him with a diminished retinue of only fourteen hundred followers. When Hoelun came to know of this, she took it so much to heart that her strength failed, and age and death came rapidly down on her.

The influence of Teb Tenggeri the shaman continued to grow. He held assemblies, at which he worshipped the spirits and was visited by them. Great crowds of people attended these, and many from the Khan's *auruq* began to slip off to them. Some of Otchigin's men went without leave; he sent his messenger Sokhor to call them back. Teb Tenggeri had Sokhor beaten, tied his saddle on his back, and sent him home on foot.

Prince Otchigin went himself to call his people back. The Qongqotadai threatened him with physical violence unless he knelt to apologise to them.

Otchigin went the next morning early to Temujin, while he was still in bed. He knelt and told the Khan how he had been treated.

Berta sat up in bed, covering her breast with the blanket. 'The Qongqotadai grow too great,' she said. 'Lately they fell on Kasar and beat him; now they make Otchigin kneel before them. How will this end? Will you let your brothers be destroyed? They stand about you like trees in a forest. If they fall, how will your own body, the tallest tree of all, be saved from falling also? And then who will rule over your people, who are like a flock of birds nesting in your branches?'

The Khan said to Otchigin: 'When Teb Tenggeri comes, you may treat him in any manner you choose.'

On the next visit of Teb Tenggeri and the Qongqotadai to the *auruq*, Otchigin waited until the shaman, his brothers, and their father Munglik were all in the palace *yurt* of the Khan, then went up to him.

'Lately you forced me to apologise to you,' he said. 'Now we will measure ourselves against each other.'

He pulled Teb Tenggeri by his coat collar towards the door. The shaman clutched at Otchigin, grasping his collar;

they struggled with each other. Teb Tenggeri's cap fell off. Munglik picked it up, smelt it, and stuck it in his bosom. He was distraught at this sudden disturbance; lately his sons had been high in favour.

The Khan was alarmed for his own safety. It was clear that a general brawl was about to break out.

'Go outside, and measure your strength out there,' he commanded.

Otchigin had stationed three strong men of his bodyguard outside the tent. The moment Otchigin and Teb Tenggeri, obeying the Khan's command, came out, they seized Teb Tenggeri, broke his back and flung his body into a corner.

Otchigin went back into the tent and said: 'Teb Tenggeri did not wish to wrestle; he has flung himself down, shamming death. He is a worthless kind of man.'

Munglik, sensing what had happened, wept. 'I have been a companion to you,' he said to the Khan, 'since the mighty earth was no bigger than a clod; since the seas and rivers were no larger than a brook.'

The six Qongqotadai brothers, who had gone out with Otchigin and Teb Tenggeri, pushed their way roughly back into the tent. Genghis Khan sprang up immediately from his seat.

'It is getting too crowded in here,' he said. 'Stand aside! I will go out.'

He thrust his way through the thronged tent and called for the guards of the day-watch, who, as he came out, surrounded him in a circle. He saw Teb Tenggeri's body lying in a corner by the wagons. Even in this confused moment he saw a threat to his power, and took steps to counter it; this death might cause a disturbance among the people, and the shaman's body must not be displayed to them. He commanded that a tent must be immediately put up over the body, and had a guard posted round it. Then he commanded horses to be brought, ordered that the camp should be struck, and rode away to establish his *auruq* some distance away, leaving a strong guard over the body.

The roof-opening of the tent in which Teb Tenggeri's body lay had been fastened, and the door securely tied; but on the third day, so it is said, the roof-hole opened of itself, and the body disappeared through it, up to Heaven. It is certain that it vanished without trace, and was never found.

Genghis Khan had his judgment on this matter proclaimed to the people.

'Because Teb Tenggeri treated my brothers with disrespect, and incited bad feeling against them, Heaven looked on him with disfavour. It has taken away his body as well as his life.'

The Khan called Munglik before him.

'You did not curb the ambitions of your sons,' he said. 'They wished even to put themselves on the same level as myself. Because of this, misfortune has come upon Teb Tenggeri. If I had known that such a thing would happen, I would have treated you in the same way that I treated Altan and Khuchar and their friends.'

He reprimanded Munglik severely and at great length, but in the end relented, saying: 'He who refutes in the evening that which he said in the morning, and denies in the morning that which he said the previous evening, is of little worth. My earlier faith in you must be allowed to weigh more than these misfortunes. In consideration of this, I pardon you, and soften my anger. But if only you had kept their unruly characters under control, who would have compared with the posterity of Father Munglik?'

From this time on, the influence of the Qongqotadai waned. The priests of the different persuasions, shamans, Buddhists, Christians and Moslems were given equal freedom to work among the Khan's people, and make their versions of the truth known; but none of them was allowed to jeopardise the position of the Khan's family, or the security of his power.

XVII

The World-Conqueror

At the time when he was made Khan of the Steppes, Temujin had twenty-one more years to live.

When a man has achieved great power, what is there left for him to achieve but more power? When he has overcome all his enemies, what does he find but more enemies?

Three powerful realms now bordered the Khan's lands on the south. The easternmost of these was the Chin Empire. West of this, in the great bend of the Yellow river, was the kingdom of the Tanguts. Westwards again was the kingdom of the Kara Kitay.

Genghis Khan first of all attacked the Tanguts, because they were the weakest. The Mongols learned much there of the way of attacking walled cities, which their steppe wars had not taught them. Three separate campaigns, over the space of six years, sufficed to bring these people to submission.[93]

WAR AGAINST CHINA

The Chin Emperor, the Golden Khan, could no longer play one ruler in the steppes off against another, since there was only one left. Genghis Khan, the weakest, had suddenly risen up and defeated the Keraits and the Naiman, who had appeared to be stronger. All the steppe nations, from the Uighurs in the west to the Tatars in the east and the forest peoples of the north, had submitted to him. The ministers of the Golden Khan came to him and told him that the Mongols were getting ready to attack his empire. The Emperor could not believe that such rebellious notions should be entertained, and clapped them in gaol.

In 1213, a year after the Tangut had been subjugated, the Mongols crossed the Wall, and after defeating the armies of the Emperor marched on Peking. The Emperor offered them treaties of friendship and poured immense wealth on them as tribute; but as soon as the Mongol armies retired, he arrested the Khan's envoys. The Mongols immediately came back again. In the Year of the Pig, 1215, Peking was taken and sacked; the Emperor fled to the south of the Yellow river.

In the following year, Genghis Khan went back to his *auruq* in the Mongol country, leaving the Go-ong Mukhali to continue the war in China.[94]

The Kara Kitay still thought themselves too great a people to submit to Genghis Khan. The Khan, however, did not think them so great that he needed to lead an expedition against them himself. Instead, he sent Jebe, the Arrow, against them; that Jebe who had once wounded his horse at Koyitan, and been pardoned for it. Jebe proved himself capable of the task.

Farther to the west lay the realms of the Sultan Mohammed, the Khwarizm-Shah.[95] Genghis Khan considered himself to be at peace with this ruler, until the news was brought to him that an embassy of a hundred of his men had been seized and slain by the governor of Otrar, in the Sultan's realms.

Genghis Khan said: 'How can I let my golden leading-rein be broken by the Moslem people?' He began to make ready a great army to subdue the Sultan Mohammed.[96]

197

As he was preparing for this war, the lady Yesui, the daughter of Yeke Charan the Tatar, put the following thoughts before him.

'The Khan is now thinking of climbing over high passes, and crossing over broad rivers; he is undertaking a distant military expedition with the purpose of keeping his many peoples in order.

'But no living creature lives for ever. When your body like a tall tree stoops to its fall, who will give your people shelter? To whom will you entrust the swarm of birds, your people? Of the four heroic sons born to you, which will you name? I have brought this forward for your consideration, having pondered long on it, for the sake of your sons, your brothers, your subjects, and even for us, the least worthy. We would all learn your will.'

Genghis Khan replied: 'Although Yesui is only a woman, her words are the wisest of all. None of you, my brothers, my sons, nor Bo'orchu, Mukhali and the others, has ever brought forward such thoughts. And I myself had forgotten to think of it, as if I did not some day have to follow after my forefathers. I have slept, as if I could never be overtaken by death.

'The eldest of my sons is Jochi. What do you say? Speak!'

But before Jochi could utter a word, Chagatai said: 'When you call on Jochi to speak, do you mean to say that you trust him? He is a bastard of the Merkit. How can we leave the government to him?'

Jochi sprang up, seized Chagatai by the collar, and said: 'Our imperial father has never made any distinction between us. How can you, then, treat me as different? You are superior to me only in stubbornness. If you surpassed me in shooting with the bow, I should hack off my thumb and throw it away. If you defeated me in wrestling, I should never rise again from the place where I fell. It is the will of our imperial father, that must be obeyed.'

198

While these two, Jochi and Chagatai, gripped each other by the collar, and Bo'orchu pulled at Jochi's hand and Mukhali at Chagatai's, trying to separate them, Genghis Khan sat silent and listened.

The worthy old counsellor Kokochos, who had been placed in charge of the wilful and evil-tempered Chagatai, intervened. The combatants having been parted, he said: 'Why, Chagatai, do you become so excited? You are one of those sons on whom your imperial father set all his hope. Before you were born, Heaven and all its stars were in confusion; the people all fought against each other. They did not even sleep at night, but robbed each other of all their possessions. Nobody lived as they wished to; there was nothing but conflict and battle. Nobody lived in love; they dealt mutual death-blows.

'Your words would make your sacred mother's soft heart curdle like butter. Were you not born out of the same warm body? It is not right that you should slander the mother who bore you.

'Your imperial father, to found this great empire, slaved like a common man. He poured out his blood; he hardly closed his eyes, or laid his head on his pillow. He quenched his thirst with his own spittle and chewed his own gums for supper. He exerted himself till the sweat of his brow moistened the soles of his feet.

'Your mother suffered those same afflictions with him. She shortened her skirts and tightened her belt; searching endlessly for food, she gave you her own share, and went empty herself. Carrying you on her shoulders, her one care was how she could make you into men. She wished always the best for you. Our sacred lady queen had a mind as bright as the sun and as limpid as a lake!'

Genghis Khan, having listened to this, stirred himself, and said to Chagatai: 'Why do you speak in this way of Jochi? He is the eldest of my sons. In future you shall speak no more of him in this way.'

Chagatai smiled and said: 'That Jochi is strong and valorous, no man denies. There are not wagons enough to carry away those he has slain with his mouth; those he has killed with his words are too numerous to be plundered.

'Jochi and I are the eldest of your sons. Both of us wish to dedicate our strength to our imperial father. If one of us departed from his allegiance, the other would hack him in pieces.

'Ogodai is a peaceful man. It is he whom we should elect. He should stay near to you, so that you can teach him the correct usages, and the ways of a ruler. This would be the right and just course.'

Genghis Khan said: 'What does Jochi say? Give utterance!'

Jochi said: 'Chagatai has spoken well. He and I both give our strength to the common good. We should elect Ogodai.'

Genghis Khan said: 'What will happen in your dealings with each other, you two? Mother Earth is wide. I will give you the rule over grazing-grounds distant the one from the other.

'You must keep your word, and give the people no cause for ridicule. What happened to Altan and Khuchar, when they made agreements and did not keep their word? Bearing these men in mind, do not be neglectful of your allegiance.

'What does Ogodai say? Speak!'

Ogodai said: 'When, through the kindness of my imperial father, I am asked to speak, what shall I say of myself? How could I dare to refuse? I shall strive eagerly, with all my might. I fear only that it may happen to my descendants, later, that they will grow fat, being too well protected and wrapped up. Some incapable man will be born, who could not shoot a Qandaqai deer, or a rat close at hand. What other thoughts than these can I express of myself?'

Genghis Khan said: 'What does Tuli say? Speak!'

Tuli, the youngest son, said: 'I will stand by the side of my elder brother, who has been nominated by my imperial father. If he forgets something I will remind him of it; if he falls asleep, I will wake him up. I will be a sworn companion, and a whip for his horse. I will not neglect the oath.

I will ride with him on the longest campaign, as in the briefest battle.'

Genghis Khan praised his words, and said: 'You have chosen well. If you change nothing and do not go against my wishes, you will never err; you will make no mistake. And as for those unworthy ones among his descendants, of whom Ogodai speaks, they will also be descendants of mine: how should they be unworthy?'

THE SEVEN-YEAR EXPEDITION TO THE WEST

In the spring of the Year of the Hare, 1219, the Khan set out for the west, taking the lady Hulan with him, and leaving Prince Otchigin in charge of the *auruq*; he did not return there for seven years. His armies assembled on the Irtish. Chagatai and Ogodai were sent to besiege Otrar; Jochi marched down the Syr Darya; the Khan took Bokhara and Samarkand.

From Samarkand, Jebe and Subetai pursued the Sultan Mohammed across Persia, until he took refuge in an island in the Caspian, and there died. Jebe and Subetai marched round the south of the Caspian and conquered the Armenians and the Georgians. They then crossed the Caucasus northwards and came into the great steppes. The Russians and the Kipchaks sent their armies against them and were defeated. Jebe and Subetai passed round to the north of the Caspian and rejoined the Khan.

In 1220 the Khan marched up the Amu Darya, the Oxus. In the following year he crossed that river and took Balkh. Tuli was sent to Khorasan, which he laid waste. Jelal al Din, the son of the Sultan Mohammed, a valiant warrior, having been pursued into India, turned at bay and defeated the Mongol army pursuing him. In retaliation for this, the only setback experienced by the Mongols in the whole of this campaign, Genghis Khan himself took his army across the Hindu Kush and descended into the plains of India. On the banks of the Indus, Jelal al Din stood to defend himself, and fought fiercely; but at last, finding himself surrounded on three sides by the Mongols, he plunged into the river behind him and swam to the farther side, so making his escape. The Khan praised his courage as an example to all his warriors.

During his long years of conquest, other matters had been troubling the Khan's mind. His experience with Teb Tenggeri had brought him some disillusion with the shamans; Ong Khan had been a Christian, and this may have diminished his regard for that faith; the Moslems had never been among his favourite subjects.

He heard from Mukhali, campaigning in China, of the reputed wisdom of the famous alchemist Ch'ang Ch'un. Before he set out on his western expedition in 1219, the Khan sent messages to the ancient sage, assuring him of his respectful esteem. He asked Ch'ang Ch'un to visit him, in order to expound to him the wisdom of the Tao.

The old man set out with the escort provided, in February 1220.[97] He left the borders of China in mid-March, and crossed the eastern extremity of the Gobi, reaching Prince Otchigin's camp on a tributary of the Kerulen late in April.

In early May he travelled down to the Kerulen and westwards up that river. He observed the life of the Mongols with curiosity: they were herdsmen and hunters, living in black wagons and white tents, wearing clothes made of hide and furs. He noted that they shared all food between them, hastened to assist those in trouble, were obedient to orders and kept their promises faithfully.

Throughout that summer and autumn the Adept and his party travelled westwards, crossing the Altai in August and reaching the Tien Shan in mid-September. In late November they came to Tashkent, and in early December to Samarkand. The bridges across the Amu Darya were broken. The journey was not resumed until April, after Chagatai had repaired them. Bo'orchu came to escort the Adept through the Iron Gates pass. They crossed the Amu Darya, and in the middle of May, fourteen months after leaving China, came to the Khan's camp.

The Khan received the Adept, and appointed a day to question him about the Way; but owing to local insurrections and outbreaks of banditry, these further meetings had to be postponed until September. The Adept then had several audiences with the Khan, accompanying him as he started on his slow journey homeward.

On 19 November 1222 the Adept pronounced his major exposition of his doctrine. The Tao, he told the Khan, produced Heaven and Earth; they in turn opened up and produced Man. When Man was first born he shone with a holy radiance of his own, and his step was so light it was as if he flew.

Gradually his body grew heavy and his holy light grew dim. This was because his appetite and longing were so keen. Those who study the Tao, the Adept said, must learn not to desire the things that other men desire. They must do without pleasant sights and sounds, and get their pleasure only out of purity and quiet.

The male is called Yang; his element is fire. The female is called Yin; her element is water. But Yin, the imperfect, quenches Yang, the perfect; water conquers fire. Therefore, the man of Tao must above all abstain from lust . . .

The Khan summoned his sons and the other princes, his high ministers and officers. He told them that the Master was indeed a Being from Heaven, and repeated all that the Master had told him. 'Heaven,' he said, 'has sent this holy immortal to tell me these things. Engrave them upon your hearts.'

The Khan, if he had engraved the Adept's injunctions on his own heart, singularly failed to read them. As far as abstaining from lust was concerned, his ministers were under standing instructions to search the cities and lands he conquered for women to fill his tents. As for not desiring the things that other men desire, at this time he had just completed the conquest of the greatest empire ever carved out by one man.

As Li Tai-po says:[98]

> A full beaker of wine at the right season
> Is worth more than all the riches of this earth.
> Dark is life: dark also is death.

THE DEATH OF GENGHIS KHAN

Ch'ang Ch'un took his final farewell of the Khan in April 1223. He was escorted into Peking by his Taoist friends in the spring of 1224 and died, greatly revered, three years later.

Genghis Khan, who had lingered in the Hindu Kush in 1222, spent the following summer around Tashkent, and the summer after that on the upper Irtish. He came back to his headquarters in the spring of 1225.

In 1226 a new expedition was necessary to pacify the Tangut. Genghis Khan took with him the lady Yesui. During that winter, while they were still on the way south, the Khan went hunting the wild horses of Arbukha. His own horse, a roan, shied when the wild horses came running across in front of him, and the Khan was thrown.

He developed a fever. His advisers wished him to abandon the expedition, but Genghis Khan refused to do so. The Tangut were duly pacified. One of Temujin's last acts was to order the execution of their ruler, Burhan.

Shortly afterwards he died, in the Year of the Pig, 1227, and, as the chroniclers say, ascended into Heaven.

In the Year of the Rat, 1228, the Princes of the Right Hand, with Chagatai and Batu at their head, the Princes of the Left Hand, with Prince Otchigin at their head, the Princes of the Centre, with Tuli at their head, the Princesses, the Sons-in-law, the leaders of ten thousands and the leaders of thousands came together in a great *kurultay* or council at the island of Kode'e on the Kerulen and, as Genghis Khan had commanded, raised up Ogodai as Khan of Khans.[99]

Notes, Tables, Bibliography
and Index

NOTES

(SH followed by a number in brackets
refers to the relevant paragraph of the *Secret History*)

1. Kälürän in the Mongol text. Kerulen is the modern spelling.
2. The temperature at Ulan Bator ranges from −45° F. in winter to 100° F. in summer. Carpini says: 'Even in summer . . . there are terrible storms, with thunder and lightning, which kill many people. In the same season, snow may even fall in great quantities. There occur also tempests of such violence, accompanied by such icy winds, that only with the greatest efforts can a man cling to his saddle . . . Hail often falls in immense grains . . . During the summer it can pass suddenly from great heat to the most intense cold.'
3. The Khitans who had previously ruled in north China were replaced in 1122–3 by the Jurchen, a people from northern Manchuria. These rulers were known as the Chin or Kin Emperors (= Golden Emperors). They ruled north China until they were driven from Peking by Genghis Khan in 1215, and their power was finally destroyed in 1233. South China was ruled throughout this period by the Sung Dynasty (960–1279), which lasted until the Mongol conquest of the whole of China established the Yüan (Mongol) dynasty.
4. Juvaini (trans. Boyle) says: 'Their clothing was of the skins of dogs and mice, and their food was the flesh of those animals and other dead things; their wine was mare's milk and their dessert the fruit of a tree shaped like the pine . . . The sign of a great emir amongst them was that his stirrups were of iron; from which one can form a picture of their other luxuries . . .'
5. Büyür-na'ur is the original form; Buir Nor is the modern spelling.
6. The Juyin Tatars were probably a special warrior élite rather than a true clan, like the Jurkin mentioned later among the Mongols.
7. The Tatars, allied with the Chin Emperors, inflicted a crushing defeat on the Mongols in 1161. It is not certain which of the thirteen battles refers to this historical event; perhaps several of them.
8. I have chosen to use the form Bahadur rather than the Mongol Ba'atur because of its familiarity in this form to many British people who have had associations with India. It is pronounced Bahádur.
9. Yesugei must have been born about 1140–5. He would be a youth or young man at the time of the Tatar battles in 1161 onwards.
10. Hoelun makes it clear in her farewell speech to Chileidu that she has been perched up on the driving-seat. There are only two of them, and Chileidu is riding. She could not have taken off her shift and held it out to him if she had been wearing anything on top of it. Yesugei has 'seen her unclothed'; he had no opportunity to peer into the wagon (SH 54–5).

11. The phrase 'black wagons' is frequently used. The adjective appears to be habitual, as in Homer; there is no indication that the wagons were ever any other colour.

12. The women belonging to various chieftains are often referred to in the *Secret History* as their wives, but it is clear throughout that the chief wife provided the heirs.

13. See note on Bektair and Belgutai, Ch. IV.

14. It is possible that the name means 'blacksmith' (cf. Turkish *'demirci'*). There are different estimates of the date of Temujin's birth; 1167, the traditional date, fits in well with the events of the chronicle.

15. The Olkunut (Olqunu'ut) were a branch of the Onggirat living east of the Gobi. The Mongols practised exogamy, marrying only outside their own group.

16. The grey wolf and the white hind were Burte Chino and Maral Qo'a, his consort. Burte Chino may have been a Tibetan prince or the personified memory of invading Tibetan rulers.

17. The Hungarians, Estonians and Finns certainly did so.

18. Berta was probably made up for the occasion. The *Pei-lu fêng-su* (trans. Serruys) says: 'The women use also vermilion and powder to make themselves up. But if they use vermilion, they are too red; if they use powder, they are too white; they do not know how to keep the proper proportions as they do here in China.' The painting of their faces by Mongol women is also noted by William of Rubrouck.

19. Travellers in Mongolia often refer to the savagery of the dogs, though it is a matter easily exaggerated. Herdsmen keep dogs the world over, and sometimes they are savage, but they would not be savage to a small boy living among them.

20. The Tatars actually say 'Yesugei the Kiyan'; Kiyat (the form used earlier by Dai Sechen) is the plural form. I have here, as in other instances, used only one form of each clan name (usually the plural) in order to avoid confusion.

21. The journey home is said to have taken three days. I have omitted the figure because it seems to me unlikely that a sick man could have covered the distance (about 500 miles) in the time. The figure three is always suspect.

22. Munglik, the son of the old man Charakha, belonged to the clan of the Qongqotat; hence he was a Qongqotadai.

23. It is probable that at the place of sacrifice meat offered to the spirits was hung up on poles stuck in the earth, a shamanistic practice still known among the Tunguses of northern Manchuria. Carpini refers to certain images in human form, made out of felt, which were set up on either side of the entrance of the yurt, and sometimes placed on decorated wagons before the yurt. William of Rubrouck says that the Mongols carried their idols with them on fine covered wagons. These idols carried on the sacred wagons were ancestral images, which were worshipped like gods. The 'shrines' overturned by Temujin and his allies on the Merkit expedition may have been these

wagons; some images of gods or ancestors may have been a feature of the holy places.

24. Her cap: the *boqtaq* worn by married women is described by Carpini as 'an object made of willow-twigs or bark, about an ell long, which, widening always from the bottom to the top, terminates at the summit in a square plate, ornamented with a little rod, long and thin, of gold, silver or wood, or else with a feather'. This hat, covered with cloth of various kinds, rested on a kind of cap which hung down to the shoulders. Married women never appeared before men without the *boqtaq*, the precious sign of their married status (which distinguished them from their husband's other women who were not wives). Hoelun may have worn a simpler hat than that worn by the court ladies of Carpini's time, but SH 74 leaves no doubt that she wore a *boqtaq*.

25. The *Secret History* does not mention the relative ages of the four boys, but it seems an inescapable deduction that Bektair and Belgutai were the older pair. Temujin and Kasar would not have had this trouble with them if they had been younger.

26. This speech by Hoelun is of great length (SH 78); I have condensed it.

27. Descriptions of Genghis Khan are unfortunately scarce. He was tall and vigorous; it is said that his forehead was broad and his beard relatively long (for a Mongol), though there is little evidence for this. As for the 'cat's eyes', it is doubtful whether this refers to their shape or their colour. They may well have been greenish in colour; or the description may well refer to an intentness of observation which would be typical of what we know of him.

28. Almost every horse mentioned in the chronicle is distinguished by some physical detail of this nature. The human beings are hardly ever granted any individual features other than a name.

29. Also known as the 'Four Heroes'. They were Bo'orchu, Mukhali, Borokhul and Chila'un Ba'atur.

30. This knot of mountains where the Onon and Kerulen rise lies at the western end of what is now called the Yablonovii range.

31. There is no direct statement in the *Secret History* that any animals other than the horses were left to Hoelun at all. Some commentators have assumed they had none; but the indirect evidence that some personal flocks were left to Hoelun is overwhelmingly strong. In SH 96 they move from the Sanggur to summer pasture; they would hardly have had to change pasture to feed nine horses. But the most significant detail is in SH 100; when the Merkit raiders come, Khoakchin has been shearing at the main yurt. There is no way in which they could have newly acquired any animals by that time.

32. It seems to have escaped the notice of commentators that horse-stealing was an unpardonable crime. There must have been some very peculiar reason to justify this theft, from a chieftain with whom the men concerned had no apparent quarrel. The tacit support of Targutai seems the only possible explanation.

33. This whole episode is a pure Mongolian Western, with characters and speeches to match. The temptation to translate Bo'orchu's speech as: 'Friend, you got problems. Seems most *hombres* got the same kinda problems, all over . . .' was almost irresistible.

34. Temujin means in this instance that whichever of them delayed to shoot the leading pursuer was in particular danger of being lassoed or overtaken if he missed. But the statement is also a dry observation that Bo'orchu is running a general risk by his sudden devotion.

35. The development of a feudal system to replace the old clan system is an important feature in the rise of Genghis Khan.

36. Käräyit. The spelling Kerait is commonly used; also Kereit and Kereyt.

37. The Keraits were converted to Christianity in 1009 by the Nestorian bishop of Merv.

38. The Khitans, a central Asian people, established themselves in northern China in the tenth century after defeating the rulers of the Sung dynasty. Their name survives in the Russian name for China (Kitai) and in the word 'Cathay'. After their overthrow by the Jurchids, they fled to the west under their leader Yeh-lü Ta-shih (1124–43). He founded a state stretching from the Gobi to the Syr Darya, ruling over the Uighurs among others. He was known as the Gur Khan. It was his defeat of the Seljuk sultan near Samarkand that gave rise to the legend of a Christian king in the East: the legend of Prester John.

39. The belief that Toghrul, Ong Khan of the Keraits, was Prester John was voiced by (among others) Marco Polo, who visited the court of the Great Khan Khubilai, Genghis Khan's grandson: he who did in Xanadu a stately pleasure-dome decree.

40. The Tangut kingdom of Hsi Hsia or Qashin lay between north China, ruled by the Chin Emperors, and the lands of the Kara Kitay; due south of the Kerait country, across the Gobi. The Tanguts were a central Asian people akin to the Turks and the Mongols. They had fled to the borders of China from Chinghai when that region was conquered by the Tibetans in the seventh century. They were at first faithful subjects of the T'ang emperors, but under the Sung dynasty made themselves independent and established the kingdom of Hsi Hsia in 1001–3. The rulers were Buddhists; the people a mixture of Mongols, Turks and Chinese.

According to Rashid-ud-Din, one of Genghis Khan's grandchildren was named Qashin. When the child died in infancy Genghis Khan commanded that the name Qashin should no longer be spoken, and that the country should henceforth be known by the name of its people, the Tangut.

41. Toghrul's camp was situated not far from the present capital of Outer Mongolia, Ulan Bator.

42. Grousset believes that the Uriangqut were first a steppe people who later moved to the upper Yenisei and took up reindeer herding. Lattimore more convincingly suggests that the people of Urianghai in the northern forest-lands, having domesticated the reindeer, moved south to the steppe

and took to domesticating horses, sheep, cattle, yaks and camels. Some Tunguses did the same.

The ancestor of the Jadaran, Jamukha's clan, was probably an Uriangqadai (SH 18, 44).

43. The Four Hounds were Khubilai, Jelmei, Jebe and Subetai.

44. On both occasions when Jamukha actually fought Temujin, at Dalan Baljut and Khalakhaljit Elet, he defeated him.

45. These numbers are probably exaggerated. The Mongol army has been estimated (on the basis of Rashid-ud-Din's account) at figures ranging from 129,000 to 230,000. Effective allies and auxiliaries may have amounted to as many again. The Mongols were nearly always outnumbered in battle. The reasons for their success must be seen in 'organisation, discipline, leadership and morale' (Martin).

46. There is no other apparent explanation for the ability of Temujin to take a body of warriors with him to join Ong Khan and Jakha-gambu. It is certain that he did not ride down to the Kimurkha (SH 107, 108) unsupported by any forces. Ong Khan may have sent him some men who had been serving under him since the death of his former *anda* Yesugei. Jamukha implies that those men of Yesugei's serving under him would be given to Temujin on his arrival, not before.

47. Temujin held firmly throughout his life to this principle, that all property taken in battle under his leadership belonged to him, and was granted to his followers as a gracious act. In the days of his conquests all booty belonged to him (SH 252).

48. In fact, since his late brother's wife Hoelun had been stolen by Yesugei, Chilger had little to reproach himself with in accepting Yesugei's son's wife Berta as part of the normal operation of social justice; but these expressions had to be put into his mouth out of respect for Berta, who by the time they were written was wife of a World-Conqueror and mother of Ogodai, Khan of Khans. But it is unlikely that he spoke them.

49. There is also, of course, a possibility that Genghis Khan himself was the son, not of Yesugei, but of Chileidu, from whom Yesugei stole her after they had been married a few days.

50. This taking of counsel is made clear in SH 117.

51. The negotiations with other chieftains during his alliance with Jamukha are an inescapable deduction from the events immediately following the break. The chieftains must have been following the course of affairs with close attention and took action immediately the time was ripe for it.

52. Wladimirtsov has a theory that Jamukha was the leader of poor shepherds and Temujin, of more aristocratic origin, of richer horseherds. It is an ingenious and improbable hypothesis with no evidence to support it. Jamukha was just as aristocratic by descent as Temujin, and more autocratic in behaviour. As a chieftain of long standing, he was undoubtedly richer at the time. The idea that the shepherds needed to camp near a stream and the horseherds needed uplands is even more far-fetched. The simple struggle for

power between two chieftains is a wholly adequate explanation for a break which was bound to take place sooner or later.

53. This is the Khubilai who became one of the Four Hounds.

54. Among the Jalair who joined Temujin was probably the future Go-ong Mukhali, one of the leading men of the Empire. At this time he was an inconsiderable grandson of Telegetu.

55. Naturally all these groups of tribesmen took up a lot of room. Temujin was now the leader of a confederation of clans rather than the head of a single group of his own. In many cases it must be assumed that the leaders came to make submission to him with a group of relations and attendants, leaving their people behind in their own grazing areas. The movement to summer pastures following these latest accessions must be taken as representing a movement of Temujin's headquarters camp, together with the principal chieftains supporting him, who were still carrying on negotiations among themselves. Later it is clear that these greater chieftains carried on their own separate existence, but acknowledging Temujin as their overlord.

56. There are many different interpretations of the title Genghis Khan, and different opinions about its pronunciation, Genghis or Chinggis. The derivation I give here seems to me overwhelmingly the most probable. Wladimirtsov thinks the name came from that of a spirit worshipped by the shamans. Pelliot opts for a palatalised version of the Turkish 'tenggiz', sea: meaning 'Oceanic' or 'Wide-spreading' Khan. The Mongols certainly called Lake Baikal 'Tenggiz', but if they had wanted to call Temujin Tenggiz Khan it seems likely that they would have called him Tenggiz, not Chenggiz. Chinese titles were familiar to the Mongols. *Chêng*, meaning right, correct or chief, seems the most probable source of the title (I have spelt it *jeng* in the book since it is so pronounced, *chêng* being the method of representing this pronunciation in the rather unfortunate academic convention). *Chêng* (pronounced *jeng*) with the Mongol adjectival ending in -s gives Jenggis. The Mongols, like the Turks, tended to use unvoiced consonants in preference to voiced; so that the title probably sounded more like 'Chenggis' or 'Chinggis'. 'Chinggis' was the form in which the scribes wrote it down, but they were probably Uighurs, for whom Mongolian was a foreign language. The question is whether we are more concerned with what the Mongols were saying, or what the Uighurs thought they were saying. It seems highly probable that what the Mongols actually said was something between 'Chinggis' and 'Chenggis'; and what they meant was 'Jenggis', the true or rightful ruler, but they very naturally said it with a Mongolian accent. By a series of accidents the form Genghis, which is most familiar to the public, and is often regarded as incorrect in favour of Chinggis, actually comes closest to representing both the original pronunciation of the title, when the Mongols took the trouble to pronounce it correctly, and its meaning.

57. These appointments are described in great detail in the *Secret History*.

58. The line continues into the modern world with Napoleon, Hitler and

others. There is a strong tendency for natural leaders of men to lead them preferentially to death and destruction.

59. They formed half his remaining army in his flight to Baljuna.

60. Until the reconstruction of the *Secret History* all accounts attributed this ghoulish massacre to Genghis Khan. He was guilty of many; it is just to clear his name of one he was not guilty of.

61. Paragraph 132 of the *Secret History*, from which this account is taken, suddenly breaks off from this trivial quarrel to introduce the much wider subject of the expedition dispatched by the Golden Khan of the Kitay (the Chin Emperor) against the Tatars. There is no doubt a long passage omitted here by some copyist; possibly he picked up the repeated phrase 'Let us make peace' at a later stage, missing out all the material between; a process not unfamiliar to any copy-typist.

62. The deposition of Toghrul took place in 1196 and his restoration in 1198. The elevation of Temujin as Khan cannot have taken place much later than 1187. There is here, therefore, a gap of nine years about which the chronicler has nothing whatever to say. The account of Toghrul's deposition and restoration, which chronologically were the first events following this gap, is not given in the appropriate place (following SH 132) but is introduced much later in SH 150–2 in a confused retrospective sequence. The suggestion of some loss of this part of the chronicle and the later faulty restoration of some of the missing material is strong. Nevertheless it is apparent that little of great importance happened during this period before the Tatar expedition. It may be, though, that the partial reconciliation hinted at later between Temujin and Jamukha took place during this time.

63. The minister is referred to in the *Secret History* as Ongging Chingsang. According to Haenisch (fn. to SH 132) the family name pronounced by the Mongols as Ongging was transliterated into Chinese in the *Yüan-ch'ao Pi-shih* as Wangking. However, this minister is named in the official history of the Yüan dynasty as Wanyen Siang; since the Chinese historians had access to other (Chinese) sources this may be assumed to be the correct name.

64. Wanyen Siang was in the position of those who confer rewards for public service on worthy British citizens. The man of established position is made a Knight Commander of St Michael and St George, while his assistant of more lowly social status, who has done at least as much useful work, gets the M.B.E.

65. Haenisch's guesswork at the derivation of *ja'utkhuri* is profoundly intelligent, but some uncertainty still remains as to the precise Chinese word of qualification which turned the potential Commissioner into a Vice-Commissioner.

66. Shigikutuku lived long enough to serve as chief policy-maker (Tuan-shih-kuan) under Genghis Khan's grandson Khubilai Khan.

67. This is where the *Secret History* was later written.

68. The age of Borokhul is something of a mystery. The destruction of the Jurkin follows immediately on the Tatar raid in 1198. Ong Khan asks

Genghis Khan to send him his Four Coursers after the expedition against the Naiman in 1202. Borokhul, if it is the same Borokhul, has had only four years to grow up and become a famous warrior. My own guess is that he was the same Borokhul, and was a youth of sixteen or eighteen when Hoelun acquired him. At that age, he would still be younger than the first two boys, Kuchu and Kokochu, who, captured in approximately 1184 and 1187, would by now be in their early twenties. Shigikutuku was, of course, much younger.

69. The name is a title, meaning 'Commander'.

70. A name meaning in fact 'member of the Borjigin clan'. But this practice is not unknown elsewhere in the *Secret History*.

71. The allied armies set up advance posts on the mountains Chekcher and Chikurku, past which Yesugei had ridden from Dai Sechen's camp to his fatal meeting with the Tatars.

72. The exact meaning of the title 'Beki' is so dubious that I have made no attempt to explain it in the book itself. *Beğ* in Turkic (cf. Turkish 'bey') means ruler or prince. Naka claims that Beki means the chieftain of a tribe, which fits Sacha Beki and Khuchar Beki well enough. Wladimirtsov says that Beki means a shaman high priest, who determines which month and year are favourable for the undertakings of the people. Waley supports this, maintaining that the title is related to the word '*bögä*', a wizard. The *Secret History* itself (SH 216) appears to support all these contentions. Genghis Khan grants Usun the Old the rank of Beki on the grounds that he is wise, or at least discreet, and of noble birth; and part of his privileges as Beki is 'to determine the favourable year and month'. So the matter appears to be satisfactorily settled, except that the chronicle mentions several young women who bear the title as part of their names.

73. Ong Khan may well have come to an agreement with Jamukha—still nominally a vassal of his—by negotiation.

74. The practice was a simple but effective hygienic measure, to prevent death from infected wounds. Only two years before this, in the west, Richard Coeur de Lion of England was wounded by an arrow from a small fortress he was attacking in France. The wound became infected and he died a few days later. If he had had a Mongol attendant to suck the wound, he might have lived longer. Magna Carta might then never have been signed, since the barons would have had a harder time with him than they did with his brother John.

75. The dried curds of buttermilk were one of the forms of food taken by the Mongols on journeys. The buttermilk left over after making butter by churning cows' milk was allowed to go sour and then boiled till it curdled. The curds were then dried. Mixed with water, they formed a rather acid but refreshing drink.

76. This is part of the *yasakh*, the collected laws of Genghis Khan.

77. Charlemagne used a somewhat similar procedure to reduce what he thought an excessive number of Saxons.

78. The part played by Jamukha in this affair is mysterious. SH 160 has

Jamukha meet Ong Khan on the latter's retreat from this battlefield, and throw doubt on Genghis Khan's loyalty; but later, when Ong Khan's forces are pillaged by the Naiman general, Jamukha has disappeared again. It is possible that he followed the allies to see which way the battle would go, and left Ong Khan when he was in trouble from the Naiman. It would be natural to suppose that during these years Jamukha and Temujin, both being vassals of Ong Khan, sometimes met, though the whole account of their final meeting suggests strongly that they never did.

79. This is the same name as Toghrul. I use the original Mongol form to avoid confusion between the two. Toghrul is a more familiar Turkified form.

80. The site of the battle of Khalakhaljit Elet is doubtful. Martin places it in the far east, beyond Buir Nor. The chronicle quite clearly implies that it followed swiftly on Temujin's decision not to attend the betrothal feast on the western borders of the country. The chronicler is often unreliable about time, but never elsewhere as unreliable as this. I have to follow his account and place the battle within a day or two's march of Jeje'er Undur.

81. Ong Khan is referring to the type of arrow called *uchumaq*, meaning a nail. Other types of arrow were the *angqu'a* and the *keiyibur* (SH 195).

82. The Tubegen chieftain, a staunch pagan, is making a slighting reference to Ong Khan's Christian practices.

83. This appears to imply some continued association between Temujin and Jamukha after their separation, presumably between the years 1186-7 and Jamukha's elevation as Gur Khan in 1201.

84. The Onon, Kerulen and Tula.

85. It is said that during the long retreat to Baljuna a red lock of hair across Genghis Khan's forehead turned white. The detail is interesting and quite probable (he was thirty-six and had led a hard life) but unsupported by any reliable evidence.

86. This Khorisu Beki and the Khorisu who slew Ong Khan at the watercourse may be the same person. He is earlier described as a scout of the Naiman, but he may well have been a commander of border forces who surprised Ong Khan at the watercourse while on patrol. The *Secret History* often fails to distinguish between a single person and that same person with a body of followers, making it seem as if the latter is acting alone.

87. This story is not given in the *Secret History* and is probably pure legend. It may well, however, be true to Genghis Khan's relations with his wife Berta.

88. The list of 95 commanders of 10,000 in SH 202 adds up in fact to only 90 names, and includes Khuyildar, who was dead at the time this list was ostensibly drawn up. Of those spoken of in this book, it includes Father Munglik, Bo'orchu, Mukhali, Khorchi, Jurchadai, Khubilai, Jelmei, Borokhul, Shigikutuku, Kokochu, Sorkhan Shira, Chimbai, Chila'un, Naya'a, Jebe, Subetai, Badai, Kishilik. Besides the two horseherds the list includes a shepherd and a carpenter among those appointed to the highest command. Among auxiliaries and allies Alakhu is mentioned, with 5,000 Onggut.

89. Most of the steppe peoples closed their doors by a hanging curtain. The forest peoples used a plank door which opened outwards, so that, since it was set in a slightly sloping wall, it closed of itself, like the sloping door of a Lapp *kåta*.

90. In 1206 Khubilai was sent against the Kharlukh. These people lived between the Naiman country and the Sartakh river, and had previously considered themselves subjects of the Kara Kitay. The Khan, Arslan, submitted immediately and accompanied Khubilai back to the court of Genghis Khan, to whom he did homage. Temujin accepted his homage and granted him one of his numerous daughters.

In 1207 Jochi went against Kuduka Beki of the Oirat, the forest peoples of the north and west. Kuduka and his people surrendered without a struggle. Jochi went on to subdue the Buriat and the Khirghiz: the Khirghiz princes came to submit to him, bringing as gifts white falcons, geldings and sables. All these tribes lived along the upper reaches of the Yenisei.

91. Even after this the Khori Tumat gave trouble. Khorchi, commanding in the north, went to collect his usual thirty women from them; they seized him and took him before their queen, Botokhui. Temujin sent Kuduka Beki of the Oirat to demand his release, since Kuduka knew the customs and usages of the forest peoples, being one of them himself. Kuduka was also arrested. The Khori Tumat had to be invaded and subjugated again. After they were finally pacified, Khorchi, released from captivity, took away his thirty women; the queen, Botokhui, was given to Kuduka of the Oirat.

The repeated uprisings of the Khori Tumat were no doubt encouraged by their knowledge that, like other subjugated peoples, they heavily outnumbered the Mongols.

92. Hoelun may be harking back here to the murder of Bektair.

93. During the war against the Tanguts, a former Khitan subject of the Chin Emperors, Yeh-lü Ch'u-ts'ai (a member of the ruling house), was captured and brought before Genghis Khan, who was impressed by his bearing. He became Genghis Khan's 'prime minister'. It was he who dissuaded the Khan from converting the whole of north China into grazing grounds. He probably saved more lives than any other single person in history.

94. Kasar, now restored to favour, was sent with the army of the left wing on a great march to the coast through the Jurchen country, finishing up in Peking.

95. Jochi, returning from his expedition to the Khirghiz, had fought a battle north-east of the Aral Sea with an army of the Sultan, but no decisive result came of it.

96. Kasar had by now returned from his march round the Chin Empire and Jochi from Khirghizia. Both were ready for the expedition against the west.

97. As mentioned in the Introduction, I am indebted to the translation by Arthur Waley for details of the Adept's account of his journey.

98. The poem is used by Mahler in *Das Lied von der Erde*.

99. Ogodai died in 1241, the year following that in which the great council was held at which the *Secret History* was written. His selection of his successor proved debatable. The princes made their way back to Mongolia to another council. Ogodai's death was timely for Europe. Batu, the son of Jochi and grandson of Genghis Khan, had just conquered eastern Europe and was about to move on to conquer the west, which would probably have proved as helpless to resist him. Instead of doing so, he turned back towards Asia to take part in the council. Having got as far as the Volga, he decided that Mongolia was unsafe for him. Sending two representatives to attend the council for him, he remained where he was and founded the Golden Horde, which dominated Russia till 1481.

CHRONOLOGICAL TABLE

938	The Khitans establish their capital at Peking.
960–1279	The Sung dynasty rules in China south of the Yellow river.
1001–3	The Tangut kingdom of Hsi Hsia (Qashin) established.
1122–3	The Jurchen (Chin Emperors) replace the Khitans as rulers of north China.
1124 onwards	The Khitan Yeh-lü Ta-shih establishes the rule of the Kara Kitay westwards of Qashin.
1135	Death of the Chin Emperor Wukimai.
	Kabul Khan attends the ceremonies on the accession of Holoma.
	Period of domination of the Mongols.
1141	Victory of the Kara Khitan Yeh-lü Ta-shih over the Seljuk Sultan, Sinjar, gives rise to the legend of Prester John.
1140/5 (?)	Birth of Yesugei.
1161	Crushing defeat of the Mongols by the Tatars in alliance with the Chin Emperor.
1167	Birth of Temujin (Genghis Khan).
1176 (?)	Betrothal of Temujin to Berta.
	Death of Yesugei.
1177–82 (?)	The years of exile in the steppes.
1182 (?)	Capture of Temujin by the Taijiut.
1184–5 (?)	The Merkit raid.
	Expedition against the Merkit with Toghrul and Jamukha.
1185 (?)	Companionship with Jamukha.
1187 (?)	Separation from Jamukha.
	Accession of the clans.
	Temujin proclaimed Khan.
	Battle of Dalan Baljut (defeat by Jamukha).
1196	Toghrul expelled from his throne; goes to the Kara Kitay.
1198	Restoration of Toghrul by Temujin.
	Chin Emperor sends an expedition led by Wanyen Siang against the Tatars. The Tatars defeated by the aid of Toghrul and Temujin.
1198 (?)	Death of Inancha Bilgei, Khan of the Naiman.
1201	The tribes raise up Jamukha as Gur-Khan.
	Battle of Koyitan (the magic thunderstorm).
	Genghis Khan pillages the Taijiuts.

1202	Further expedition against the Tatars by Genghis Khan alone. Battle of Dalan Namurgas.
	Ong Khan attacks Tokhto'a of the Merkit.
	Expedition of the two Khans against Buyiruk Khan of the Naiman.
	Ong Khan deserts from the battle against Kokse'u Sabrakh.
	Genghis Khan sends his Four Coursers to aid Ong Khan.
	Renewal of the oath between the two Khans.
1203	Conspiracy of Jamukha and others against Genghis Khan.
	Battle of Khalakhaljit Elet.
	Genghis Khan retires to Baljuna.
1203 or 1204 (?)	Return of Genghis Khan from Baljuna.
	Defeat of Ong Khan at Mount Jeje'er.
	Death of Ong Khan.
1204	Battle of Chakirma'ut. Defeat of Tayang Khan of the Naiman.
	Attack on the Merkit; Hulan brought to Genghis Khan.
1205	Death of Jamukha.
	The Merkit and Naiman refugees defeated on the Irtish.
	Death of Tokhto'a.
1206	Genghis Khan made Khan of all the steppe peoples.
	Submission of the Uighurs.
	Khubilai sent against the Kharlukh.
1207	Jochi sent against Kuduka Beki of the Oirat.
	Expedition against the Khori Tumat; Borokhul killed.
1207–10 (?)	The rise and fall of Teb Tenggeri.
1209	Attack on the Tangut.
1211	Further attacks on the Tangut.
	Expedition against the Chin Empire. The whole area north of the Great Wall is overrun.
1212	Final submission of the Tangut.
1213	The Mongols cross the Great Wall.
1214	Further expedition against the Chin Empire.
1215	Capture and sack of Peking. All territory north of the Yellow river is lost to the Chin Emperors.
1216	Genghis Khan returns to his headquarters leaving Mukhali to carry on the campaign in China.
1218	The Kara Kitay brought to submission by Jebe.
1219	Beginning of the seven-year expedition to the West.
1220	Fall of Bukhara and Samarkand.
	Tuli lays waste Khorasan.
1221	Jebe and Subetai set out on their march round the Caspian.

	Genghis Khan crosses the Hindu Kush and defeats Jelal al Din on the banks of the Indus.
1223	Jebe and Subetai storm cities in Crimea and south Russia.
1224	Jebe and Subetai rejoin Genghis Khan.
1225	Genghis Khan returns from the expedition to the West and takes up quarters in autumn in the Black Forest on the Tula.
1226	Further expedition against the Tangut; Genghis Khan falls from his horse.
1227	Death of Genghis Khan.
1228	Ogodai elected Khan of Khans.
1237–8	Batu extends his conquests in Russia.
1240	The council on the Kerulen; the *Secret History* written. Fall of Kiev.
1241	Batu and Subetai invade Poland, Hungary and Germany. Death of Ogodai.
1242	The Mongols under Batu and Subetai complete the conquest of Hungary and advance into Dalmatia, Croatia and Austria. Advance forces reach Korneuburg and Wiener Neustadt, thirty miles south of Vienna.
	On learning of the death of Ogodai, Batu discontinues the campaign against western Europe.

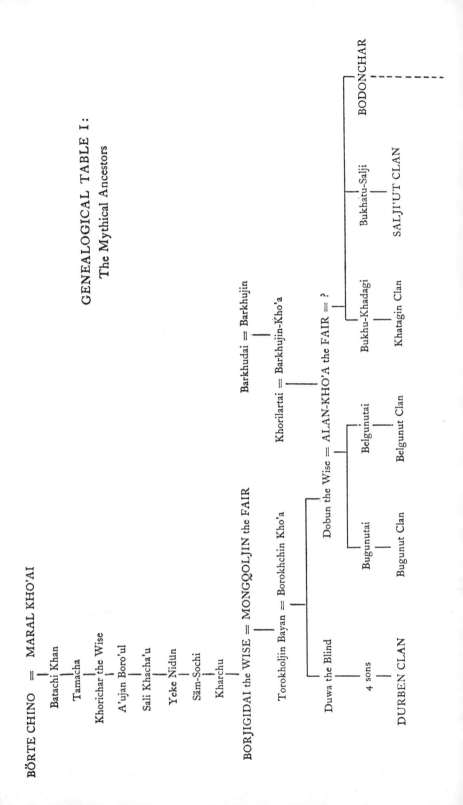

GENEALOGICAL TABLE I:
The Mythical Ancestors

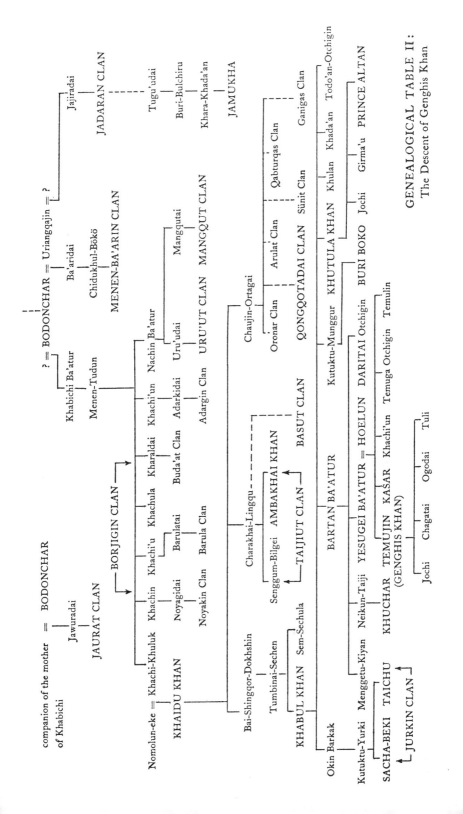

GENEALOGICAL TABLE II:
The Descent of Genghis Khan

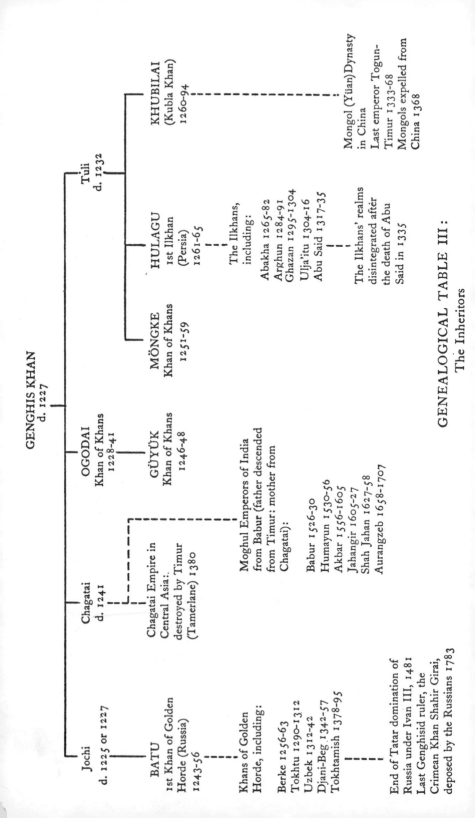

GENGHIS KHAN
d. 1227

Jochi
d. 1225 or 1227

BATU
1st Khan of Golden
Horde (Russia)
1243-56

Khans of Golden
Horde, including:

Berke 1256-63
Tokhtu 1290-1312
Uzbek 1312-42
Djani-Beg 1342-57
Tokhtamish 1378-95

End of Tatar domination of
Russia under Ivan III, 1481
Last Genghisid ruler, the
Crimean Khan Shahir Girai,
deposed by the Russians 1783

Chagatai
d. 1241

Chagatai Empire in
Central Asia:
destroyed by Timur
(Tamerlane) 1380

Moghul Emperors of India
from Babur (father descended
from Timur: mother from
Chagatai):

Babur 1526-30
Humayun 1530-56
Akbar 1556-1605
Jahangir 1605-27
Shah Jahan 1627-58
Aurangzeb 1658-1707

OGODAI
Khan of Khans
1228-41

GÜYÜK
Khan of Khans
1246-48

Tuli
d. 1232

MÖNGKE
Khan of Khans
1251-59

HULAGU
1st Ilkhan
(Persia)
1261-65

The Ilkhans,
including:

Abakha 1265-82
Arghun 1284-91
Ghazan 1295-1304
Ulja'itu 1304-16
Abu Said 1317-35

The Ilkhans' realms
disintegrated after
the death of Abu
Said in 1335

KHUBILAI
(Kubla Khan)
1260-94

Mongol (Yüan) Dynasty
in China
Last emperor Togun-
Timur 1333-68
Mongols expelled from
China 1368

GENEALOGICAL TABLE III:
The Inheritors

BIBLIOGRAPHY

THE MONGOL CHRONICLE ALTAN TOBČI. Text, translation and critical notes by Charles R. Bawden. Wiesbaden: Otto Harrassowitz, 1955.

GIOVANNI DA PIAN DEL CARPINE: *Viaggio a' Tartari (Historia Mongolorum)*. Edited Giorgio Pullé. Milan: Edizioni 'Alpes', 1929.

JOHANN DE PLANO CARPINI. *Geschichte der Mongolen und Reisebericht*, 1245–1247. Translated and edited by Dr Friedrich Risch. Leipzig: Pfeiffer, 1930.

CH'ANG CH'UN: *The Travels of an Alchemist*. The Journey of the Taoist Ch'ang Ch'un from China to the Hindu Kush at the Summons of Chingiz Khan. Recorded by his disciple LI CHIH-CH'ANG. Translated and with an Introduction by ARTHUR WALEY. London: Routledge, 1931.

CHRISTOPHER DAWSON (Ed.): *The Mongol Mission*. Narratives and Letters of the Franciscan Missionaries in Mongolia and China in the thirteenth and fourteenth centuries. Translated by a nun of Stanbrook Abbey. London and New York: Sheed and Ward, 1955.

GRIGOR OF AKANC': *History of the Nation of the Archers* (hitherto ascribed to MAGHAKIA the Monk). The Armenian text edited with an English translation and notes by Robert P. Blake and Richard N. Frye. Harvard University Press, 1954.

RENÉ GROUSSET: *Conqueror of the World*. Translated by Denis Sinor and Marian MacKellar from *Le Conquérant du Monde*, 1946. Edinburgh and London: Oliver and Boyd, 1967.

RENÉ GROUSSET: *L'Empire des Steppes*. Paris: Payot, 1939.

RENÉ GROUSSET: *L'Empire Mongol (1re. Phase)*. Tome VIII of Histoire du Monde, ed. Cavaignac. Paris: E. de Boccard, 1941.

ERICH HAENISCH: *Die Geheime Geschichte der Mongolen* (aus einer mongolischen Niederschrift des Jahres 1240 von der Insel Kode'e im Keluren-Fluss). Leipzig: Otto Harrassowitz, 1948.

C. DE HARLEZ: *Histoire de l'Empire du Kin ou Empire d'Or* (Aisin Gurun-i Suduri Bithe). Translated from the Manchu by C. de Harlez. Louvain: Charles Peeters, 1887.

HENRY H. HOWORTH: *History of the Mongols*. London: Longmans, Green & Co., 1876.

THE ENCYCLOPAEDIA OF ISLAM. Leiden: E. J. Brill, 1965.

'ALA-AD-DIN 'ATA-MALIK JUVAINI: *The History of the World-Conqueror*. Translated from the text of MIRZA MUHAMMAD QAZVINI by JOHN ANDREW BOYLE, Ph.D. Manchester University Press, 1958.

OWEN LATTIMORE: *Studies in Frontier History*. Collected Papers, 1928–58. Oxford University Press, 1962.

H. DESMOND MARTIN: *The Rise of Chingis Khan and his Conquest of North China*. Baltimore: The Johns Hopkins Press, 1950.

MOURADJA OHSSON (C. D'OHSSON): *Histoire des Mongols depuis Tchinguiz*

Khan jusqu'à Timour Bey ou Tamerlan. Amsterdam: Frederick Muller, 1852.

Kuo-yi Pao: *Studies on the Secret History of the Mongols*. Indiana University Publications: Uralic and Altaic Series, Vol. 58, 1965.

Paul Pelliot: *Oeuvres Posthumes: Histoire Secrète des Mongols*. Restitution du texte Mongol et traduction française des chapitres I à VI. Paris: Librairie d'Amérique et d'Orient. Adrien-Maisonneuve, 1949.

Paul Pelliot and Louis Hambis: *Histoire des Campagnes de Gengis Khan* (Cheng-wou Ts'in-tcheng Lou). Translated and annotated by P. Pelliot and L. Hambis. Leiden: E. J. Brill, 1951.

Marco Polo: *The Travels of Marco Polo*. Translated and with an introduction by Ronald Latham. London: Penguin Books, 1958.

Pavel Poucha. *Die Geheime Geschichte der Mongolen als Geschichtsquelle und Literaturdenkmal*. Prague: Československá Akademie Věd: Archiv Orientální, Supplementa IV (1956).

Michael Prawdin: *The Mongol Empire: its Rise and Legacy*. Translated from Tschingis-Chan und sein Erbe (1938) by Eden and Cedar Paul. London: Allen and Unwin, 1961.

Steven Runciman: *A History of the Crusades*. Cambridge University Press, 1954.

Sanang Setsen: *Geschichte der Ost-Mongolen und ihres Fürstenhauses*. Translated from the Mongolian by Isaac Jacob Schmidt. St Petersburg, 1829.

The Tarikh-i-rashidi of Mirza Muhammad Haidar Dughlat: *A History of the Moguls of Central Asia*. Translated by E. Denison Ross. Edited by N. Elias. London: Sampson Low, Marston & Co. Ltd., 1895.

William of Rubruck: *The Journey of William of Rubruck to the Eastern Parts of the World, 1253–55, as Narrated by Himself*. Translated and edited by William Woodville Rockhill. London: Hakluyt Society, 1900.

B. Ya. Vladimirtsov: *The Life of Chingis-Khan*. Translated from the Russian by Prince D. S. Mirsky. London: Routledge, 1930.

INDEX